THE SECRET OF THE AGES

The Art of War with Study Guide
The Magic of Believing with Study Guide
The Prince with Study Guide
The Richest Man In Babylon with Study Guide
The Science of Getting Rich with Study Guide
The Science of Mind with Study Guide
The Secret of the Ages
Think and Grow Rich with Study Guide

THE SECRET OF THE AGES

ROBERT COLLIER

WITH STUDY GUIDE
BY THERESA PUSKAR

Published 2019 by Gildan Media LLC
aka G&D Media
www.GandDmedia.com

THE SECRET OF THE AGES. Copyright © 2019 by G&D Media. All rights reserved.

No part of this book may be reproduced or transmitted in any form, by any means, (electronic, photocopying, recording, or otherwise) without the prior written permission of the author. No liability is assumed with respect to the use of the information contained within. Although every precaution has been taken, the author and publisher assume no liability for errors or omissions. Neither is any liability assumed for damages resulting from the use of the information contained herein.

FIRST EDITION 2019

Front Cover design by David Rheinhardt of Pyrographx

Interior design by Meghan Day Healey of Story Horse, LLC

Library of Congress Cataloging-in-Publication Data is available upon request

ISBN: 978-1-7225-0162-4

10   9   8   7   6   5   4   3   2   1

Contents

Foreword...9
Study Guide Introduction 11

VOLUME ONE

I   The World's Greatest Discovery 17
II The Genie-of-Your-Mind....................... 27

VOLUME TWO

III The Primal Cause...............................55
IV   Desire—The First Law of Gain................. 86

VOLUME THREE

V   Aladdin & Company 107
VI   See Yourself Doing It.......................... 123
VII "As a Man Thinketh" 135
VIII The Law of Supply............................ 147

VOLUME FOUR

- IX The Formula of Success 169
- X "This Freedom"................................. 184
- XI The Law of Attraction 195
- XII The Three Requisites.......................... 208
- XIII That Old Witch—Bad Luck 216

VOLUME FIVE

- XIV Your Needs Are Met......................... 235
- XV The Master of Your Fate 250
- XVI Unappropriated Millions..................... 263
- XVII The Secret of Power......................... 268
- XVIII This One Thing I Do 273

VOLUME SIX

- XIX The Master Mind 287
- XX What Do You Lack? 296
- XXI The Sculptor and the Clay 306
- XXII Why Grow Old? 316

VOLUME SEVEN

- XXIII The Medicine Delusion 337
- XXIV The Gift of the Magi....................... 348

"A fire-mist and a planet,
A crystal and a cell,
A jellyfish and a saurian,
A cave where the cave men dwell;
Then a sense of law and order,
A face upturned from the clod;
Some call it Evolution, And others call it God."

—REPRINTED FROM
THE NEW ENGLAND JOURNAL.

Foreword

If you had more money than time, more millions than you knew how to spend, what would be your pet philanthropy? Libraries? Hospitals? Churches? Homes for the Blind, Crippled or Aged? Mine would be "Homes"—but not for the aged or infirm. *For young married couples!*

I have often thought that, if ever I got into the "Philanthropic Billionaire" class, I'd like to start an Endowment Fund for helping young married couples over the rough spots in those first and second years of married life—especially the second year, when the real troubles come. Take a boy and a girl and a cozy little nest—add a cunning, healthy baby—and there's nothing happier on God's green footstool. But instead of a healthy babe, fill in a fretful, sickly baby—a wan, tired, worn-out little mother—a worried, dejected, heartsick father—and, there's nothing more pitiful.

A nurse for a month, a few weeks at the shore or mountains, a "lift" on that heavy doctor's bill—any one of these things would spell H-E-A-V-E-N to that tiny family. But do they get it? Not often! And the reason? Because they are not poor enough for charity. They are not rich enough to afford it themselves. They belong to that great "Middle Class" which has to bear the burdens of both the poor and the rich—and take what is left for itself.

It is to them that I should like to dedicate this book. If I cannot endow libraries or colleges for them, perhaps I can point the way to get all good gifts for them.

For men and women like them do not need "charity"—or even sympathy. What they do need is inspiration—and opportunity—the kind of inspiration that makes a man go out and create his own opportunity. And that, after all, is the greatest good one can do anyone. Few people appreciate free gifts. They are like the man whom admiring townsfolk presented with a watch. He looked it over critically for a minute. Then—"Where's the chain?" he asked.

But a way to win for themselves the full measure of success they've dreamed of but almost stopped hoping for—that is something every young couple would welcome with open arms. And it is something that, if I can do it justice, will make the "Eternal Triangle" as rare as it is today common, for it will enable husband and wife to work together—not merely for domestic happiness, but for business success as well.

Robert Collier.

Study Guide Introduction

Robert Collier wrote *The Secret of the Ages* almost a century ago. He was a pioneer in his day, and the philosophy that he taught was new and provocative. He writing style is conversation, however he frequently uses bible quotes throughout the book. While they may throw you at times, the messages that are rooted in the quotes are valuable and applicable to his philosophy and teachings.

While I've read many books on personal empowerment, what struck me most about this particular book was the power of the Perfection within each of us, and the freedom that comes with realizing that we are all a part of the Infinite Universal Mind of Creation. Denying our part in that mind, is denying the power of a divine creator. While writing this study guide, I realized that denying myself all that I desire, is denying the Creator His truth power, creativity and generosity.

I also better understood the power that comes with making a commitment to a solitary desire, and the potency of single-minded focus. I discovered that a part of the way in which I sabotage myself is through lack of committing to laser, solitary focus. Now that I have come to this realization, I am excited to integrate the teachings, utilize the tools ,and practice the techniques that the author has outlines for us in this wonderful book.

The study guide questions are located at the end of each chapter. They have been created to enhance your experience with this book. While you can gain a great deal by simply reading the book, going through the questions in the study guide, allows you to integrate Robert Collier's teaching into your own life. I believe doing so makes your reading experience much richer, and your retention much greater.

At times I pose a question earlier in the study guide, and then ask a similar question at a later time. Having read through the book, you may find that your perceptions have shifted. Re-visiting certain questions, gives you an opportunity to track your progress, and re-evaluate your position after gaining additional insights.

While I encourage you to work through the study guide in tandem with reading the book, follow your own inner guidance. You may wish to peruse the book, and then complete the study guide at a later time. Be aware, however, that planning to "do the study guide at a later time" could be the means by which your self-saboteur plots to avoid actually working through your issues and challenges. While reading self-empowerment books may be useful, you will gain much more out of the experience if you apply the lessons to your own life.

Give yourself time to "play" with this study guide. Allow your childlike-self to explore your imagination. You will discover that targeted and specific daydreaming could become your greatest ally and deepest joy!

Theresa Puskar
Writer, Study Guide

*A word of caution: At times Collier encourages you to release yourself from a reliance on modern medicine so that you can fully claim your perfection and draw healing from the Universal Mind. While the exercises and action steps I created follow Collier's encouragement, I suggest that you use your own best judgment. The medical resources that are available to us now were not invented in Collier's day. Give yourself permission to explore and practice his teaching, but also maintain an open mind. After all, the Universal Mind also had a hand in creating medical innovations.

VOLUME ONE

I

The World's Greatest Discovery

"You can do as much as you think you can,
But you'll never accomplish more;
If you're afraid of yourself, young man,
There's little for you in store.
For failure comes from the inside first,
It's there if we only knew it,
And you can win, though you face the worst,
If you feel that you're going to do it."
—Edgar A. Guest*

What, in your opinion, is the most significant discovery of this modern age?

The finding of dinosaur eggs on the plains of Mongolia, laid—so scientists assert—some 10,000,000 years ago?

The unearthing of the Tomb of Tutankh-Amen, with its matchless specimens of a bygone civilization?

The radioactive time clock by which Professor Lane of Tufts College estimates the age of the earth at 1,250,000,000 years?

Wireless? The Aeroplane? Man-made thunderbolts?

---

* From "A Heap o' Livin'." The Reilly & Lee Co.

No—not any of these. The really significant thing about them is that from all this vast research, from the study of all these bygone ages, men are for the first time beginning to get an understanding of that "Life Principle" which—somehow, some way—was brought to this earth thousands or millions of years ago. They are beginning to get an inkling of the infinite power it puts in their hands—to glimpse the untold possibilities it opens up.

This is the greatest discovery of modern times—that every man can call upon this "Life Principle" at will, that it is as much the servant of his mind as was ever Aladdin's fabled "genie-of-the-lamp" of old; that he has but to understand it and work in harmony with it to get from it anything he may need—health or happiness, riches or success.

To realize the truth of this, you have but to go back for a moment to the beginning of things.

In the Beginning

It matters not whether you believe that mankind dates back to the primitive ape-man of 500,000 years ago, or sprang full-grown from the mind of the creator. In either event, there had to be a first cause—a creator. Some power had to bring to this earth the first germ of life, and the creation is no less wonderful if it started with the lowliest form of plant life and worked up through countless ages into the highest product of today's civilization, than if the whole were created in six days.

In the beginning, this earth was just a fire mist—six thousand or a billion years ago— what does it matter which?

The one thing that does matter is that some time, some way, there came to this planet the germ of life—the life principle that animates all nature—plant, animal, and man. If we accept the scientists' version of it, the first form in which life appeared upon earth was the humble algae—a jelly-like mass that floated upon the waters. This, according to the scientists, was the beginning, the dawn of life upon the earth.

Next came the first bit of animal life—the lowly amoeba, a sort of jelly fish, consisting of a single cell, without vertebrae, and with very little else to distinguish it from the water round about. But it had *life*—the first bit of *animal* life—and from that life, according to the scientists, we could trace everything we have and are today.

All the millions of forms and shapes and varieties of plants and animals that have since appeared are but different manifestations of *life*—formed to meet differing conditions. For millions of years this "Life Germ" was threatened by every kind of danger—from floods, from earthquakes, from droughts, from desert heat, from glacial cold, from volcanic eruptions—but to it each new danger was merely an incentive to finding a new resource, to putting forth Life in some new shape.

To meet one set of needs, it formed the dinosaur—to meet another, the butterfly. Long before it worked up to man, we see its unlimited resourcefulness shown in a thousand ways. To escape danger in the water, it sought land. Pursued on land, it took to the air. To breathe in the sea, it developed gills. Stranded on land, it perfected lungs. To meet one kind of danger it grew a shell. For another, a sting. To protect itself from glacial cold, it grew fur, in temperate climates, hair. Subject to alternate heat and cold, it produced feathers. But ever, from the beginning, it showed its power to meet every changing condition, to answer every creature need.

Had it been possible to kill this "Life Idea," it would have perished ages ago, when fire and flood, drought and famine followed each other in quick succession. But obstacles, misfortunes, cataclysms, were to it merely new opportunities to assert its power. In fact, it required obstacles to awaken it, to show its energy and resource.

The great reptiles, the monster beasts of antiquity passed on. But the "Life Principle" stayed, changing as each age changed, always developing, and always improving.

Whatever power it was that brought this "Life Idea" to the earth, it came endowed with unlimited resource, unlimited energy, unlimited LIFE! No other force can defeat it. No obstacle can hold it back. All through the history of life and mankind you can see its directing intelligence—call it nature, call it providence, call it what you will—rising to meet every need of life.

The Purpose of Existence

No one can follow it down through the ages without realizing that the whole purpose of existence is GROWTH. Life is dynamic—not static. It is ever moving forward—not standing still. The one unpardonable sin of nature is to stand still, to stagnate. The Giganotosaurus, that was over a hundred feet long and as big as a house; the Tyrannosaurus, that had the strength of a locomotive and was the last word in frightfulness; the Pterodactyl or Flying Dragon—all the giant monsters of Prehistoric Ages—are gone. They ceased to serve a useful purpose. They did not know how to meet the changing conditions. They stood still—stagnated—while the life around them passed them by.

Egypt and Persia, Greece and Rome, all the great Empires of antiquity, perished when they ceased to grow.

China built a wall about her and stood still for a thousand years. Today she is the football of the powers. In all nature, to cease to grow is to perish.

It is for men and women who are not ready to stand still, who refuse to cease to grow, that this book is written. It will give you a clearer understanding of your own potentialities, show you how to work with and take advantage of the infinite energy all about you.

The terror of the man at the crossways, not knowing which road to take, will be no terror to you. Your future is of your own making. For the only law of infinite energy is the law of supply. The "Life Principle" is your principle. To survive, to win through, and to triumphantly surmount all obstacles has been its everyday practice since the beginning of time. It is no less resourceful now than ever it was. You have but to supply the urge, to work in harmony with it, to get from it anything you may need.

For if this "Life Principle" is so strong in the lowest forms of animal life that it can develop a shell or a poison to meet a need; if it can teach the bird to circle and dart, to balance and fly; if it can grow a new limb on a spider to replace a lost one, how much more can it do for you—a reasoning, rational being, with a mind able to work with this "Life Principle," with an energy and an initiative to urge it on!

The evidence of this is all about you. Take up some violent form of exercise—rowing, tennis, and swimming, riding. In the beginning your muscles are weak, easily tired. But keep on for a few days. The "Life Principle" promptly strengthens them, toughens them, to meet their new need. Do rough manual labor—and what happens? The skin of your hands becomes tender, blisters, and hurts. Keep it up, and does the skin all wear off? On the contrary, the "Life Principle" provides extra thicknesses, extra toughness—calluses, we call them—to meet your need.

All through your daily life you will find this "Life Principle" steadily at work. Embrace it, work with it, take it to yourself, and there is nothing you cannot do. The mere fact that you have obstacles to overcome is in your favor, for when there is nothing to be done, when things run along too smoothly; this "Life Principle" seems to sleep. It is when you need it, when you call upon it urgently, that it is most on the job.

It differs from "Luck" in this, that fortune is a fickle jade that smiles most often on those who need her least. Stake your last penny on the turn of a card—have nothing between you and ruin but the spin of a wheel or the speed of a horse—and it's a thousand to one "Luck" will desert you! But it is just the opposite with the "Life Principle." As long as things run smoothly, as long as life flows along like a song, this "Life Principle" seems to slumber, secure in the knowledge that your affairs can take care of themselves.

But let things start going wrong, let ruin and disgrace stare you in the face—*then* is the time this "Life Principle" will assert itself if you but give it a chance.

The "Open, Sesame!" of Life

There is a Napoleonic feeling of power *that insures success* in the knowledge that this invincible "Life Principle" is behind your every act. Knowing that you have working with you a force, which never yet has failed in anything it has undertaken, you can go ahead in the confident knowledge that it will not fail in your case, either. The ingenuity, which overcame every obstacle in making you what you are, is not likely to fall short when you have immediate need for it. It is the reserve strength of the athlete, the "second wind" of the runner, the power that, in moments of great stress or excitement, you unconsciously call upon to do the deeds which you ever after look upon as superhuman.

But they are in no wise superhuman. They are merely beyond the capacity of your conscious self. Ally your conscious self with that sleeping giant within you, rouse him daily to the task, and those "superhuman" deeds will become your ordinary, everyday accomplishments.

W. L. Cain, of Oakland, Oregon, writes: "I know that there is such a power, for I once saw two boys, 16 and 18 years of age, lift a great log off their brother, who had been caught under it. The next day, the same two boys, with another man and me, tried to lift the end of the log, but could not even budge it."

How was it that the two boys could do at need what the four were unable to do later on, when the need had passed? Because they never stopped to question whether or not it *could* be done. They saw only the urgent need. They concentrated all their thought, all their energy on that one thing—never doubting, never fearing—and the genie which is in all of us waiting only for such a call, answered their summons and gave them the strength—not of two men, but of ten!

It matters not whether you are banker or lawyer, businessman or clerk. Whether you are the custodian of millions, or have to struggle for your daily bread. This "Life Principle" makes no distinction between rich and poor, high and low. The greater your need, the more readily will it respond to your call. Wherever there is an unusual task, wherever there is poverty or hardship or sickness or despair, there is this servant of your mind, ready and willing to help, asking only that you call upon him.

And not only is it ready and willing, but it is always ABLE to help. Its ingenuity and resource are without limit. It is Mind. It is thought. It is the Telepathy that carries messages without the spoken or written word. It is the Sixth Sense that warns you of unseen dangers. No matter how stupendous and complicated, nor how simple your problem may be—the solution of it is somewhere in Mind, in Thought. And since the solution does exist, this Mental Giant can find it for you. It can KNOW, and it can DO, every right thing. Whatever it is necessary for you to know, whatever it is necessary for you to do, you can know and you can do if you will but seek the help of this genie-of-your-mind and work with it in the right way.

STUDY GUIDE

I *The World's Greatest Discovery*

1. What does the Edgar A. Guest poem at the beginning of this chapter mean to you? Are you afraid of yourself? Do you feel a failure?

2. What do you believe to be man's top three greatest discoveries?

3. What is the "Life Principle" that Collier is referring to at the beginning of the book?

In the Beginning
4. The author asserts that how the world began does not really matter. The dangers that were faced incentivized the evolution of Life into new forms and shapes. What current situations do you believe are incentivizing humankind to continue to evolve?

5. Collier asserts that the whole purpose of existence is growth? Do you believe this to be true? Why or why not?

The Purpose Of Existence
6. Prehistoric animals and great Empires of antiquity became stagnant and were unable to meet changing conditions. Where do you see other examples of energetic stagnation throughout history?

7. The author states that you need to 1) supply the urge, 2) work in harmony with it, and 3) get from this anything you may need from the Life Principle to "win through, and triumphantly surmount all obstacles". Please explain what he means by this in your own words.

8. The author shares examples of the Life Principle is all about you—from your strengthening muscles to your callused hands. List at least three areas where you have seen these principles manifest in your life.

9. According to Collier, obstacles actually work in your favor, for without them, the Life Principle seems to sleep. Provide an example in your life of how an obstacle propelled you forward in a positive way.

10. Life Principle is described as "invincible", as it has never failed anyone yet. Do you struggle with the sense of absolute success that is being asserted? Why or why not?

The "Open, Sesame?" Of Life

11. This principle can call upon superhuman power to get things done. The author uses the example of two boys able to lift a heavy log to save their brother. Research and describe at least two other accounts of such superhuman feats.

12. Your social status does not make a difference with this powerful force. The greater your need, the more readily it will respond to your call. On a scale from one to ten (1 being very little, and 10 being a great deal), rate how much your need is to pursue your life's passion.

1——2——3——4——5——6——7——8——9——10

13. *"There is this servant of your mind, ready and willing to help, asking only that you call upon him . . . No matter how stupendous and complicated, nor how simple your problem may be – the solution of it is somewhere in Mind, In Thought."* Do you ever reach out to ask for help, or do you tend to struggle through things alone?

II

The Genie-of-Your-Mind

"It matters not how strait the gate,
How charged with punishment the scroll,
I am the Master of my Fate;
I am the Captain of my Soul."
—Henley

First came the Stone Age, when life was for the strong of arm or the fleet of foot. Then there was the Iron Age—and while life was more precious, still the strong lorded it over the weak. Later came the Golden Age, and riches took the place of strength—but the poor found little choice between the slave drivers' whips of olden days and the grim weapons of poverty and starvation.

Now we are entering a new age—the Mental Age—when every man can be his own master, when poverty and circumstance no longer hold power and the lowliest creature in the land can win a place side by side with the highest.

To those who do not know the resources of mind these will sound like rash statements; but science proves beyond question that in the wellsprings of every man's mind are unplumbed depths—undiscovered deposits of energy, wisdom and ability. Sound these depths—bring these treasures to the surface—and you gain an astounding wealth of new power.

From the rude catamaran of the savages to the giant liners of today, carrying their thousands from continent to continent is but a step in the development of Mind. From the lowly cave man, cowering in his burrow in fear of lightning or fire or water, to the engineer of today, making servants of all the forces of Nature, is but a measure of difference in mental development.

Man, without reasoning mind, would be as the monkeys are—prey of any creature fast enough and strong enough to pull him to pieces. At the mercy of wind and weather. A poor timid creature, living for the moment only, fearful of every shadow.

Through his superior mind, he learned to make fire to keep himself warm; weapons with which to defend himself from the savage creatures round about; habitations to protect himself from the elements. Through mind he conquered the forces of Nature.

Through mind he has made machinery do the work of millions of horses and billions of hands. What he will do next, no man knows, for man is just beginning to awaken to his own powers. He is just getting an inkling of the unfathomed riches buried deep in his own mind. Like the gold seekers of '49, he has panned the surface gravel for the gold swept down by the streams. Now he is starting to dig deeper to the pure vein beneath.

We bemoan the loss of our forests. We worry over our dwindling resources of coal and oil. We decry the waste in our factories. But the greatest waste of all, we pay no attention to—the waste of our own potential mind power. Professor Wm. James, the world-famous Harvard psychologist, estimated that the average man uses only 10% of his mental power. He has unlimited power—yet he uses but a tithe of it. Unlimited wealth all about him—and he doesn't know how to take hold of it. With God-like powers slumbering within him, he is content to continue in his daily grind—eating, sleeping, working—plodding through an existence little more eventful than the animals, while all of Nature, all of life, calls upon him to awaken, to bestir himself.

The power to be what you want to be, to get what you desire, to accomplish whatever you are striving for, abides within you. It rests with you only to bring it forth and put it to work. Of course you must know *how* to do that, but before you can learn how to use it, you must *realize* that you *possess* this power. So our first objective is to get acquainted with this power.

For Psychologists and Metaphysicians the world over, are agreed in this—that Mind is all that counts. You can be whatever you make up your mind to be. You need not be sick. You need not be unhappy. You need not be poor. You need not be unsuccessful. You are not a mere clod. You are not a beast of burden, doomed to spend your days in unremitting labor in return for food and housing. You are one of the Lords of the Earth, with unlimited potentialities. Within you is a power, which, properly grasped and directed, can lift you out of the rut of mediocrity and place you among the Elect of the earth—the lawyers, the writers, the statesmen, the big business men—the DOERS and the THINKERS. It rests with you only to learn to use this power, which is yours—this Mind that can do all things.

Your body is for all practical purposes merely a machine, which the mind uses. This mind is usually thought of as consciousness; but the *conscious part* of your mind is in fact the *very smallest part of it*. Ninety per cent of your mental life is subconscious, so when you make active use of only the conscious part of your mind you are using but a fraction of your real ability; you are running on low gear. And the reason why more people do not achieve success in life is because so many of them are content to run on low gear all their lives—on SURFACE ENERGY. If these same people would only throw into the fight the resistless force of their subconscious minds they would be amazed at their undreamed of capacity for winning success.

Conscious and subconscious are, of course, integral parts of the one mind. But for convenience sake let us divide your mind into three parts—the conscious mind, the subconscious mind, and the Infinite, Subliminal or Universal Mind.

The Conscious Mind

When you say, "I see—I hear—I smell—I touch," it is your conscious mind that is saying this, for it is the force governing the five physical senses. It is the phase of mind with which you feel and reason—the phase of mind with which everyone is familiar. It is the mind with which you do business. It controls, to a great extent, all your voluntary muscles. It discriminates between right and wrong, wise and foolish. It is the generalissimo, in charge of all your mental forces. It can plan ahead and get things done as it plans. Or it can drift along haphazardly, a creature of impulse, at the mercy of events—a mere bit of flotsam in the current of life.

For it is only through your conscious mind that you can reach the subconscious and the Universal Mind. Your conscious mind is the porter at the door, the watchman at the gate. It is to the conscious mind that the subconscious looks for all its impressions. It is on it that the subconscious mind must depend for the teamwork necessary to get successful results. You wouldn't expect much from an army, no matter how fine its soldiers, whose general never planned ahead, who distrusted his own ability and that of his men, and who spent all his time worrying about the enemy instead of planning how he might conquer them. You wouldn't look for good scores from a ball team whose pitcher was at odds with the catcher. In the same way, you can't expect results from the subconscious when your conscious mind is full of fear or worry, or when it does not know what it wants.

The one most important province of your conscious mind is to center your thoughts on the thing you want, and to shut the door on every suggestion of fear or worry or disease.

If you once gain the ability to do that, nothing else is impossible to you.

For the subconscious mind does not reason inductively. It takes the thoughts you send in to it and works them out to their logical conclusion. Send to it thoughts of health and strength, and it will work out health and strength in your body. Let suggestions of disease, fear of sickness or accident, penetrate to it, either through your own thoughts or the talk of those around you, and you are very likely to see the manifestation of disease working out in yourself.

Your mind is master of your body. It directs and controls every function of your body. Your body is in effect a little universe in itself, and mind is its radiating center—the sun that gives light and life to all your system, and around which the whole revolves. And your *conscious thought* is master of this sun center. As Emile Coué puts it—"The conscious can put the subconscious mind over the hurdles."

The Subconscious Mind

Can you tell me how much water, how much salt, how much of each different element there should be in your blood to maintain its proper specific gravity if you are leading an ordinary sedentary life? How much and how quickly these proportions must be changed if you play a fast game of tennis, or run for your car, or chop wood, or indulge in any other violent exercise?

Do you know how much water you should drink to neutralize the excess salt in salt fish? How much you lose through perspiration? Do you know how much water, how much salt, how much of each different element in your food should be absorbed into your blood each day to maintain perfect health?

No? Well, it need not worry you. Neither does anyone else. Not even the greatest physicists and chemists and mathematicians. But your subconscious mind knows.

And it doesn't have to stop to figure it out. It does it almost automatically. It is one of those "Lightning Calculators." And this is but one of thousands of such jobs it performs every hour of the day. The greatest mathematicians in the land, the most renowned chemists, could never do in a year's time the abstruse problems, which your subconscious mind, solves every minute.

And it doesn't matter whether you've ever studied mathematics or chemistry or any other of the sciences. From the moment of your birth your subconscious mind solves all these problems for you. While you are struggling along with the three R's, it is doing problems that would leave your teachers aghast. It supervises all the intricate processes of digestion, of assimilation, of elimination, and all the glandular secretions that would tax the knowledge of all the chemists and all the laboratories in the land. It planned and built your body from infancy on up. It repairs it. It operates it. It has almost unlimited power, not merely for putting you and keeping you in perfect health but for acquiring all the good things of life. Ignorance of this power is the sole reason for all the failures in this world. If you would intelligently turn over to this wonderful power all your business and personal affairs in the same way that you turn over to it the mechanism of your body, no goal would be too great for you to strive for.

Dr. Geo. C. Pitzer sums up the power of the subconscious mind very well in the following:

"The subconscious mind is a distinct entity. It occupies the whole human body, and, when not opposed in any way, it has absolute control over all the functions, conditions, and sensations of the body. While the objective (conscious) mind has control over all of our voluntary functions and motions, the subconscious mind controls all of the silent, involuntary, and vegetative functions. Nutrition, waste, all secretions and excretions, the action of the heart in the circulation of the blood, the lungs in respiration or breathing, and all cell life, cell changes and development, are positively under the complete control of the subconscious mind. This was the only mind animal had before the evolution of the brain; and it could not, nor can it yet, reason inductively, but its power of deductive reasoning is perfect. And more, it can see without the use of physical eyes. It perceives by intuition. It has the power to communicate with others without the aid of ordinary physical means. It can read the thoughts of others. It receives intelligence and transmits it to people at a distance. Distance offers no resistance against the successful missions of the subconscious mind. It never dies. We call this the 'soul mind.' It is the living soul."

In "Practical Psychology and Sex Life," by David Bush, Dr. Winbigler is quoted as going even further. To quote him:

"It is this mind that carries on the work of assimilation and upbuilding whilst we sleep . . .

It reveals to us things that the conscious mind has no conception of until the consummations have occurred.

It can communicate with other minds without the ordinary physical means.

It gets glimpses of things that ordinary sight does not behold.

It makes God's presence an actual, realizable fact, and keeps the personality in peace and quietness.

It warns of approaching danger.

It approves or disapproves of a course of conduct and conversation.

It carries out all the best things, which are given to it, providing the conscious mind does not intercept and change the course of its manifestation.

It heals the body and keeps it in health, if it is at all encouraged."

It is, in short, the most powerful force in life, and when properly directed, the most beneficent. But, like a live electric wire, its destructive force is equally great. It can be either your servant or your master. It can bring to you evil or good.

The Rev. William T. Walsh, in a new book just published, explains the idea very clearly:

"The subconscious part in us is called the subjective mind, because it does not decide and command. It is a subject rather than a ruler. Its nature is to do what it is told, *or what really in your heart of hearts you desire.*

"The subconscious mind directs all the vital processes of your body. You do not think consciously about breathing. Every time you take a breath you do not have to reason, decide, command. The subconscious mind sees to that. You have not been at all conscious that you have been breathing while you have been reading this page. So it is with the mind and the circulation of blood. The heart is a muscle like the muscle of your arm. It has no power to move itself or to direct its action. Only mind, only something that can think, can direct our muscles, including the heart. You are not conscious that you are commanding your heart to beat. The subconscious mind attends to that. And so it is with the assimilation of food, the building and repairing of the body. In fact, all the vital processes are looked after by the subconscious mind."

"Man lives and moves and has his being" in this great subconscious mind. It supplies the "intuition" that so often carries a woman straight to a point that may require hours of cumbersome reasoning for a man to reach. Even in ordinary, every-day affairs, you often draw upon its wonderful wisdom.

But you do it in an accidental sort of way without realizing what you are doing.

Consider the case of "Blind Tom." Probably you've heard or read of him. You know that he could listen to a piece of music for the first time and go immediately to a piano and reproduce it. People call that abnormal. But as a matter of fact he was in this respect more normal than any of us. We are abnormal because we cannot do it.

Or consider the case of these "lightning calculators" of whom one reads now and then. It may be a boy seven or eight years old; but you can ask him to divide 7,649.437 by 326.2568 and he'll give you the result in less time than it would take you to put the numbers down on a piece of paper. You call him phenomenal. Yet you ought to be able to do the same yourself. Your subconscious mind can.

Dr. Hudson, in his book "The Law of Psychic Phenomena," tells of numerous such prodigies. Here are just a few instances:

"Of mathematical prodigies there has been upwards of a score whose calculations have surpassed, in rapidity and accuracy, those of the greatest educated mathematicians. These prodigies have done their greatest feats while but children from three to ten years old. In no case had these boys any idea how they performed their calculations, and some of them would converse upon other subjects while doing the sum. Two of these boys became men of eminence, while some of them showed but a low degree of objective intelligence.

Whateley spoke of his own gift in the following terms:

"There was certainly something peculiar in my calculating faculty. It began to show itself at between five and six, and lasted about three years. I soon got to do the most difficult sums, always in my head, for I knew nothing of figures beyond numeration. I did these sums much quicker than anyone could upon paper, and I never remember committing the smallest error. When I went to school, at which time the passion wore off, I was a perfect dunce at ciphering, and have continued so ever since."

"Professor Safford became an astronomer. At the age of ten he worked correctly a multiplication sum whose answer consisted of thirty-six figures. Later in life he could perform no such feats."

"Benjamin Hall Blyth, at the age of six, asked his father at what hour he was born. He was told that he was born at four o'clock. Looking at the clock to see the present time, he informed his father of the number of seconds he had lived. His father made the calculation and said to Benjamin, 'You are wrong 172,000 seconds.' The boy answered, 'Oh, papa, you have left out two days for the leap years 1820 and 1824,' which was the case."

"Then there is the celebrated case of Zerah Colburn, of whom Dr. Schofield writes:

"'Zerah Colburn could instantaneously tell the square root of 106,929 as 327, and the cube root of 268,336,125 as 645. Before the question of the number of minutes in forty-eight years could be written he said 25,228,810. He immediately gave the factors of 247,483 as 941 and 263, which are the only two; and being asked then for those of 36,083, answered none; it is a prime number. He could not tell how the answer came into his mind. He could not, on paper, do simple multiplication or division.'"

The time will come when, as H. G. Wells envisioned in his "Men Like Gods," schools and teachers will no longer be necessary except to show us how to get in touch with the infinite knowledge our subconscious minds possess from infancy.

"The smartest man in the world," says Dr. Frank Crane in a recent article in *Liberty* "is the Man Inside. By the

Man Inside I mean that Other Man within each one of us that does most of the things we give ourselves credit for doing. You may refer to him as Nature or the Subconscious Self or think of him merely as a Force or a Natural Law, or, if you are religiously inclined, you may use the term God.

"I say he is the smartest man in the world. I know he is infinitely more clever and resourceful than I am or than any other man is that I ever heard of. When I cut my finger it is he that calls up the little phagocytes to come and kill the septic germs that might get into the wound and cause blood poisoning. It is he that coagulates the blood, stops the gash, and weaves the new skin.

"I could not do that. I do not even know how he does it. He even does it for babies that know nothing at all; in fact, does it better for them than for me.

"No living man knows enough to make toenails grow, but the Man Inside thinks nothing of growing nails and teeth and thousands of hairs all over my body; long hairs on my head and little fuzzy ones over the rest of the surface of the skin.

"When I practice on the piano I am simply getting the business of piano playing over from my conscious mind to my subconscious mind: in other words, I am handing the business over to the Man Inside.

"Most of our happiness, as well as our struggles and misery, come from this Man Inside. If we train him in ways of contentment, adjustment, and decision he will go ahead of us like a well-trained servant and do for us easily most of the difficult tasks we have to perform."

Dr. Jung, celebrated Viennese specialist, claims that the subconscious mind contains not only all the knowledge that it has gathered during the life of the individual, but that in addition it contains all the wisdom of past ages. That by drawing upon its wisdom and power the individual may possess any good thing of life, from health and happiness to riches and success.

You see, the subconscious mind is the connecting link between the Creator and us, between Universal Mind and our conscious mind. It is the means by which we can appropriate to ourselves all the good gifts, all the riches and abundance that Universal Mind has created in such profusion.

Berthelot, the great French founder of modern synthetic chemistry, once stated in a letter to a close friend that the final experiments which led to his most wonderful discoveries had never been the result of carefully followed and reasoned trains of thought, but that, on the contrary, "they came of themselves, so to speak, from the clear sky."

Charles M. Barrows, in "Suggestion Instead of Medicine," tells us that:

"If man requires another than his ordinary consciousness to take care of him while asleep, not less useful is this same psychical provision when he is awake. Many persons are able to obtain knowledge, which does not come to them through their senses, in the usual way, but arrives in the mind by direct communication from another conscious intelligence, which apparently knows more of what concerns their welfare than their ordinary reason does. I have known a number of persons who, like myself, could tell the contents of letters in their mail before opening them. Several years ago a friend of mine came to Boston for the first time, arriving at what was then the Providence railroad station in Park Square. He wished to walk to the Lowell station on the opposite side of the city. Being utterly ignorant of the streets as well as the general direction to take, he confidently set forth without asking the way, and reached his destination by the most direct path. In doing this he trusted solely to 'instinctive guidance,' as he called it, and not to any hints or clews obtained through the senses."

The geniuses of literature, of art, commerce, government, politics and invention are, according to the scientists, but ordinary men like you and me who have learned somehow, some way, to draw upon their subconscious minds.

Sir Isaac Newton is reported to have acquired his marvelous knowledge of mathematics and physics with no conscious effort. Mozart said of his beautiful symphonies "they just came to him." Descartes had no ordinary regular education. To quote Dr. Hudson:

"This is a power which transcends reason, and is independent of induction. Instances of its development might be multiplied indefinitely. Enough is known to warrant the conclusion that when the soul is released from its objective environment it will be enabled to perceive all the laws of its being, to 'see God as He is,' by the perception of the laws which He has instituted. It is the knowledge of this power which demonstrates our true relationship to God, which confers the warranty of our right to the title of 'sons of God,' and confirms our inheritance of our rightful share of his attributes and powers—our heir ship of God, our joint heir ship with Jesus Christ."

Our subconscious minds are vast magnets, with the power to draw from Universal Mind unlimited knowledge, unlimited power, unlimited riches.

"Considered from the standpoint of its activities," says Warren Hilton in "Applied Psychology," "the subconscious is that department of mind, which on the one hand directs the vital operations of the body, and on the other conserves, subject to the call of interest and attention, all ideas and complexes not at the moment active in consciousness.

"Observe, then, the possibility that lies before you. On the one hand, if you can control your mind in its subconscious activities, you can regulate the operation of your bodily functions, and can thus assure yourself of bodily efficiency and free yourself of functional disease. On the other hand, if you can determine just what ideas shall be brought forth from sub consciousness into consciousness, you can thus select the materials out of which will be woven your conscious judgments, your decisions and your emotional attitudes.

"To achieve control of your mind is, then, to attain (a) health, success, and (c) happiness."

Few understand or appreciate, however, that the vast storehouse of knowledge and power of the subconscious mind can be drawn upon at will. Now and then through intense concentration or very active desire we do accidentally penetrate to the realm of the subconscious and register our thought upon it. Such thoughts are almost invariably realized. The trouble is that as often as not it is our negative thoughts—our fears—that penetrate. And these are realized just as surely as the positive thoughts. What you must manage to do is learn to communicate only such thoughts as you wish to see realized to your subconscious mind, for it is exceedingly amenable to suggestion. You have heard of the man who was always bragging of his fine health and upon whom some of his friends decided to play a trick. The first one he met one morning commented upon how badly he looked and asked if he weren't feeling well. Then all the others as they saw him made similar remarks. By noontime the man had come to believe them, and before the end of the day he was really ill.

That was a rather glaring example. But similar things are going on every day with all of us. We eat something that someone else tells us isn't good for us and in a little while we think we feel a pain. Before we know it we have indigestion, when the chances are that if we knew nothing about the supposed indigestible properties of the food we could eat it the rest of our days and never feel any ill effects.

Let some new disease be discovered and the symptoms described in the daily paper. Hundreds will come down with it at once. They are like the man who read a medical encyclopedia and ended up by concluding he had everything but "housemaid's knee." Patent medicine advertisers realize this power of suggestion and cash in upon it. Read one of their ads. If you don't think you have everything the matter with you that their nostrums are supposed to cure, you are the exception and not the rule.

That is the negative side of it. Emile Coué based his system on the positive side—which you suggest to your subconscious mind that whatever ills it thinks you have are getting better. And it is good psychology at that. Properly carried out it will work wonders. But there arc better methods. And I hope to be able to show them to you before we reach the end of this book.

Suffice it now to say that your subconscious mind is exceedingly wise and powerful. That it knows many things that is not in books. When properly used it has infallible judgment, un-failing power. It never sleeps never tires.

Your conscious mind may slumber. It may be rendered impotent by anesthetics or a sudden blow. But your subconscious mind works on, keeping your heart and lungs, your arteries and glands ever on the job.

Under ordinary conditions, it attends faithfully to its duties, and leaves your conscious mind to direct the outer life of the body. But let the conscious mind meet some situation with which it is unable to cope, and, if it will only call upon the subconscious, that powerful Genie will respond immediately to its need.

You have heard of people who had been through great danger tell how, when death stared them in the face and there seemed nothing they could do, things went black before them and, when they came to, the danger was past. In the moment of need, their subconscious mind pushed the conscious out of the way, the while it met and overcame the danger. Impelled by the subconscious mind, their bodies could do things absolutely impossible to their ordinary conscious selves.

For the power of the subconscious mind is unlimited. Whatever it is necessary for you to do in any right cause, it can give you the strength and the ability to do.

Whatever of good you may desire, it can bring to you. "The Kingdom of Heaven is within you."

The Universal Mind

Have you ever dug up a potato vine and seen the potatoes clustering underneath? How much of intelligence do you suppose one of these potatoes has? Do you think it knows anything about chemistry or geology? Can it figure out how to gather carbon gas from the atmosphere, water and all the necessary kinds of nutriment from the earth round about to manufacture into sugar and starch and alcohol? No chemist can do it. How do you suppose the potato knows? Of course it doesn't. It has no sense. Yet it does all these things. It builds the starch into cells, the cells into roots and vines and leaves—and into more potatoes.

"Just old Mother Nature," you'll say. But old Mother Nature must have a remarkable intelligence if she can figure out all these things that no human scientist has ever been able to figure. There must be an all-pervading Intelligence behind Mother Nature—the Intelligence that first brought life to this planet—the Intelligence that evolved every form of plant and animal—that holds the winds in its grasp—that is all-wise, all-powerful. The potato is but one small manifestation of this Intelligence. The various forms of plant life, of animals, of man—all are mere cogs in the great scheme of things.

But with this *difference*—that man is an active part of this Universal Mind. That he partakes of its creative wisdom and power and that by working in harmony with Universal Mind he can *do* anything *have* anything, *be* anything.

There is within you—within everyone—this mighty resistless force with which you can perform undertakings that will dazzle your reason, stagger your imagination. There constantly resides within you a Mind that is all-wise, all-powerful, a Mind that is entirely apart from the mind which you consciously use in your everyday affairs yet which is one with it.

Your subconscious mind partakes of this wisdom and power, and it is through your subconscious mind that you can draw upon it in the attainment of anything you may desire. When you can intelligently reach your subconscious mind, you can be in communication with the Universal Mind.

Remember this: the Universal Mind is omnipotent. And since the subconscious mind is part of the Universal Mind, there is no limit to the things, which it can do when it is given the power to act. Given any desire that is in harmony with the Universal Mind and you have but to hold that desire in your thought to attract from the invisible domain the things you need to satisfy it.

For mind does its building solely by the power of thought. Its creations take form according to its thought. Its first requisite is a mental image, and your desire held with unswerving purpose will form that mental image.

An understanding of this principle explains the power of prayer. The results of prayer are not brought about by some special dispensation of Providence. God is not a finite being to be cajoled or flattered into doing, as you desire. But when you pray earnestly you form a mental image of the thing that you desire and you hold it strongly in your thought. Then the Universal Intelligence, which is your intelligence—Omnipotent Mind—, begins to work with and for you, and this is what brings about the manifestation that you desire.

The Universal Mind is all around you. It is as all-pervading as the air you breathe. It encompasses you with as little trouble as the water in the sea encompasses the fish. Yet it is just as thoroughly conscious of you as the water would be, were it intelligent, of every creature within it. "Are not two sparrows sold for a farthing? And one of them shall not fall on the ground without your Father. But the very hairs of your head are all numbered. Fear ye not, therefore, ye are of more value than many sparrows."

It seems hard to believe that a Mind busied with the immensities of the universe can consider such trivial affairs as our own when we are but one of the billions of forms of life which come into existence. Yet consider again the fish in the sea. It is no trouble for the sea to encompass them. It is no more trouble for the Universal Mind to encompass us. Its power, it's thought, is as much at our disposal as the sunshine and the wind and the rain. Few of us take advantage to the full of these great forces. Fewer still take advantage of the power of the Universal Mind. If you have any lack, if you are prey to poverty or disease, it is because you do not believe or do not understand the power that is yours. It is not a question of the Universal giving to you. It offers everything to everyone—there is no partiality. "Ho, everyone that thirsteth, come ye to the waters." You have only to take. "Whosoever will let him take of the water of life freely."

"With all thy getting, get understanding," said Solomon. And if you will but get understanding, everything else will be added unto you.

To bring you to a realization of your indwelling and unused power, to teach you simple, direct methods of drawing upon it, is the beginning and the end of this course.

STUDY GUIDE

II *The Genie-of-Your-Mind*

1. What does the Henley poem at the beginning of this chapter mean to you?

2. Collier asserts that there are undiscovered deposits of energy, wisdom and ability within the depths of the mind, that when brought to the surface can gain you *"an astounding wealth of new power"*. Describe in as much detail as possible what your life would be like as the astounding wealth of new power arises.

3. Humankind only uses about 10% of his mind power. How do you believe he may someday be able to expand it?

4. Before learning how to use it, you must first believe that you possess extraordinary power within you. On a scale from one to ten (1 being very little, and 10 being a great deal), rate how much you truly believe in the God-like powers that lie dormant within you.

   1——2——3——4——5——6——7——8——9——10

5. The author divides the mind into three segments: the conscious mind, the subconscious mind, and the Infinite, Subliminal or Universal Mind. How much do you believe each of these minds functions in your daily life?

The Conscious Mind:
6. Your senses (sight, hearing, smell, taste and touch), reasoning, planning capacities are all governed by your conscious mind. It is also the gatekeeper to the subconscious and Universal Mind. If it is full of fear or worry, you cannot expect results from the subconscious. On a scale from one to ten (1 being very little, and 10 being a great

deal), rate how much you experience fear in your conscious mind.

7. *"The one most important province of your conscious mind is to center your thoughts on the thing you want, and to shut the door on every suggestion of fear or worry or disease. If you once gain the ability to do that, nothing else is impossible to you."* Do you have difficulty shutting the door on fearful or worrisome suggestions? Is there something you do to expand beyond those feelings?

The Subconscious Mind:

8. If you send your subconscious mind thoughts of health and strength, it will work out health and strength in your body. However, if it is penetrated with suggestions of disease, fear of sickness or accident (through your thoughts or talk of those around you), you will likely see disease manifesting in your life. Do many of the people in your life focus on fear and disease or the opposite?

9. If your mind is the sun that gives light and life to all your systems, is your body experiencing more darkness or light? For the day, focus on the thoughts that are entering your mind, along with the conversations you are having. Track how many negative you experience, compared to positive.

10. Your subconscious mind is likened to a "Lightening Calculator" that responds to all of your body's needs automatically. According to the author, ignorance of this power is the sole reason for all the failures in the world. Could you explain why?

11. Collier asserts that if you turn over the wonderful power of your subconscious in dealing with all your business and personal affairs, no goals would be too great. Where do you think mankind/your lost your trust in your subconscious mind?

12. Consider Collier's argument that your body, mind and spirit naturally have all needed to keep you in perfect health and for acquiring all the good things of life. He states, *"Ignorance of this power is the sole reason for all the failures in this world."* This is a strong, sweeping statement. Do you believe it to be true? Why or why not?

13. If the above statement is true, then how do you believe disease and aging exist?

14. If you turned your natural power over to all your business and personal affairs in the same way that your body's mechanisms are managed, no goal would be too great. Write a list of the goals that you currently believe are too great, and then list why.

15. Dr. Geo C. Pitzer states that the body has absolute control over all its function, if not opposed. How do you believe you may be opposing your body's natural abilities?

16. He also states that the subconscious mind does not need eyes to see and never dies. Have you considered your subconscious mind as linked to your intuition? Why or why not?

17. According to David Bush, the subconscious mind *"carries on the work of assimilation and upbuilding while we sleep."* Do you get enough sound sleep each night? On a scale from one to ten (1 being very little, and 10 being a great deal), rate how much sound sleep you get on a regular basis.

    1——2——3——4——5——6——7——8——9——10

18. Bush also claims, *"It carries out all the best things, which are given to it, providing the conscious mind does not intercept and change the course of its manifestation"*. List at least five ways in which you believe your conscious mind is intercepting the course of manifestation in your life.

19. According to Rev. William T. Walsh, the nature of the subjective mind is to do what it is told. Do you pay strict attention to what you put into your subjective mind? Do you often feed it negativity through thoughts, images, or media input? Please explain.

20. Walsh also states that *"it (the subconscious mind) supplies the 'intuition' that so often carries a woman straight to a point that may require hours of cumbersome reasoning for a man to reach."* Do you believe this statement biased and offensive, or true? Why?

21. According to Walsh, when we fully utilize our subconscious mind, we are all capable of what would be considered extraordinary feats. Do you believe this to be true? Why or why not? Have your experienced evidence of this in your own life?

22. Collier shares several examples of young children who possessed extraordinary abilities. Most lost their abilities later in their lives. What do you attribute that loss to?

23. Dr. Frank Crane refers to the orchestrator of this phenomenon as the *"Man Inside"*. It has also been referred to as *"that Other Man, Nature, the Subconscious Self, a Force or a Natural Law, or God."* How do you refer to it?

24. According to Dr. Crane, *"Most of our happiness, as well as our struggle and misery come from this Man Inside. If we train him in ways to contentment, adjustment, and decision, he will go ahead of us like as well-trained service and do for us easily most of the difficult tasks we have to perform."* On a scale from one to ten (1 being very little, and 10 being a great deal), rate how effectively your Man Inside has been trained.

1——2——3——4——5——6—— 7 —8——9——10

25. According to Carl Jung, your subconscious mind contains the wisdom of past ages within it. What time in history do you find most interesting and why?

26. Synthetic chemist, Berthelot claimed his most wonderful discoveries came of themselves, and did not follow a reasoned train of thought. Describe a situation in which you got an innovative idea seemingly out of nowhere.

27. Charles M. Barrows describes a situation where a friend finds a train station at the other end of town solely by following his intuition. Have you ever had a similar situation where you followed your own inner guidance, and actually got to the target destination?

28. Collier claims that the geniuses of literature, art, commerce, government, politics and invention all drew upon their subconscious minds for inspiration. Have you ever felt inspired with an idea, perhaps an invention, a piece of music or another innovation?

29. *"Our subconscious minds are vast magnets, with the power to draw from Universal Mind unlimited knowledge, unlimited power, unlimited riches."* If you accessed, unlimited knowledge, what would you be most excited about knowing? If you accessed, unlimited power, what would you be most excited about gaining power over? If you accessed, unlimited riches, what would you be most excited about owning?

30. *"Now and then through intense concentration or very active desire we do accidentally penetrate to the realm of the subconscious and register our thought upon it."* Have you ever tapped into the realm of subconscious through intense concentration or desire?

31. That which you focus on can become manifest. Often we experience this with negativity. Illness, as an example. How has the power of suggestion become manifest in you in a negative way? Positive way?

32. While your conscious mind may slumber through anesthetic or a sudden blow, your subconscious mind never does. Have you ever experienced slumber of your conscious mind? What was it like?

33. When necessary, for example when in danger, the subconscious mind pushed the conscious out of the way, while meeting and overcoming the danger. Their bodies could do things that are absolutely impossible to their ordinary conscious self. Research and write about such a scenario.

The Universal Mind:

34. Stop and contemplate the beauty and perfection of Mother Nature and the Intelligence behind Her. What do you most appreciate when you consider the wisdom of nature?

35. The author asserts that the Universal Mind is omnipotent. What does that mean to you in relation to what is possible in your life?

36. The first requisite for your mind to build prior to thought is mental image. Not everyone has the capacity to visualize. Do you have the ability to do so?

37. *"When you pray earnestly, you form a mental image of the thing that you desire and you hold it strongly in your thought. Then the Universal Intelligence…begins to work with and for you, and this is what brings about the manifestation that you desire."* What was your understanding of prayer prior to reading this description?

38. Collier asserts that few take full advantage of the power of the Universal Mind? On a scale from one to ten (1 being very little, and 10 being a great deal), rate how much you believe you take full advantage of the Universal Mind.

    1——2——3——4——5——6——7——8——9——10

39. The author often references bible quotes. Does doing so further support your appreciation and understanding of these lessons, or does it get in the way? Why?

VOLUME TWO

"And the earth was
Without form and void;
And darkness was upon
The face of the deep.
And the Spirit of God moved
Upon the face of the waters."
GENESIS 1:2.

III

The Primal Cause

This city, with all its houses, palaces, steam engines, cathedrals and huge, immeasurable traffic and tumult, what is it but a Thought, but millions of Thoughts made into one—a huge immeasurable Spirit of a Thought, embodied in brick, in iron, smoke, dust, Palaces, Parliaments, coaches, docks and the rest of it! Not a brick was made but some man had to think of the making of that brick.
—CARLYLE.

For thousands of years the riddle of the universe has been the question of causation. Did the egg come first, or the chicken? "The globe," says an Eastern proverb, "rests upon the howdah of an elephant. The elephant stands upon a tortoise, swimming in a sea of milk." But then what?

And what is life? As the Persian poet puts it—

"What without asking, hither hurried whence,
And without asking whither hurried hence?"

It has been said that every man, consciously or unconsciously, is either a materialist or an idealist. Certainly throughout the ages the schools of philosophy as well as individuals have argued and quarreled, but always human thought through one or the other of these channels "has rolled down the hill of speculation into the ocean of doubt."

The materialist, roughly speaking, declares that nothing exists but matter and the forces inherent therein.

The idealist declares that all is mind or energy, and that matter is necessarily unreal.

The time has come when people have become dissatisfied with these unceasing theories, which get them nowhere. And today, as the appreciation of a Primal Cause becomes more clearly defined, the spiritual instinct asserts itself determinedly.

"Give me a base of support," said Archimedes, "and with a lever I will move the world."

And the base of support is that all started with *mind*. In the beginning was nothing—a fire mist. Before anything could come of it there had to be an idea, a model on which to build. *Universal Mind* supplied that idea, that model. Therefore the primal cause is mind. Everything must start with an idea. Every event, every condition, everything is first an idea in the mind of someone.

Before you start to build a house, you draw up a plan of it. You make an exact blueprint of that plan, and your house takes shape in accordance with your blueprint. Every material object takes form in the same way. Mind draws the plan. Thought forms the blueprint, well drawn or badly done, as your thoughts are clear or vague. It all goes back to the one cause. The creative principle of the universe is mind, and thought is the eternal energy.

But just as the effect you get from electricity depends upon the mechanism to which the power is attached, so the effects you get from mind depend upon the way you use it. We are all of us dynamos. The power is there—unlimited power. But we've got to connect it up to something—set it some task—give it work to do—else are we no better off than the animals.

The "Seven Wonders of the World" was built by men with few of the opportunities or facilities that are available to you. They conceived these gigantic projects first in their own minds, pictured them so vividly that their subconscious minds came to their aid and enabled them to overcome obstacles that most of us would regard as insurmountable. Imagine building the Pyramids of Gizeh, enormous stone upon enormous stone, with nothing but bare hands. Imagine the labor, the sweat, the heartbreaking toil of erecting the Colossus of Rhodes, between whose legs a ship could pass! Yet men built these wonders, in a day when tools were of the crudest and machinery was undreamed of, by using the unlimited power of Mind.

Mind is creative, but it must have a model on which to work.

It must have thoughts to supply the power.

There are in Universal Mind ideas for millions of wonders far greater than the "Seven Wonders of the World." And those ideas are just as available to you as they were to the artisans of old, as they were to Michael Angelo when he built St. Peter's in Rome, as they were to the architect who conceived the Woolworth Building, or the engineer who planned the Hell Gate Bridge.

Every condition, every experience of life is the result of our mental attitude. We can *do* only what we think we can do. We can *be* only what we think we can be. We can *have* only what we think we can have. What we do, what we are, what we have, all depend upon what we think. We can never express anything that we do not first have in mind. The secret of all power, all success, all riches, is in first thinking powerful thoughts, successful thoughts, and thoughts of wealth, of supply. We must build them in our own mind first.

William James, the famous psychologist, said that the greatest discovery in a hundred years was the discovery of the power of the sub-conscious mind. It is the greatest discovery of all time. It is the discovery that man has within himself the power to control his surroundings that he is not at the mercy of chance or luck that he is the arbiter of his own fortunes that he can carve out his own destiny. He is the master of all the forces round about him. As James Allen puts it:

"Dream lofty dreams, and as you dream, so shall you become. Your vision is the promise of what you shall one day be; your Ideal is the prophecy of what you shall at last unveil."

For matter is in the ultimate but a product of thought. Even the most material scientists admit that matter is not what it appears to be. According to physics, matter (be it the human body or a log of wood—it makes no difference which) is made up of an aggregation of distinct minute particles called atoms. Considered individually, these atoms are so small that they can be seen only with the aid of a powerful microscope, if at all.

MATTER—Dream or Reality?

Until recently these atoms were supposed to be the ultimate theory regarding matter. We ourselves —and all the material world around us—were supposed to consist of these infinitesimal particles of matter, so small that they could not be seen or weighed or smelled or touched individually—but still particles of matter *and indestructible.*

Now, however, these atoms have been further analyzed, and physics tells us that they are not indestructible at all—that they are mere positive and negative buttons of force or energy called protons and electrons, without hardness, without density, without solidity, without even positive actuality. In short, they are vortices in the ether—whirling bits of energy—dynamic, never static, pulsating with life, but the life is *spiritual!* As one eminent British scientist put it—"Science now explains matter by *explaining it away!*"

And that, mind you, is what the solid table in front of you is made of, is what your house, your body, the whole world is made of—*whirling bits of energy!*

To quote the New York *Herald-Tribune* of March 11, 1926: "We used to believe that the universe was composed of an unknown number of different kinds of matter, one kind for each chemical element. The discovery of a new element had all the interest of the unexpected. It might turn out to be anything, to have any imaginable set of properties.

"That romantic prospect no longer exists. We know now that instead of many ultimate kinds of matter there are only two kinds. Both of these are really kinds of electricity. One is negative electricity, being, in fact, the tiny particle called the electron, familiar to radio fans as one of the particles vast swarms of which operate radio vacuum tubes. The other kind of electricity is positive electricity. Its ultimate particles are called protons. From these protons and electrons all of the chemical elements are built up. Iron and lead and oxygen and gold and all the others differ from one another merely in the number and arrangement of the electrons and protons, which they contain. That is the modern idea of the nature of matter. *Matter is really nothing but electricity.*"

Can you wonder then that scientists believe the time will come when mankind *through mind* can control all this energy, can be absolute master of the winds and the waves, can literally follow the Master's precept—"If ye have faith as a grain of mustard seed, ye shall say unto this mountain, Remove hence to yonder place; and it shall remove; and nothing shall be impossible unto you."

For Modern Science is coming more and more to the belief that what we call *matter is a force subject wholly to the control of mind.*

How tenuous matter really is, is perhaps best illustrated by the fact that a single violin string, tuned to the proper pitch, could start a vibration that would shake down the Brooklyn Bridge! Oceans and mountains, rocks and iron, all can be reduced to a point little short of the purely spiritual. Your body is *85* per cent water, 15 per cent ash and phosphorus! And they in turn can be dissipated into gas and vapor. Where do we go from there?

Is not the answer that, to a great degree at least, and perhaps altogether, this world round about us is one of our mind's own creating? And that we can put into it, and get from it, pretty much what we wish? You see this illustrated every day. A panorama is spread before you. To you it is a beautiful picture; to another it appears a mere collection of rocks and trees. A girl comes out to meet you. To you she is the embodiment of loveliness; to another all that grace and beauty may look drab and homely. A moonlit garden, with its fragrant odors and dew-drenched grass, may mean all that is charming to you, while to another it brings only thoughts of asthma or fever or rheumatism. A color may be green to you that to another is red. A prospect may be inviting for you that to another is rugged and hard.

To quote "Applied Psychology," by Warren Hilton:

"The same stimulus acting on different organs of sense will produce different sensations. A blow upon the eye will cause you to 'see stars'; a similar blow upon the ear will cause you to hear an explosive sound. In other words, the vibratory effect of a touch on eye or ear is the same as that of light or sound vibrations.

"The notion you may form of any object in the outer world depends solely upon what part of your brain happens to be connected with that particular nerve-end that receives an impression from the object.

"You see the sun without being able to hear it because the only nerve-ends tuned to vibrate in harmony with the ether-waves set in action by the sun are nerve-ends that are connected with the brain center devoted to sight. 'If,' says Professor James, 'we could splice the outer extremities of our optic nerves to our ears, and those of our auditory nerves to our eyes, we should hear the lightning and see the thunder, see the symphony and hear the conductor's movements.'

"In other words, the kind of impressions we receive from the world about us, the sort of mental pictures we form concerning it, in fact, the character of the outer world, the nature of the environment in which our lives are cast—all these things depend for each one of us simply upon how he happens to be put together, upon his individual mental make-up."

In short, it all comes back to the old fable of the three blind men and the elephant. To the one who caught hold of his leg, the elephant was like a tree.

To the one who felt of his side, the elephant was like a wall. To the one who seized his tail, the elephant was like a rope. The world is to each one of us the world of *his individual perceptions*.

You are like a radio receiving station. Every moment thousands of impressions are reaching you. You can tune in on whatever ones you like—on joy or sorrow, on success or failure, on optimism or fear. You can select the particular impressions that will best serve you, you can hear only what you want to hear, you can shut out all disagreeable thoughts and sounds and experiences, or you can tune in on discouragement and failure and despair.

Yours is the choice. You have within you a force against which the whole world is powerless. By using it, you can make what you will of life and of your surroundings.

"But," you will say, "objects themselves do not change. It is merely the difference in the way you look at them." Perhaps. But to a great extent, at least, we find what we look for, just as, when we turn the dial on the radio, we tune in on whatever kind of entertainment or instruction we may wish to hear. And who can say that it is not our thoughts that put it there? Who, for the matter of that, can prove that our surroundings in waking hours are not as much the creature of our minds as are our dreams? You've had dreams many a time where every object seemed just as real as when you were awake. You've felt of the objects, you've pinched yourself, yet still you were convinced that you were actually *living* those dreams. May not your waking existence be largely the creation of your own mind, just as your dream pictures are?

Many scientists believe that it is, and that in proportion as you try to put into your surroundings the good things you desire, rather than the evil ones you fear, *you will find those good things.* Certain it is that you can do this with your own body. Just as certain that many people are doing it with the good things of life. They have risen above the conception of life in which matter is the master.

Just as the most powerful forces in nature are the invisible ones—heat, light, air, electricity—so the most powerful forces of man are his invisible forces, his thought forces. And just as electricity can fuse stone and iron, so can your thought forces control your body, so can they make or mar your destiny.

The Philosopher's Charm

There was once a shrewd necromancer who told a king that he had discovered a way to make gold out of sand. Naturally the king was interested and offered him great rewards for his secret. The necromancer explained his process. It seemed quite easy, except for one thing. Not once during the operation must the king think of the word Abracadabra. If he did, the charm was broken and the gold would not come. The king tried and tried to follow the directions, but he could not keep that word Abracadabra out of his mind. And he never made the gold.

Dr. Winbigler puts the same idea in another way: "Inspiration, genius, power, are often interfered with by the conscious mind's interposing, by man's failing to recognize his power, afraid to assist himself, lacking the faith in himself necessary to stimulate the subconscious so as to arouse the genius asleep in each."

From childhood on we are assured on every hand—by scientists, by philosophers, by our religious teachers, that "ours is the earth and the fullness thereof." Beginning with the first chapter of Genesis, we are told that "God said, Let us make man in our image, after our likeness; and let them have dominion over the fish of the sea, and over the fowl of the air, and over the cattle, and over all the earth—and over every living thing that moveth upon the earth." All through the Old and the New Testament, we are repeatedly adjured to use these God-given powers. "He that believeth on me," said Jesus, "the works that I do shall he do also; and greater works than these shall he do." "If ye abide in me, and my words abide in you, ye shall ask what ye will, and it shall be done unto you." "For verily I say unto you, that whosoever shall say unto this mountain, Be thou removed, and be thou cast into the sea; and shall not doubt in his heart, but shall believe that those things which he saith shall come to pass; he shall have whatsoever he saith." "The kingdom of God is within you."

We hear all this; perhaps we even think we believe, but always, when the time comes to use these God-given talents, there is the "doubt in our heart."

Baudouin expressed it clearly: "To be ambitious for wealth and yet always expecting to be poor; to be always doubting your ability to get what you long for, is like trying to reach east by traveling west. There is no philosophy, which will help a man to succeed when he always doubts his ability to do so, and thus attracting failure.

"You will go in the direction in which you face . . .

"There is a saying that every time the sheep bleats, it loses a mouthful of hay. Every time you allow yourself to complain of your lot, to say, 'I am poor; I can never do what others do; I shall never be rich; I have not the ability that others have; I am a failure; luck is against me;' you are laying up so much trouble for yourself.

"No matter how hard you may work for success, if your thought is saturated with the fear of failure, it will kill your efforts, neutralize your endeavors, and make success impossible."

And that is responsible for all our failures. We are like the old lady who decided she wanted the hill behind her house removed. So she got down on her knees and prayed the good Lord to remove it. The next morning she got up and hurried to the window. The hill was still in its same old place. "I knew it!" she snapped. "I gave Him his chance. But I knew all the time there was nothing to this prayer business."

Neither is there, as it is ordinarily done. Prayer is not a mere asking of favors. Prayer is not a paean of praise. Rather prayer is a realization of the God-power within you—of your right of dominion over your own body, your environment, your business, your health, your prosperity. It is an understanding that you are "heir of God and co-heir with Christ." And that as such, no evil has power over you, whereas you have all power for good. And "good" means not merely holiness. Good means happiness—the happiness of everyday people. Good means everything that is good in this world of ours—comforts and pleasures and prosperity for us, health and happiness for those dependent upon us. There are no limits to "Good" except those we put upon it ourselves.

What was it made Napoleon the greatest conqueror of his day? Primarily his magnificent faith in Napoleon. He had a sublime belief in his destiny, an absolute confidence that the obstacle was not made which Napoleon could not find a way through, or over, or around. It was only when he lost that confidence, when he hesitated and vacillated for weeks between retreat and advance, that winter caught him in Moscow and ended his dreams of world empire. Fate gave him every chance first. The winter snows were a full month late in coming. But Napoleon hesitated—and was lost. It was not the snows that defeated him. It was not the Russians. It was his loss of faith in himself.

The Kingdom of Heaven

"The Kingdom of Heaven is within you." Heaven is not some far-away state—the reward of years of tribulation here. Heaven is right here—here and now! When Christ said that Heaven was within us, He meant just what He said—that the power for happiness, for good, for everything we need of life, is within each one of us.

That most of us fail to realize this Heaven—that many are sickly and suffering, that more are ground down by poverty and worry—is no fault of His. He gave us the power to overcome these evils; He stands ready and waiting to help us use it. If we fail to find the way, the fault is ours. To enjoy the Heaven that is within us, to begin here and now to live the life eternal, takes only a fuller understanding of the Power-that-is-within-us.

Even now, with the limited knowledge at our command, we can control circumstances to the point of making the world without an expression of our own world within, where the real thoughts, the real power, resides. Through this world within you can find the solution of every problem, the cause for every effect. Discover it—and all power, all possession is within your control.

For the world without is but a reflection of that world within. Your thought *creates* the conditions your mind images. Keep before your mind's eye the image of all you want to be and you will see it reflected in the world without. Think abundance, feel abundance, BELIEVE abundance, and you will find that as you think and feel and believe, abundance will manifest itself in your daily life. But let fear and worry be your mental companions, thoughts of poverty and limitation dwell in your mind, and worry and fear, limitation and poverty will be your constant companions day and night.

Your mental concept is all that matters. Its relation to matter is that of idea and form. There has got to be an idea before it can take form. As Dr. Terry Walter says:

"The impressions that enter the subconscious form indelible pictures, which are never forgotten, and whose power can change the body, mind, manner, and morals; can, in fact, revolutionize a personality.

"All during our waking hours the conscious mind, through the five senses, acts as constant feeder to the subconscious; the senses are the temporal source of supply for the content of the soul mind; therefore it is most important that we know and realize definitely and explicitly that every time we think a thought or feel an emotion, we are adding to the content of this powerful mind, good or bad, as the case may be. Life will be richer or poorer for the thoughts and deeds of today."

Your thoughts supply you with limitless energy, which will take whatever form your mind demands. The thoughts are the mold, which crystallizes this energy into good, or ill according to the form you impress upon it. You are free to choose which. But whichever you choose, the result is sure. Thoughts of wealth, of power, of success, can bring only results commensurate with your idea of them. Thoughts of poverty and lack can bring only limitation and trouble.

"A radical doctrine," you'll say, and think me wildly optimistic. Because the world has been taught for so long to think that some must be rich and some poor, that trials and tribulations are our lot. That this is at best a vale of tears.

The history of the race shows that what is considered to be the learning of one age is ignorance to the next age.

Dr. Edwin E. Slosson, Editor of *Science Service*, speaking of the popular tendency to fight against new ideas merely because they were *new*, said: "All through the history of science, we find that new ideas have to force their way into the common mind in disguise, as though they were burglars instead of benefactors of the race."

And Emerson wrote: "The virtue in most request is conformity. Self-reliance is its aversion. It loves not realities and creators, but names and customs."

In the ages to come man will look back upon the poverty and wretchedness of so many millions today, and think how foolish we were not to take advantage of the abundance all about us. Look at Nature; how profuse she is in everything. Do you suppose the Mind that imaged that profuseness ever intended you to be limited, to have to scrimp and save in order to eke out a bare existence?

There are hundreds of millions of stars in the heavens. Do you suppose the Mind, which could bring into being worlds without number in such prodigality intended to stint you of the few things necessary to your happiness?

What is money but a mere idea of mind, a token of exchange? The paper money you have in your pockets is supposed to represent so much gold or silver currency. There are billions upon billions of this paper money in circulation, yet all the gold in the world amounts to only about $8,000,000,000. Wealth is in ideas, not in money or property. You can control those ideas through mind.

Reduced to the ultimate—to the atom or to the electron—everything in this world is an idea of mind. All of it has been brought together through mind. If we can change the things we want back into mental images, we can multiply them as often as we like, possessing all that we like.

"To Him That Hath"—

Take as an example the science of numbers. Suppose all numbers were of metal—that it was against the law to write figures for ourselves. Every time you wanted to do a sum in arithmetic you'd have to provide yourself with a supply of numbers, arrange them in their proper order, work out your problems with them. If your problems were too abstruse you might run out of numbers, have to borrow some from your neighbor or from the bank.

"How ridiculous," you say. "Figures are not things; they are mere ideas, and we can add them or divide them or multiply them or subtract them as often as we like. Anybody can have all the figures he wants."

To be sure he can. And when you get to look upon money in the same way, you will have all the money you want.

"To him that hath shall be given, and from him that hath not shall be taken away even that which he hath." To him that hath the right idea everything shall be given, and from him who hath not that right idea shall be taken away everything he hath.

Thought externalizes itself. What we are depends entirely upon the images we hold before our mind's eye. Every time we think, we start a chain of causes, which will create conditions similar to the thoughts, which originated it. Every thought we hold in our consciousness for any length of time becomes impressed upon our subconscious mind and creates a pattern, which the mind weaves into our life or environment.

All power is from within and is therefore under our own control. When you can direct your thought processes, you can consciously apply them to any condition, for all that comes to us from the world without is what we've already imaged in the world within.

Do you want more money? Sit you down now quietly and realize that money is merely an idea. That your mind is possessed of unlimited ideas. That being part of Universal Mind, there is no such thing as limitation or lack. That somewhere, somehow, the ideas that shall bring you all the money you need for any right purpose are available for you. That you have but to put it up to your subconscious mind to find these ideas.

Realize that—*believe* it—and your need will be met. "What things so ever ye desire, when ye pray, believe that ye receive it and ye shall have it." Don't forget that *"believe that ye receive it."* This it is that images the thing you want on your subconscious mind. And this it is that brings it to you. Once you can image the belief clearly on your subconscious mind, "whatsoever it is that ye ask for . . . ye shall have it."

For the source of all good, of everything you wish for, is the Universal Mind, and you can reach it only through the subconscious.

And Universal Mind will be to you whatever you believe it to be—the kind and loving Father whom Jesus pictured, always looking out for the well-being of his children—or the dread Judge that so many dogmatists would have us think.

When a man realizes that his mind is part of Universal Mind, when he realizes that he has only to take any right aspiration to this Universal Mind to see it realized, he loses all sense of worry and fear. He learns to dominate instead of to cringe. He rises to meet every situation, secure in the knowledge that everything necessary to the solution of any problem is in Mind, and that he has but to take his problem to Universal Mind to have it correctly answered.

For if you take a drop of water from the ocean, you know that it has the same properties as all the rest of the water in the ocean, the same percentage of sodium chloride. The only difference between it and the ocean is in volume. If you take a spark of electricity, you know that it has the same properties as the thunderbolt, the same power that moves trains or runs giant machines in factories. Again the only difference is in volume. It is the same with your mind and Universal Mind. The only difference between them is in volume. Your mind has the same properties as the Universal Mind, the same creative genius, the same power over all the earth, the same access to all knowledge. Know this, believe it, use it, and "yours is the earth and the fullness thereof." In the exact proportion that you believe yourself to be part of Universal Mind, sharing in its all-power, in that proportion can you demonstrate the mastery over your own body and over the world about you?

All growth, all supply is from the world-within. If you would have power, if you would have wealth, you have but to image it on this world within, on your subconscious mind, through belief and understanding.

If you would remove discord, you have but to remove the wrong images—images of ill health, of worry and trouble from within. The trouble with most of us is that we live entirely in the world without. We have no knowledge of that inner world which is responsible for all the conditions we meet and all the experiences we have. We have no conception of "the Father that is within us."

The inner world promises us life and health, prosperity and happiness—dominion over all the earth. It promises peace and perfection for its entire offspring. It gives you the right way and the adequate way to accomplish any normal purpose. Business, labor, professions, exist primarily in thought. And the outcome of your labors in them is regulated by thought. Consider the difference, then, in this outcome if you have at your command only the limited capacity of your conscious mind, compared with the boundless energy of the subconscious and the Universal Mind. "Thought, not money, is the real business capital," says Harvey S. Firestone, "and if you know absolutely that what you are doing is right, then you are bound to accomplish it in due season.

Thought is a dynamic energy with the power to bring its object out from the invisible substance all about us. Matter is inert, unintelligent. Thought can shape and control. Every form in which matter is today is but the expression of some thought, some desire, and some idea.

You have a mind. You can originate thought. And thoughts are creative. Therefore you can create for yourself that which you desire. Once you realize this you are taking a long step toward success in whatever undertaking you have in mind.

More than half the prophecies in the Scriptures refer to the time when man shall possess the earth, when tears and sorrow shall be unknown, and peace and plenty shall be everywhere. That time will come. It is nearer than most people think possible. You are helping it along. Every man who is honestly trying to use the power of mind in the right way is doing his part in the great cause. For it is only through Mind that peace and plenty can be gained. The earth is laden with treasures as yet undiscovered. But they are every one of them known to Universal Mind, for it was Universal Mind that first imaged them there. And as part of Universal Mind, they can be known to you.

How else did the Prophets of old foretell, thousands of years ago, the aeroplane, the cannon, the radio? What was the genius that enabled Ezekiel to argue from his potter's wheel, his water wheel and the stroke of the lightning to an airplane, with its wheels within wheels, driven by electricity and guided by man? How are we to explain the descriptions of artillery in the Apocalypse and the astonishing declaration in the Gospels that the utterances of the chamber would be broadcast from the housetops?

"To the Manner Born"

Few of us have any idea of our mental powers. The old idea was that man must take this world as he found it. He'd been born into a certain position in life, and to try to rise above his fellows was not only the height of bad taste, but sacrilegious as well. An all-wise Providence had decreed by birth the position a child should occupy in the web of organized society. For him to be discontented with his lot, for him to attempt to raise himself to a higher level, was tantamount to tempting Providence. The gates of Hell yawned wide for such scatterbrains, who were lucky if in this life they incurred nothing worse than the ribald scorn of their associates.

That is the system that produced aristocracy and feudalism. That is the system that feudalism and aristocracy strove to perpetuate.

The new idea—the basis of all democracies—is that man is not bound by any system, that he need not accept the world as he finds it. He can remake the world to his own ideas. It is merely the raw material. He can make what he wills of it.

It is this new idea that is responsible for all our inventions, all our progress. Man is satisfied with nothing. He is constantly remaking his world. And now more than ever will this be true, for psychology teaches us that each one has within himself the power to become what he wills.

Learn to control your thought. Learn to image upon your mind only the things you want to see reflected there.

You will never improve yourself by dwelling upon the drawbacks of your neighbors. You will never attain perfect health and strength by thinking of weakness or disease. No man ever made a perfect score by watching his rival's target. You have got to think strength, think health, think riches. To paraphrase Pascal—"Our achievements today are but the sum of our thoughts of yesterday."

For thought is energy. Mental images are concentrated energy. And energy concentrated on any definite purpose becomes power. To those who perceive the nature and transcendency of force, all physical power sinks into insignificance.

What is imagination but a form of thought? Yet it is the instrument by which all the inventors and discoverers have opened the way to new worlds. Those who grasp this force, be their state ever so humble, their natural gifts ever so insignificant, becomes our leading men. They are our governors and supreme lawgivers, the guides of the drifting host, which follows them as by an irrevocable decree. To quote Glenn Clark in the *Atlantic Monthly*, "Whatever we have of civilization is their work, theirs alone. If progress was made they made it. If spiritual facts were discerned, they discerned them. If justice and order were put in place of insolence and chaos, they wrought the change. Never is progress achieved by the masses. Creation ever remains the task of the individual."

Our railroads, our telephones, our automobiles, our libraries, our newspapers, our thousands of other conveniences, comforts and necessities are due to the creative genius of but two per cent of our population.

And the same two per cent own a great percentage of the wealth of the country. The question arises, who are they? What are they? The sons of the rich? College men? No—few of them had any early advantages. Many of them have never seen the inside of a college. It was grim necessity that drove them, and somehow, some way, they found a method of drawing upon their Genie-of-the-Mind, and through that inner force they have reached success.

You don't need to stumble and grope. You can call upon your inner forces at will. There are three steps necessary:

First, to realize that you have the power; Second, to know what you want.

Third, to center your thought upon it with singleness of purpose.

To accomplish these steps takes only a fuller understanding of the Power-that-is-within-you.

But what is this power? Where should you go to locate it? Is it a thing, a place, an object? Has it bounds, form or material shape? No! Then how shall you go about finding it?

If you have begun to *realize* that there is a power within you, if you have begun to arouse in your conscious mind the ambition and desire to use this power—you have started in the pathway of wisdom. If you are willing to go forward, to endure the mental discipline of mastering this method, nothing in the world can hinder you or keep you from overcoming every obstacle.

Begin at once, today, to use what you have learned. All growth comes from practice. All the forces of life are active—peace—joy—power. The unused talent decays. Open the door—"Behold I stand at the door and knock; if ANY MAN hear my voice and open the door, I will come in to him, and will sup with him and he with me."

So let us make use of this dynamo, which is *you*. What is going to start it working? Your *Faith*, the faith that is begotten of understanding. Faith is the impulsion, the propulsion of this power within. Faith is the confidence, the assurance, the enforcing truth, the knowing that the right idea of life will bring you into the reality of existence and the manifestation of the All power.

All cause is in Mind—and Mind is everywhere. All the knowledge there is, all the wisdom there is, all the power there is, is all about you—no matter where you may be. Your Mind is part of it. You have access to it. If you fail to avail yourself of it, you have no one to blame but yourself. For, as the drop of water in the ocean shares in all the properties of the rest of the ocean water so you share in that all-power, all-wisdom of Mind. If you have been sick and ailing, if poverty and hardship have been your lot, don't blame it on "fate." Blame yourself. "Yours is the earth and everything that's in it." But you've got to *take* it. The power is there—but *you* must *use* it. It is round about you like the air you breathe. You don't expect others to do your breathing for you. Neither can you expect them to use your Mind for you. Universal Intelligence is not only the mind of the Creator of the universe, but it is also the mind of MAN, *your* intelligence, *your* mind. "Let this mind be in you, which was also in Christ Jesus!"

So start today by KNOWING that you can do anything you wish to do, have anything you wish to have, be anything you wish to be. The rest will follow.

"Ye shall ask what ye will and it shall be done unto you."

STUDY GUIDE

III *The Primal Cause*

1. In Carlyle's quote it is stated *"Not a brick was made but some man had to think of the making of that brick."* Have you ever considered the reality that there had to be intention beyond every grain of sand or every brick laid on this earth? How does this reality make you feel?

2. It is said that every man is either a materialist or idealist. How would you label yourself? Why?

3. Provide a brief description of Primal Cause in your own words.

4. If mind is the primal cause, then why do so many metaphysical seekers see it as the enemy to the raising of our consciousness, something to transcend?

5. The "Seven Wonders of the World" were all built with nothing but the bare hands of men. What would you consider the three most powerful man-made modern-day Wonders of the World? Would they be structures, or perhaps in the realm of information technology?

   If thoughts supply the power, then focus on your thought throughout the past day. What have they been focusing most of their attention upon?

6. If you can *do* what you think you can, what limitations have you placed on yourself?

7. If you can *be* what you think you can, what restrictions have you put upon yourself?

8. If you can *have* what you think you can, what blocks have you placed upon your ability to have what you desire?

9. William James states that the greatest discovery of all time was the human mind. Do you concur? Why or why not?

10. James Allen stated, *"Dream lofty dreams, and as you dream, so shall you become. Your vision is the promise of what you shall one day be; your Ideal is the prophecy of what you shall at last unveil."* Describe in as much detail as possible your ideal day.

MATTER—Dream or Reality?

11. Atoms are described as *"Vortices of ether . . . pulsating with life, but the life is spiritual . . . whirling bits of energy."* If this is the case, then "spiritually or energetically" how do you account for some items as being apparently solid and dense, while other liquid or gas?

12. This book was written close to a century ago, and science has progressed since. The author talks about the possibility of mind control. While it is still not widely accepted, there is more information about it. Do you believe in mind control? Have you seen evidence of it in your life?

13. Our responses to stimulus vary, as they are subjective and dependent upon *"that particular nerve-end that receives an impression from the object."* An example provided is one's reaction to a moonlit garden. While one individual may find peace and beauty in it, another may experience allergic reactions to it. Provide three examples in your life where you find yourself in aversion towards something that others might find pleasant and visa-versa.

14. Do you belief you mental make-up to be more optimistic or pessimistic? Why?

15. The author poses a suggestion that our surroundings when we awaken could as much be the creation of our minds as our dreams are. What are your thoughts on this suggestion?

16. Have you experienced dreams that seemed absolutely vivid and real? Do you believe your dream state to be just as real as your waking? Why or why not?

The Philosopher's Charm

17. Inspiration and genius are interfered with by your conscious mind's doubt and inability to recognize your power. Provide an example of how you conscious sabotaged a potential opportunity with your doubt.

18. What thoughts and feelings come to mind when you hear the phrase *"the Kingdom of God is within you"*? Do you believe this to be true? If not, why not?

19. The author instructs that every time you complain, you are creating negativity and trouble for yourself. Do you believe this to absolutely true? Do you believe every thought that comes your way has the power to sway your life? Please explain your point of view on this.

20. *"No matter how hard you may work for success, if your thought is saturated with the fear of failure, it will kill your efforts, neutralize your endeavors, and make success impossible."* Do you believe you have fear of failure, or perhaps fear of success? What is the difference?

21. *"Prayer is not a mere asking of favors . . . Rather prayer is a realization of the God-power within you—of your right of domination over your own body, your environment, your business, your health, your prosperity."* Do you pray with this knowing, or do you ask the universe for favors? How do you cultivate this realization? Do you believe it to be a grace or something you can develop within yourself?

22. Do you believe that evil has power over you? Why or why not?

23. According to Collier, Napoleon's faith in himself created his success. He claims that ultimately his defeat come from his loss of faith in himself. Reflect on your life. Was

there a circumstance like Napoleon's where you believed in yourself and experience victory, only to undermine yourself with a lack of confidence? Write out the scenario, then see it again in your mind's eye, as if you were completely successful. How do you feel after re-experiencing it with a positive outcome?

The Kingdom of Heaven

24. The author emphasizes that Heaven is right here within you. Do you believe this to be true? If so, how do you experience it? If not, why not?

25. What percentage of your day do you focus on fear and worry, as compared to joy and abundance?

26. If your thoughts supply your limitless energy, then what do you do when you note yourself having a negative thought?

27. If you judge yourself when you think a negative thought, are you not adding to the negativity? Is it possible for you to simply witness the negativity, then focus on self-love and self-care?

28. The author references the power of your thoughts as *"A radical doctrine"*. While it was when the book was originally written, it no longer is. How do you surmise that the Law of Attraction became more popularized?

29. Emerson wrote, *"The virtue in most request is conformity. Self-reliance is its aversion. It loves not realities and creator, but names and customs."* Why do you think the masses are still skeptical of the realization that we each create our reality?

30. Collier makes a powerful argument that the Mind that created a natural world of abundance would not deny us the happiness that is our birthright. If you consider it, all in nature grows in abundance, whether a mold or a blade of grass. List three forces of nature that you see as abundant.

31. The author references money as *"a mere idea of mind, a token of exchange"*. If you are comfortable bartering a skill or item for someone else's, can you give money that same reference point in your mind? Why or why not?

32. Collier asserts that wealth is an idea that you can control through your mind. What small step can you take to shift your perception of money, so that is it more attainable?

"To Him That Hath"—

33. Collier asserts that you can view money as you would number figures. *"Anybody can have all the figures he wants."* Do you think that the "unattainable" attitude that so many have around money is the reason for the sense of lack so many suffer from? Is this the case with you?

34. *"Thought externalizes itself . . . Every time we think, we start a chain of causes, which will create conditions similar to the thoughts, which originated it."* Experiment with the following exercise. Every time you think that you lack what you desire, take at least one minute, and imagine yourself having it in abundance. Track your progress for at least a week as you do this exercise.

35. The author asserts that every thought you have becomes a pattern which you weave into your life or environment. When you were a child, were you raised in an environment that was supportive and positive? On a scale from one to ten (1 being very little, and 10 being a great deal), rate how much supportive your childhood environment was.

    1——2——3——4——5——6——7——8——9——10

36. What specific action step can you take to rid your mind of limitation and lack? Write about it and being practicing it immediately.

37. Can you see the image of the perfect home, car, partner, family and career for yourself? Take at least 3 minutes and see the ideal within your mind's eye.

38. Many were raised with the belief that there is a punitive, angry God that created and oversees the world. Have you overcome this belief? If so, how? If not, what might you do to shift it?

39. All you need do is take your problem to the Universal Mind to have it correctly answered. Do frequently do you take your issues to the Universal Mind for resolution? Try to take your daily challenges to that source, and record any shifts you encounter.

40. Likening your mind to a spark of electricity and the Universal Mind to a thunder bolt, the only difference is volume. You have access to the same power and knowledge as the Creator. If you absolutely had faith that you have access to all knowledge and power, in which area of your life would you most wish to apply it?

41. According to Collier, all you need do is remove discord and the wrong images from your mind. The tricky thing is that they may be so ingrained that you do not clearly see them for the blocks that they are. Set an intention to become conscious of more of them, asking the Universal Mind to reveal them to you. Note any insights you gain by doing this exercise.

42. Focusing solely on the outer world around you further obstructs you from manifesting all that you desire. What small action step can you take daily to check in with your inner self? Write it down and practice it daily.

43. Collier states, *"More than half the prophecies in the Scriptures refer to the time when man shall possess the earth, when tears and sorrow shall be unknown, and peace and plenty shall be everywhere. That time will come. It is nearer than most people think possible."* Do you believe this statement to be true? Do you believe you will experience a substantial shift during your lifetime? Why or why not?

44. If you don't believe a major shift is upon us, are you basing your belief on the current external conditions in your world, or your inner world?

"To the Manner Born"

45. Collier reminds us that in earlier times, trying to move beyond your birth status was considered temping Providence, and worthy of being sent to Hell. While you are currently not bound by any such system, do you believe there may be residue of the old state system within your mind or body?

46. You are encouraged to *"Learn to control your thought"*. Do you believe it is possible to control your thoughts? Do they not simply appear within your mind? If so, how can you control them?

47. Concentrated energy becomes power. On a scale from one to ten (1 being very little, and 10 being a great deal), rate how much potent is your ability to concentrate?

    1——2——3——4——5——6——7——8——9——10

48. Collier asserts that progress is never achieved by the masses. It remains the task of the individual, and only 2 percent of the population are successful achievers. Do you think you have the potential to be one of those 2 percent? Why or why not?

49. To call upon your inner forces, you need to follow these three steps:
    1. Realize that you have the power.
    2. Know what you want.
    3. Center your thought upon it with singleness of purpose.

    Do you believe you have the power? Do you know what you want? Can you focus upon your desire with a singleness of purpose?

50. It is emphasized that you need mental discipline to harness your mental power. On a scale from one to ten (1 being very little, and 10 being a great deal), rate how much mental discipline you believe you currently have.

51. It is suggested that you begin by practicing once a day. Faith is key to your success. Do you have faith that you are ready to take action on using your Mind to transform your life at this time? Why or why not?

52. You need to shame blame from fate or being victim of others, to yourself. *"Start today by KNOWING that you can do anything you wish to do, have anything you wish to have, be anything you wish to be. The rest will follow."* Write a list of issues that have arisen for which you blame fate or others. Then with each, write a statement that reflects your personal ownership and responsibility for the situation.

IV

Desire—The First Law of Gain

"Ah, Love! Could Thou and I with Fate conspire
To grasp this sorry Scheme of Things entire,
Would we not shatter it to bits—and then
Re-mold it nearer to the Heart's Desire!"
—THE RUBAIYAT OF OMAR KHAYYAM.

If YOU had a fairy-wishing ring, what one thing would you wish for? Wealth? Honor? Fame? Love? What one thing do you desire above everything else in life? Whatever it is, you can have it. Whatever you desire wholeheartedly, with singleness of purpose—you can have. But the first and all-important essential is to know what this one thing is. Before you can win your heart's desire, you've got to get clearly fixed in your mind's eye what it is that you want.

It may sound paradoxical, but few people do know what they want. Most of them struggle along in a vague sort of way, hoping—like Micawber—for something to turn up. They are so taken up with the struggle that they have forgotten—if they ever knew—what it is they are struggling for. They are like a drowning man—they use up many times the energy it would take to get them somewhere, but they fritter it away in aimless struggles—without thought, without direction, exhausting themselves, while getting nowhere.

You've got to know what you want before you stand much chance of getting it. You have an unfailing "Messenger to Garcia" in that Genie-of-your Mind—but YOU have got to formulate the message. Aladdin would have stood a poor chance of getting anything from his Genie if he had not had clearly in mind the things he wanted the Genie to get.

In the realm of mind, the realm in which is all practical power, you can possess what you want at once. You have but to claim it, to visualize it, to bring it into actuality—and it is yours for the taking. For the Genie-of-your-Mind can give you power over circumstances. Health, happiness and prosperity. And all you need to put it to work is an earnest, intense desire.

Sounds too good to be true? Well, let us go back for a moment to the start. You are infected with that "divine dissatisfaction with things as they are" which has been responsible for all the great accomplishments of this world—else you would not have gotten thus far in this book. Your heart is hungering for something better. "Blessed are they which do hunger and thirst after righteousness (right-wise ness) for they shall be filled." You are tired of the worry and grind, tired of the deadly dull routine and daily tasks that lead nowhere. Tired of all the petty little ills and ailments that have come to seem the lot of man here on earth.

Always there is something within you urging you on to bigger things, giving you no peace, no rest, no chance to be lazy. It is the same "something" that drove Columbus across the ocean; that drove Hannibal across the Alps; that drove Edison onward and upward from a train boy to the inventive wizard of the century; that drove Henry Ford from a poor mechanic at forty to probably the richest man in the world at sixty.

This "something" within you keeps telling you that you can do anything you want to do, be anything you want to be, have anything you want to have—and you have a sneaking suspicion that it may be right.

That "something" within you is your subconscious self, your part of Universal Mind, your Genie-of-the-brain. Men call it ambition, and "Lucky is the man," says Arthur Brisbane, "whom the Demon of Ambition harnesses and drives through life. This wonderful little coachman is the champion driver of the entire world and of all history.

"Lucky you, if he is *your* driver. "He will keep you going until you do something worthwhile—working, running and moving ahead.

"And that is how a real man ought to be driven.

"This is the little Demon that works in men's brains, that makes the blood tingle at the thought of achievement and that makes the face flush and grow white at the thought of failure.

"Every one of us has this Demon for a driver, IN YOUTH AT LEAST.

"Unfortunately the majority of us he gives up as very poor, hopeless things, not worth driving, by the time we reach twenty-five or thirty.

"How many men look back to their teens, when they were harnessed to the wagon of life with Ambition for a driver? When they could not wait for the years to pass and for opportunity to come?

"It is the duty of ambition to drive, and it is your duty to *keep Ambition alive and driving.*

"If you are doing nothing, if there is no driving, no hurrying, no working, *you may count upon it that there will be no results. Nothing much worthwhile in the years to come.*

"Those that are destined to be the big men twenty years from now, when the majority of us will be nobodies *are those whom this demon is driving relentlessly, remorselessly, through the hot weather and the cold weather, through early hours and late hours.*

"Lucky YOU if you are in harness and driven by the Demon of Ambition."

Suppose you *have* had disappointments, disillusionments along the way. Suppose the fine point of your ambition has become blunted. Remember, there is no obstacle that there is not some way around, or over, or through—and if you will depend less upon the 10 per cent of your abilities that reside in your conscious mind, and leave more to the 90 per cent that constitutes your subconscious, you can overcome all obstacles. Remember this—there is no condition so hopeless, no life so far gone, that mind cannot redeem it.

Every untoward condition is merely *a lack* of something. Darkness, you know, is not real. It is merely a lack of light. Turn on the light and the darkness will be seen to be nothing. It vanishes instantly. In the same way poverty is simply a lack of necessary supply. Find the avenue of supply and your poverty vanishes. Sickness is merely the absence of health. If you are in perfect health, sickness cannot hurt you. Doctors and nurses go about at will among the sick without fear—and suffer as a rule far less from sickness than does the average man or woman.

So there is nothing you have to *overcome*. You merely have to *acquire* something. And always Mind can show you the way. You can obtain from Mind anything you want, if you will learn how to do it. "I think we can rest assured that one can do and be practically what he desires to be," says Farnsworth in "Practical Psychology." And psychologists all over the world have put the same thought in a thousand different ways.

"It is not will, but desire," says Charles W. Mears, "that rules the world." "But," you will say, "I have had plenty of desires all my life. I've always wanted to be rich. How do you account for the difference between my wealth and position and power and that of the rich men all around me?"

The Magic Secret

The answer is simply that you have never focused your desires into one great dominating desire. You have a host of mild desires. You mildly wish you were rich, you wish you had a position of responsibility and influence; you wish you could travel at will. The wishes are so many and varied that they conflict with each other and you get nowhere in particular. You lack one *intense* desire, to the accomplishment of which you are willing to subordinate everything else.

Do you know how Napoleon so frequently won battles in the face of a numerically superior foe? By concentrating his men at the actual *point of contact!* His artillery was often greatly outnumbered, but it accomplished far more than the enemy's because instead of scattering his fire, he *concentrated it all on the point of attack!*

The time you put in aimlessly dreaming and wishing would accomplish marvels if it were concentrated on one definite object. If you have ever taken a magnifying glass and let the sun's rays play through it on some object, you know that as long as the rays were scattered they accomplished nothing. But focus them on one tiny spot and see how quickly they start something.

It is the same way with your mind. You've got to concentrate *on one idea at a time.*

"But how can I learn to concentrate?" many people write me. Concentration is not a thing to be learned. It is merely a thing to do. You concentrate whenever you become sufficiently interested in anything. Get so interested in a ball game that you jump up and down on your hat, slap a man you have never seen before on the back, embrace your nearest neighbor—*that* is concentration. Become so absorbed in a thrilling play or movie that you no longer realize the orchestra is playing or there are people around you—*that* is concentration.

And that is all concentration ever is—getting so interested in some one thing that you pay no attention to anything else that is going on around you.

If you want a thing badly enough, you need have no worry about your ability to concentrate on it. Your thoughts will just naturally center on it like bees on honey.

Hold in your mind the thing you most desire. Affirm it. Believe it to be an existing fact. Let me quote again the words of the Master, because there's nothing more important to remember in this whole book. "Therefore I say unto you, what things so ever ye desire, when ye pray, *believe that ye receive them* and ye shall have them."

And again I say, the most important part is the *"believe that ye receive them."* Your subconscious mind is exceedingly amenable to suggestion. If you can truly believe that you have received something, can impress that belief upon your subconscious mind, depend upon it, it will see that you have it. For being a part of Universal Mind, it shares that Universal Mind's all power. "The Father that is within me, He doeth the works." Your mind will respond to your desire in the exact proportion in which you believe. "As thy faith is, so be it unto thee."

The people who live in beautiful homes, who have plenty to spend, who travel about in yachts and fine cars, are for the most part people who started out to accomplish *some one definite thing*. They had one clear goal in mind, and everything they did centered on that goal.

Most men just jog along in a rut, going through the same old routine day after day, eking out a bare livelihood, with no definite desire other than the vague hope that fortune will some day drop in their lap. Fortune doesn't often play such pranks. And a rut, you know, differs from a grave only in depth. A life such as that is no better than the animals live. Work all day for money to buy bread, to give you strength to work all the next day to buy more bread. There is nothing to it but the daily search for food and sustenance. No time for aught but worry and struggle. No hope of anything but the surcease of sorrow in death.

You can have anything you want—if you want it badly enough. You can be anything you want to be, have anything you desire, accomplish anything you set out to accomplish—if you will hold to that desire with singleness of purpose; if you will understand and BELIEVE in your own powers to accomplish.

What is it that you wish in life? Is it health? In the chapter on health I will show you that you can be radiantly well—without drugs, without tedious exercises. It matters not if you are crippled or bedridden or infirm. Your body rebuilds itself entirely every eleven months. You can start now rebuilding along perfect lines.

Is it wealth you wish? In the chapter on success I will show you how you can increase your income, how you can forge rapidly ahead in your chosen business or profession.

Is it happiness you ask for? Follow the rules herein laid down and you will change your whole outlook on life. Doubts and uncertainty will vanish, to be followed by calm assurance and abiding peace. You will possess the things your heart desires. You will have love and companionship. You will win to contentment and happiness.

But desire must be impressed upon the subconscious before it can be accomplished. Merely conscious desire seldom gets you anything. It is like the daydreams that pass through your mind. Your desire must be visualized, must be persisted in, must be concentrated upon, and must be impressed upon your subconscious mind. Don't bother about the means for accomplishing your desire—you can safely leave that to your subconscious mind. It knows how to do a great many things besides building and repairing your body. If you can visualize the thing you want, if you can impress upon your subconscious mind the *belief that you have it*, you can safely leave to it the finding of the means of getting it. Trust the Universal Mind to show the way.

The mind that provided everything in such profusion must joy in seeing us take advantage of that profusion. "For herein is the Father glorified—that ye bear much fruit."

You do not have to wait until tomorrow, or next year, or the next world, for happiness. You do not have to die to be saved. "The Kingdom of Heaven is within you." That does not mean that it is up in the heavens or on some star or in the next world. It means *here* and *now!* All the possibilities of happiness are always here and always available.

At the open door of every man's life there lies this pearl of great price—the understanding of man's dominion over the earth. With that understanding and conviction you can do everything, which lies before you to do, and you can do it to the satisfaction of everyone and the well-being of yourself. God and good are synonymous. And God-good-is absent only to those who believe He is absent.

Find your desire, impress it upon your thought, and you have opened the door for opportunity. And remember, in this new heaven and new earth, which I am trying to show you, *the door of opportunity is never closed.* As a matter of fact, you constantly have *all that you will take.* So keep yourself in a state of receptivity. It is your business to receive abundantly and perpetually. The law of opportunity enforces its continuance and availability. "Every good gift and every perfect gift is from above and cometh down from the Father of light, with whom is *no variableness, neither shadow of turning."*

Infinite Mind saith to every man, "Come ye to the open fountain." The understanding of the law of life will remedy every discord, giving "Beauty for ashes, the oil of joy for mourning, and the garment of praise for the spirit of heaviness.

Believe that you share in that goodness and bounty. Act the part you wish to play in this life. Act healthy, act prosperous, and act happy. Make such a showing with what you have that you will carry the conviction to your subconscious mind that all good and perfect gifts ARE yours. Register health, prosperity and happiness on your inner mind and some fine morning soon you will wake to find that *you are* healthy, prosperous and happy, that you *have* your dearest wish in life.

The Soul's Sincere Desire

Do you know what prayer is? Just an earnest desire that we take to God—to Universal Mind—for fulfillment. As Montgomery puts it—"Prayer is the soul's *sincere desire,* uttered or unexpressed." It is our Heart's Desire. At least, the only prayer that is worth anything is the prayer that asks for our real desires. That kind of prayer is heard. That kind of prayer is answered.

Mere lip prayers get you nowhere. It doesn't matter what your lips may say. The thing that counts is what your heart desires, what your mind images on your subconscious thought, and through it on Universal Mind. "Thou, when thou prayest, be not as the hypocrites are; for they love to pray standing in the synagogue and at the corners of the streets, that they may be seen of men. Verily I say unto you, they have their reward."

What was it these hypocrites that Jesus speaks of really wanted? "To be seen of men." And their prayers were answered. Their sincere desire was granted. They were seen of men. "They have their reward." But as for what their lips were saying, neither God nor they paid any attention to it.

"Thou, when thou prayest enter into thy closet, and when thou hast shut the door, pray to thy Father which is in secret, and thy Father which seeth in secret, shall reward thee openly." Go where you can be alone, where you can concentrate your thoughts on your one innermost sincere desire, where you can impress that desire upon your subconscious mind without distraction, and so reach the Universal Mind (the Father of all things).

But even sincere desire is not enough by itself. There must be BELIEF, too. "What things so ever ye desire, when ye pray, believe that ye receive them and ye shall have them." You must realize God's ability to give you every good thing. You must believe in his readiness to do it. Model your thoughts after the Psalmists of old. They first asked for that which they wanted, then killed all doubts and fears by affirming God's power and His willingness to grant their prayers. Read any of the Psalms and you will see what I mean. So when you pray, ask for the things that you want. Then affirm God's readiness and His Power to grant your prayer. Glenn Clark, in "The Soul's Sincere Desire," gives some wonderfully helpful suggestions along these lines. To quote him:

"For money troubles, realize: There is no want in Heaven, and affirm:

"Our Heavenly Father, we know that thy Love is as infinite as the sky is infinite, and Thy Ways of manifesting that love are as unaccountable as the stars of the heavens.

"Thy Power is greater than man's horizon, and Thy Ways of manifesting that Power are more numerous than the sands of the sea.

"As Thou keepest the stars in their courses, so shalt Thou guide our steps in perfect harmony, without clash or discord of any kind, if we keep our trust in Thee. For we know Thou wilt keep him in perfect peace whose mind is stayed on Thee, because he trusteth in Thee. We know that, if we acknowledge Thee in all our ways, Thou wilt direct our paths. For Thou art the God of Love, Giver of every good and perfect gift, and there is none beside Thee. Thou art omnipotent, omniscient, and omnipresent, in all, through all, and over all, the only God. And Thine is the Kingdom, and the Power, and the Glory, forever, Amen.

"For aid in thinking or writing, realize: There is no lack of ideas, and affirm:

"Thy wisdom is greater than all hidden treasures, and yet as instantly available for our needs as the very ground beneath our feet."

"For happiness: There is no unhappiness in Heaven, so affirm:

"Thy joy is brighter than the sun at noonday and Thy Ways of expressing that Joy as countless as the sunbeams that shine upon our path."

This is the kind of prayer the Psalmists of old had recourse to in their hours of trouble—this is the kind of prayer that will bring you every good and perfect gift.

Make no mistake about this—*prayer is effective.* It *can* do anything. It doesn't matter how trivial your desires may be—if it is RIGHT for you to have them, it is RIGHT for you to pray for them.

According to a United Press dispatch of May 3, 1926:

"Prayer belongs to the football field as much as to the pulpit, and a praying team stands a good chance of getting there," Tim Lowry, Northwestern University football star, told a large church audience here.

"Just before the Indiana-Northwestern game last year," Tim said. 'We worried a great deal about the outcome. Then we saw that bunch of big husky Indiana players coming toward us and we knew something had to be done quickly.

"'Fellows,' I said, 'I believe in prayer and we better pray.' We did and won a great victory.

"When the next game came, every fellow prayed again.

"You don't need to think that churches have a copyright on prayer."

In "Prayer as a Force," A. Maude Royden compares the man who trusts his desires to prayer with the swimmer who trusts himself to the water:

"Let me give you a very simple figure which I think may perhaps convey my meaning. If you are trying to swim you must believe that the sea is going to keep you afloat. You must give yourself to the sea. There is the ocean and there are you in it, and I say to you, 'According to your faith you will be able to swim!' I know perfectly well that it is literally according to your faith. A person who has just enough confidence in the sea and in himself to give one little hop from the ground will certainly find that the water will lift him but not very much; he will come down again. Persons who have enough confidence really to start swimming but no more, will not swim very far, because their confidence is so very small and they swim with such rapid strokes, and they hold their breath to such an extent, that by and by they collapse; they swim five or six, or twelve or fourteen strokes, but they do not get very far, through lack of confidence.

"Persons who know with assurance that the sea will carry them if they do certain things, will swim quite calmly, serenely, happily, and will not mind if the water goes right over them. 'Oh,' you say, 'that person is doing the whole thing!' *He can't do it without the sea!* You might hypnotize people into faith; you might say, 'You are now in the ocean; swim off the edge of this precipice' (which is really a cliff). You might make them do it, they might have implicit faith in you, you might hypnotize them into thinking they were swimming; but if they swam off the edge of the cliff they would fall. You can't swim without the sea! I might say to you, 'It lies with you whether you swim or not, according to your faith be it unto you'; but if the sea is not there you can't swim. That is exactly what I feel about God. 'According to your faith be it unto you.' Yes, certainly, if you try to swim in that ocean which is the love of God your faith will be rewarded, and according to your faith it will be to you. In exact proportion to your faith you will find the answer, like a scientific law. There is not one atom of faith you put in God that will not receive its answer."

But remember: you would not plant a valuable seed in your garden, and then, a day or a week later, go out and dig it up to see if it were sprouting. On the contrary, you would nourish it each morning with water. It is the same with your prayers. Don't plant the seed of your desire in your subconscious mind and then go out the next morning and tear it up with doubts and fears. Nourish it by holding in thought the thing you desire, by believing in it, visualizing it, SEEING it as an accomplished fact.

If you ask for my own formula for successful prayer, I would say—

1st. Center your thoughts on the thing that you want.

Visualize it. Make a mental image of it. You are planting the seed of Desire. But don't be content with that. Planting alone will not make a seed of corn grow. It has to be warmed by sunshine, nurtured by rain. So with the seed of your Desire. It must be warmed by Faith, nurtured by constant Belief. So—

2nd. Read the 91st and the 23rd Psalms, just as a reminder of God's power and His readiness to help you in all your needs.

3rd. Don't forget to be thankful, not merely for past favors, *but for the granting of this favor you are now asking!* To be able to thank God for it sincerely, in advance of its actual material manifestation, is the finest evidence of belief.

4th. BELIEVE! Picture the thing that you want so clearly, see it in your imagination so vividly, that for the moment, at least, you will actually BELIEVE THAT YOU HAVE IT!

It is this sincere conviction, registered upon your subconscious mind, and through it upon Universal Mind that brings the answer to your prayers. Once convince your subconscious mind that you HAVE the thing you want, and you can forget it and go on to your next problem. Mind will attend to the bringing of it into being.

STUDY GUIDE

IV *Desire—The First Law of Grain*

1. What does the opening poem mean to you, and how might you relate it to your life?

2. *"If YOU had a fairy-wishing ring, what one thing would you wish for? Wealth? Honor? Fame? Love?"* Be sure to focus on the one thing that you most desire.

3. Many aren't clear on what it is they want and exhaust themselves in aimless struggles. Is this the case with you?

4. Once you are clear on your greatest desire *"You have but to claim it, to visualize it, to bring into actuality—and it is yours for the taking."* Have you done so? Each day, spend at least 30 seconds visualizing it.

5. What is the greatest *"divine dissatisfaction"* that you currently have?

6. Collier speaks of the Demon of Ambition that drove us in our youth, which many of us have given up. Reflect back on your youth. List the goals and aspirations you had back then?

7. It is your duty to *"keep ambition alive and driving"*. Does referencing ambition as a "demon" preventing you from keeping it alive in any way?

8. The author reminds you that darkness is not real. It is merely a lack of light. He likens it to poverty as being a lack of necessary supply, and sickness as the absence of health. As such, there is nothing to overcome. You simply have to acquire. Have you seen yourself as having

to overcome poverty, sickness or otherwise until now? What does shifting your thinking from having to overcome to simply having to acquire change your perception of your issues?

The Magic Secret

9. The answer is to why you have not succeeded is that you have not focused all of your energy on one intense desire. You have to be willing to subordinate everything else. If you could choose only one desire among the many you may have, which would it be?

10. Can you become so absorbed in this desire that you have no interest in paying attention to anything else?

11. You must truly believe that you have received that which you desire. When you do this, your subconscious believes it, as if it were already real.

12. According to Collier, your body completely rebuild itself in eleven months. Do you believe this to be true? Why or why not?

13. You are told not to bother about the means for accomplishing your desire because your subconscious will take care of doing so. You need to impress upon your subconscious mind the *belief that you already have it.* In as much detail as possible (using all five of your senses), describe that which you desire as if you already have it.

14. One of the terms is that you act with the wellbeing of others as well as yourself in mind when focusing upon your desire. Does the manifestation of your desire support others as well as yourself? If so, how?

15. The door of opportunity is always open, so you should always keep yourself in a state of receptivity. Look deep within, and note if there is any part of you that struggles to complete receive.

16. You are encouraged to act healthy, prosperous, and happy, and register those traits within your subconscious mind. In doing so, you will eventually awaken to your wishes becoming a reality.

"The Soul's Sincere Desire"

17. According to Montgomery, *"Prayer is the soul's sincere desire, uttered or unexpressed."* Prayers that are worth answering are those with ask for your real desires. It is suggested that you do them alone, where you can impress that desire upon your subconscious mind without distraction, and in doing so, reach the Universal Mind. Do you have a time and place where you can say your prayers alone and in a focused way? It is suggested that you kill all doubts and fears by affirming God's power and His willingness to grant your prayer. Have you ever considered that by denying yourself your desires?

18. The author wrote several of Glenn Clark's prayers, suggesting that you recite them to manifest your greatest desire. Re-write each (1: Opening Prayer, 2: For Aid in Thinking or Writing, 3: For Happiness) in your own words, being sure that while staying true to the intent of the prayers, you can recite them so that they are comfortable to you.

19. Collier states, *"Make no mistake about this—prayer is effective. It can do anything. It doesn't matter how trivial your desires may be—if it is RIGHT for you to have them, it is RIGHT for you to pray for them."* Have you ever felt that your desires are not "right" for you for some reason? Is there any shame or sense unworthiness to have what you truly desire? Take a minute and go to your heart. Ask if there is any sense of your desires not being right for you. Write your response.

20. A. Maude Royden compared the man who trusts his desires to prayer, to the swimmer who trusts himself to the water. Most of us are afraid of the water prior to learn-

ing how to swim. Were you? If so, how did you overcome your fear? What advice would the swimmer give to you in relation to trusting in your desires?

21. After planting a seed, you nourish it each day with water. What additional steps can you take to nourish your desire?

22. In his four steps, Collier suggests for step #2 that you read the 91st and 23rd psalms. Take some to time find these psalms and write them out. Do they have any affect on you and your desire? If so, how?

23. What challenges have you faced in your life? List the three top issues you've had to overcome. Can you be thankful for them?

24. Sincere conviction registered upon your subconscious mind bring the answer to your prayers. Look deep and be honest with yourself. Is there any part of you that feels you are not sincere in your conviction? If so, what is in the way of complete sincerity?

VOLUME THREE

V

Aladdin & Company

*"But the feeble hands and helpless,
Groping blindly in the darkness,
Touch God's right hand in that darkness,
And are lifted up and strengthened."*
—LONGFELLOW.

It is not always the man who struggles hardest who gets on in the world. It is the direction as well as the energy of struggle that counts in making progress. To get ahead—you must swim with the tide. Men prosper and succeed who work in accord with natural forces. A given amount of effort with these forces carries a man faster and farther than much more effort used against the current. Those who work blindly, regardless of these forces, make life difficult for themselves and rarely prosper.

It has been estimated by wise observers that on the average something like 90 per cent of the factors producing success or failure lie outside a man's conscious efforts—separate from his daily round of details. To the extent that he cooperates with the wisdom and power of Universal

Mind he is successful, well and happy. To the extent that he fails to cooperate, he is unsuccessful, sick and miserable.

All down the ages some have been enabled to "taste and see that the Lord is good." Prophets and Seers being blessed with the loving kindness of God, have proclaimed a God of universal goodness saying: "The earth is full of the goodness of the Lord"; "Thou wilt show me the path of life; in Thy presence is fullness of joy."

Now we know that this Infinite Good is not more available to one than it is to all. We know that the only limit to it is in our capacity to receive. If you had a problem in mathematics to work out, you would hardly gather together the necessary figures and leave them to arrange themselves in their proper sequence. You would know that while the method for solving every problem has been figured out, *you* have got to *work* it. The principles are there, but *you* have got to *apply* them.

The first essential is to understand the principle—to learn how it works—how to use it. The second—and even more important part—is to APPLY that understanding to the problem in hand.

In the same way, the Principle of Infinite Energy, Infinite Supply, is ever available. But that Energy, that Supply, is static. You've got to make it dynamic. You've got to understand the law. You've got to apply your understanding in order to solve your problems of poverty, discord, and disease.

Science shows that it is possible to accomplish any good thing. But distrust of your ability to reach the goal desired often holds you back and failure is the inevitable result.

Only by understanding that there is but one power—and that this power is Mind, not circumstances or environment—is it possible to bring your real abilities to the surface and put them to work.

Few deny that intelligence governs the universe. It matters not whether you call this intelligence Universal Mind or Providence or God or merely Nature. All admit Its directing power. All admit that It is a force for good, for progress. But few realize that our own minds are a part of this Universal Mind in just the same way that the rays of the sun are part of the sun.

If we will work in harmony with It, we can draw upon Universal Mind for all power, all intelligence, in the same way that the sun's rays draw upon their source for the heat and light they bring the earth.

It is not enough to know that you have this power. You must put it into practice—not once, or twice, but every hour and every day. Don't be discouraged if at first it doesn't always work. When you first studied arithmetic, your problems did not always work out correctly, did they? Yet you did not on that account doubt the principle of mathematics. You knew that the fault was with your methods, not with the principle. It is the same in this. The power is there. Correctly used, it can do anything.

All will agree that the Mind, which first brought the Life Principle to this earth—which imaged the earth, itself and the trees and the plants and the animals—is all-powerful. All will agree that to solve any problem, to meet any need, Mind has but to realize the need and it will be met. What most of us do not understand or realize is that we ourselves, being part of Universal Mind, have this same power. Just as the drop of water from the ocean has all the properties of the great bulk of the water in the ocean. Just as the spark of electricity has all the properties of the thunderbolt. And having the power, we have only to realize it and use it to get from life any good we may desire.

In the beginning all was void—space—nothingness. How did Universal Mind construct the planets, the firmaments, the earth and all things on and in it from this formless void? *By first making a mental image on which to build.*

That is what you, too, must do. You control your destiny, your fortune, your happiness to the exact extent to which you can think them out, VIZUALIZE them, SEE them, and allow no vagrant thought of fear or worry to mar their completion and beauty. The quality of your thought is the measure of your power. Clear, forceful thought has the power of attracting to itself everything it may need for the fruition of those thoughts. As W. D. Wattles puts it in his "Science of Getting Rich":

"There is a thinking stuff from which all things are made and which, in its original state, permeates, penetrates, and fills the interspaces of the universe. A thought in this substance produces the thing that is imagined by the thought. Man can form things in his thought, and, by impressing his thought upon formless substance, can cause the thing he thinks about to be created."

The connecting link between your conscious mind and the Universal is thought, and every thought that is in harmony with progress and good, every thought that is freighted with the right idea, can penetrate to Universal Mind. And penetrating to it, it comes back with the power of Universal Mind to accomplish it. You don't need to originate the ways and means. The Universal Mind knows how to bring about any necessary results. There is but one right way to solve any given problem. When your human judgment is unable to decide what that one right way is, turn to Universal Mind for guidance. You need never fear the outcome, for if you heed its advice you cannot go wrong.

Always remember—your mind is but a conductor—good or poor as you make it—for the power of Universal Mind. And thought is the connecting energy. Use that conductor, and you will improve its conductivity. Demand much, and you will receive the more. The Universal is not a niggard in any of its gifts. "Ask and ye shall receive, seek and ye shall find, knock and it shall be opened unto you."

That is the law of life. And the destiny of man lies not in poverty and hardship, but in living up to his high estate in unity with Universal Mind, with the power that governs the universe.

To look upon poverty and sickness as sent by God and therefore inevitable, is the way of the weakling. God never sent us anything but good. What is more, He has never yet failed to give to those who would use them the means to overcome any condition not of His making. Sickness and poverty are not of His making. They are not evidences of virtue, but of weakness. God gave us everything in abundance, and he expects us to manifest that abundance. If you had a son you loved very much, and you surrounded him with good things which he had only to exert himself in order to reach, you wouldn't like it if he showed himself to the world half-starved, ill-kempt and clothed in rags, merely because he was unwilling to exert himself enough to reach for the good things you had provided. No more, in my humble opinion, does God.

Man's principal business in life, as I see it, is to establish a contact with Universal Mind. It is to acquire an understanding of this power that is in him. "With all thy getting, get understanding," said Solomon.

*"Happy is the man that findeth wisdom,
And the man that getteth understanding.
For the gaining of it is better than the gaining of silver.
And the profit thereof than fine gold.
She is more precious than rubies:
And none of the things thou canst desire are to be
　compared unto her.
Length of days is in her right hand:
In her left hand are riches and honor.
Her ways are ways of pleasantness,
And all her paths are peace.
She is a tree of life to them that lay hold upon her.
And happy is every one that retaineth her."*
—Proverbs.

When you become conscious, even to a limited degree, of your oneness with Universal Mind, your ability to call upon It at will for anything you may need, it makes a different man of you. Gone are the fears gone are the worries. You know that your success, your health, your happiness will be measured only by the degree to which you can impress the fruition of your desires upon mind.

The toil and worry, the wearisome grind and the backbreaking work, will go in the future as in the past to those who will not use their minds. The less they use them, the more they will sweat. And the more they work only from the neck down, the less they will be paid and the more hopeless their lot will become. It is Mind that rules the world.

But to use your mind to the best advantage doesn't mean to toil along with the mere conscious part of it. It means hitching up your conscious mind with the Man Inside You, with the little "Mental Brownies," as Robert Louis Stevenson called them, and then working together for a definite end.

"My Brownies! God bless them!" said Stevenson, "Who do one-half of my work for me when I am fast asleep, and in all human likelihood do the rest for me as well when I am wide awake and foolishly suppose that I do it myself. I had long been wanting to write a book on man's double being. For two days I went about racking my brains for a plot of any sort, and on the second night I dreamt the scene in Dr. Jekyll and Mr. Hyde at the window; and a scene, afterward split in two, in which Hyde, pursued, took the powder and underwent the change in the presence of his pursuer."

Many another famous writers have spoken in similar strain, and every man who has problems to solve has had like experiences. You know how, after you have studied a problem from all angles, it sometimes seems worse jumbled than when you started on it. Leave it then for a while—forget it—and when you go back to it, you find your thoughts clarified, the line of reasoning worked out, your problem solved for you. It is your little "Mental Brownies" who have done the work for you!

The flash of genius does not originate in your own brain. Through intense concentration you've established a circuit through your subconscious mind with the Universal, and it is from It that the inspiration comes. All genius, all progress, is from the same source. It lies with you merely to learn how to establish this circuit at will so that you can call upon It at need. It can be done.

"In the Inner Consciousness of each of us," quotes Dumont in "The Master Mind," "there are forces which act much the same as would countless tiny mental brownies or helpers who are anxious and willing to assist us in our mental work, if we will but have confidence and trust in them. This is a psychological truth expressed in the terms of the old fairy tales. The process of calling into service these Inner Consciousness helpers is similar to that which we constantly employ to recall some forgotten fact or name. We find that we cannot recollect some desired fact, date, or name, and instead of racking our brains with an increased effort, we (if we have learned the secret) pass on the matter to the Inner Consciousness with a silent command, 'Recollect this name for me,' and then go on with our ordinary work. After a few minutes—or it may be hours—all of a sudden, pop! will come the missing name or fact before us—flashed from the planes of the Inner Consciousness, by the help of the kindly workers or 'brownies' of those planes. The experience is so common that we have ceased to wonder at it, and yet it is a wonderful manifestation of the Inner Consciousness' workings of the mind. Stop and think a moment, and you will see that the missing word does not present itself accidentally, or 'just because.' There are mental processes at work for your benefit, and when they have worked out the problem for you they gleefully push it up from their plane on to the plane of the outer consciousness where you may use it.

"We know of no better way of illustrating the matter than by this fanciful figure of the 'mental brownies,' in connection with the illustration of the 'subconscious storehouse.' If you would learn to take advantage of the work of these Subconscious Brownies, we advise you to form a mental picture of the Subconscious Storehouse in which is stored all sorts of knowledge that you have placed there during your lifetime, as well as the impressions that you have acquired by race inheritance—racial memory, in fact. The information stored away has often been placed in the storage rooms without any regard for systematic storing, or arrangement, and when you wish to find something that has been stored away there a long time ago, the exact place being forgotten, you are compelled to call to your assistance the little brownies of the mind, which perform faithfully your mental command, 'Recollect this for me!' These brownies are the same little chaps that you charge with the task of waking you at four o'clock tomorrow morning when you wish to catch an early train—and they obey you well in this work of the mental alarm-clock. These same little chaps will also flash into your consciousness the report, 'I have an engagement at two o'clock with Jones'—when looking at your watch you will see that it is just a quarter before the hour of two, the time of your engagement.

"Well then, if you will examine carefully into a subject which you wish to master, and will pass along the results of your observations to these Subconscious Brownies, you will find that they will work the raw materials of thought into shape for you in a comparatively short time. They will analyze, systematize, collate, and arrange in consecutive order the various details of information which you have passed on to them, and will add thereto the articles of similar information that they will find stored away in the recesses of your memory. In this way they will group together various scattered bits of knowledge that you have forgotten. And, right here, let us say to you that you never absolutely forget anything that you have placed in your mind. You may be unable to recollect certain things, but they are not lost—sometime later some associative connection will be made with some other fact, and lo! the missing idea will be found fitted nicely into its place in the larger idea—the work of our little brownies. Remember Thompson's statement: 'In view of having to wait for the results of these unconscious processes, I 'have proved the habit of getting together material in advance, and then leaving the mass to digest itself until I am ready to write about it.' This subconscious 'digestion' is really the work of our little mental brownies.

"There are many ways of setting the brownies to work. Nearly everyone has had some experience, more or less, in the matter, although often it is produced almost unconsciously, and without purpose and intent. Perhaps the best way for the average person—or rather the majority of persons—to get the desired results is for one to get as clear an idea of what one really wants to know—as clear an idea or mental image of the question you wish answered. Then after rolling it around in your mind—mentally chewing it, as it were—giving it a high degree of voluntary attention, you can pass it on to your Subconscious Mentality with the mental command: *'Attend to this for me—work out the answer!'* or some similar order. This command may be given silently, or else spoken aloud—either will do. Speak to the Subconscious Mentality—or its little workers—just as you would speak to persons in your employ, kindly but firmly. Talk to the little workers, and firmly command them to do your work. And then forget all about the matter—throw it off your conscious mind, and attend to your other tasks. Then in due time will come your answer—flashed into your consciousness—perhaps not until the very minute that you must decide upon the matter, or need the information. You may give your brownies orders to report at such and such a time—just as you do when you tell them to awaken you at a certain time in the morning so as to catch the early train, or just as they remind you of the hour of your appointment, if you have them all well trained."

Have you ever read the story by Richard Harding Davis of "The Man Who Could Not Lose?" In it the hero is intensely interested in racing. He has studied records and "dope" sheets until he knows the history of every horse backward and forward.

The day before the big race he is reclining in an easy chair, thinking of the morrow's race, and he drops off to sleep with that thought on his mind. Naturally, his subconscious mind takes it up, with the result that he dreams the exact outcome of the race.

That was mere fiction, of course, but if races were run solely on the speed and stamina of the horses, it would be entirely possible to work out the results in just that way. Unfortunately, other factors frequently enter into every betting game.

But the idea behind Davis' story is entirely right. The way to contact with your subconscious mind, the way to get the help of the "Man Inside You" in working out any problem is:

First, fill your mind with every bit of information regarding that problem that you can lay your hands on.

Second, pick out a chair or lounge or bed where you can recline in perfect comfort, where you can forget your body entirely.

Third, let your mind dwell upon the problem for a moment, not worrying, not fretting, but placidly, and then turn it over to the "Man Inside You." Say to him—"This is your problem. You can do anything. You know the answer to everything. Work this out for me!" And utterly relax.

Drop off to sleep, if you can. At least, drop into one of those half-sleepy, half-wakeful reveries that keep other thoughts from obtruding upon your consciousness, Do as Aladdin did—summon your Genii, give him your orders, then forget the matter, secure in the knowledge that he will attend to it for you. When you waken, *you will have the answer!*

For whatever thought, whatever problem you can get across to your subconscious mind at the moment of dropping off to sleep, that "Man Inside You," that Genie-of-your-Mind will work out for you.

Of course, not everyone can succeed in getting the right thought across to the subconscious at the first or the second attempt. It requires understanding and faith, just as the working out of problems in mathematics requires an understanding of and faith in the principles of mathematics. But keep on trying, and you WILL do it. And when you do, *the results are sure.*

If it is something that you want, VISUALIZE it first in your mind's eye, see it in every possible detail, see yourself going through every move it will be necessary for you to go through when your wish comes into being. Build up a complete story, step by step, just as though you were acting it all out. Get from it every ounce of pleasure and satisfaction that you can. Be *thankful* for this gift that has come to you. Then relax; go on to sleep if you can; give the "Man Inside You" a chance to work out the consummation of your wish without interference.

When you waken, hold it all pleasurably in thought again for a few moments. Don't let doubts and fears creep in, but go ahead, confidently, knowing that your wish is working itself out. Know this, believe it—and if there is nothing harmful in it, IT WILL WORK OUT!

For somewhere in Universal Mind there exists the correct solution of every problem. It matters not how stupendous and complicated, nor how simple a problem may appear to be. There always exists the right solution in Universal Mind. And because this solution does exist, there also exists the ability to ascertain and to prove what that solution is. You can know, and you can do, every right thing. Whatever it is necessary for you to know, whatever it is necessary for you to do, you can know and you can do, if you will but seek the help of Universal Mind and be governed by its suggestions.

Try this method every night for a little while, and the problem does not exist that you cannot solve.

STUDY GUIDE

V *Aladdin & Company*

1. In Longfellow's poem, he references touching God's right hand. When have you reached out in the darkness and touched God's hand? What was the outcome?

2. Collier states that it is not always the man who struggles hardest who is successful. Do you know of anyone who became successful with little effort?

3. You must work in accord with nature—swim with the tide to get ahead. Do you ever catch yourself swimming upstream against the current? If so, how?

4. Collier asserts that those who work blindly rarely prosper. What do you think he means by "blindly"?

5. Energy is static and you have to make it dynamic. How are your currently doing so in your life?

6. Have you tried any techniques to block your beliefs that you are under the power of circumstances or environment? If so, what were they and did they work?

7. Do you believe the Creator first had a mental image of the world prior to creating it? Why or why not?

8. Collier emphasizes that clear, forceful thought has the power to attract everything it may need. How do you feel about this premise? What do you think he means by "forceful thought"? Do you believe you have to "push" in order to succeed? Why or why not?

9. Have you ever felt yourself conflicted about a desire you want to manifest? If so, did you seek guidance to remove the conflict through prayer? If not, why not?

10. Take a moment and image your mind as a conductor of energy. Like a magnet, imagine that which you desire coming to you automatically and effortlessly. Write about how you feel after doing this exercise.

11. Do you have any fears that you will become arrogant or ungrateful if your desires are fulfilled? If so, you are already one step closer to avoiding such a pitfall. How might you reassure yourself that you will maintain humility and gratitude?

12. Have you every cursed God or been angry at the Universe for something that has gone wrong in your life? If so, did you feel guilt and see an angry Creator judging you for your feelings? Would you judge your son or daughter if they had a moment of anger towards you? Do you believe the Creator is benevolent and requires no guilt or remorse from you?

13. Re-write the quote from Proverbs in your own words. What message does it bring to you personally?

14. Do you believe your "Mental Brownies" work on your behalf while you are asleep? Do you have any evidence to substantiate your position on this?

15. Could you imagine little inner helpers clearing and cleaning your physical body? Does doing so support better physical health and wellbeing within you?

16. Have you ever found yourself searching for a word or phrase, only to find that it appears in your mind's eye at a later time? Where do you believe it comes from?

17. Collier references your mental alarm clock. Have you ever found yourself waking up just prior to your alarm clock going off? You may wish to experiment with your inner knowing about time by choosing a day and time that you wish to be awakened, then focus on that time just prior to going to sleep. Note if you awaken at or just before the prescribed time (you may wish to first practice this at a

time when you do not have responsibilities that need to be met). Note your success.

18. Have you ever found yourself going to sleep with an unresolved issue, only to find yourself dreaming the resolution? If so, write about your experience. If not, set an intention to experience this phenomenon.

19. How has subconscious digestion worked on your behalf in your life? If you haven't practiced it, set an intention to do so within the next week. Don't forget to encourage and talk to the little workers within you. Write about anything you experience.

20. Take some time to peruse Richard Harding Davis' book, "The Man Who Could Not Lose". What was the key message and how might the story apply to your life?

21. Collier suggests three steps to work through any problem. Focus on an issue you are currently struggling with, and go through the three steps. Write about the outcome.

22. Practice the exercise above every night, until you find yourself trusting in the process. Be sure to write about any insights you gain while doing so.

VI

See Yourself Doing It

You say big corporations scheme
To keep a fellow down;
They drive him, shame him, starve him, too,
If he so much as frown.
God knows I hold no brief for them;
Still, come with me to-day
And watch those fat directors meet,
For this is what they say:
"In all our force not one to take
The new work that we plan!
In all the thousand men we've hired
Where shall we find a man?"
—St. Clair Adams.*

You've often heard it said that a man is worth $2 a day from the neck down. How much he's worth from the neck up depends upon how much he is able to SEE.

"Without vision the people perish" did not refer to good eyesight. It was the eyes of the mind that counted in days

---

* From "It Can Be Done." Copyright 1921, George Sully & *mechanical labor.*

of old just as they do today. Without them you are just so much power "on the hoof," to be driven as a horse or an ox is driven. And you are worth only a little more than they.

But given vision—imagination—the ability to visualize conditions and things a month or a year ahead; given the eyes of the mind—there's no limit to your value or to your capabilities.

The locomotive, the steamboat, the automobile, the aeroplane—all existed complete in the imagination of some man before ever they became facts. The wealthy men, the big men, the successful men, envisioned their successes in their minds' eyes before ever they won them from the world. From the beginning of time, nothing has ever taken on material shape without first being visualized in mind. The only difference between the sculptor and the mason is in the mental image behind their work. Rodin employed masons to hew his blocks of marble into the general shape of the figure he was about to form. *That was mere* Thinker."

Then Rodin took it in hand and from that rough-hewn piece of stone there sprang the wondrous figure of "The Company.

That was art!

The difference was all in the imagination behind the hands that wielded mallet and chisel. After Rodin had formed his masterpiece, ordinary workmen copied it by the thousands. Rodin's work brought fabulous sums. The copies brought day wages. Conceiving ideas—*creating something*—is what pays, in sculpture as in all else. Mere handwork is worth only hand wages.

"The imagination," says Glenn Clark in "The Soul's Sincere Desire," "is of all qualities in man the most Godlike—that which associates him most closely with God.

The first mention we read of man in the Bible is where he is spoken of as an 'image.' 'Let us make man in our image, after our likeness.' The only place where an image can be conceived is in the imagination. Thus man, the highest creation of God, was a creation of God's imagination.

"The source and center of all man's creative power—the power that above all others lifts him above the level of brute creation, and that gives him dominion, is his power of making images, or the power of the imagination. There are some who have always thought that the imagination was something, which makes-believe that which is not. This is fancy—not imagination. Fancy would convert that which is real into pretense and sham; imagination enables one to see through the appearance of a thing to what it really is."

There is a very real law of cause and effect, which makes the dream of the dreamer come true. It is the law of visualization—the law that calls into being in this outer material world everything that is real in the inner world. Imagination pictures the thing you desire. VISION idealizes it. It reaches beyond the thing that is, into the conception of what can be. Imagination gives you the picture. Vision gives you the impulse to make the picture your own.

Make your mental image clear enough, picture it vividly in every detail, and the Genie-of-your-Mind will speedily bring it into being as an everyday reality.

That law holds true of everything in life. There is nothing you can rightfully desire that cannot be brought into being through visualization.

Suppose there's a position you want—the general manager-ship of your company. See yourself—just as you are now—sitting in the general manager's chair. See your name on his door. See yourself handling his affairs as you would handle them. Get that picture impressed upon your subconscious mind. See it! *Believe* it! The Genie-of-your-Mind will find the way to make it come true.

The keynote of successful visualization is this: See things, as you would have them be instead of as they are. Close your eyes and make clear mental pictures. Make them look and act just as they would in real life. In short, daydream—but day dream with a purpose. Concentrate on the one idea to the exclusion of all others, and continue to concentrate on that one idea until it has been accomplished.

Do you want an automobile? A home? A factory? They can all be won in the same way. They are in their essence all of them ideas of mind, and if you will but build them up in your own mind first, stone by stone, complete in every detail, you will find that the Genie-of-your-Mind can build them up similarly in the material world.

"The building of a trans-continental railroad from a mental picture," says C. W. Chamberlain in "The Uncommon Sense of Applied Psychology," "gives the average individual an idea that it is a big job. The fact of the matter is, the achievement, as well as the perfect mental picture, is made up of millions of little jobs, each fitting in its proper place and helping to make up the whole.

"A skyscraper is built from individual bricks, the laying of each brick being a single job which must be completed before the next brick can be laid."

It is the same with any work, any study. To quote Professor James:

"As we become permanent drunkards by so many separate drinks, so we become saints in the moral, and authorities and experts in the practical and scientific spheres, by so many separate acts and hours of working. Let no youth have any anxiety about the upshot of his education whatever the line of it may be. If he keeps faithfully busy each hour of the working day he may safely leave the final result to itself. He can with perfect certainty count on waking some fine morning, to find himself one of the competent ones of his generation, in whatever pursuit he may have singled out. . . . Young people should know this truth in advance. The ignorance of it has probably engendered more discouragement and faintheartedness in youths embarking on arduous careers than all other causes taken together."

Remember that the only limit to your capabilities is the one you place upon them. There is no law of limitation. The only law is of supply. Through your subconscious mind you can draw upon universal supply for anything you wish. The ideas of Universal Mind are as countless as the sands on the seashore. Use them. And use them lavishly, just as they are given. There is a little poem by Jessie B. Rittenhouse* that so well describes the limitations that most of us put upon ourselves that I quote it here:

"I bargained with Life for a penny,
And Life would pay no more,
However I begged at evening
When I counted my scanty store.

"For Life is a just employer;
He gives you what you ask,
But once you have set the wages,
Why, you must bear the task.

---

* From "The Door of Dreams," Houghton, Muffin & Co., Boston.

*"I worked for a menial's hire,
Only to learn, dismayed,
That any wage I had asked of Life,
Life would have paid."*

Aim high! If you miss the moon, you may hit a star. Everyone admits that this world and all the vast firmament must have been thought into shape from the formless void by some Universal Mind. That same Universal Mind rules today, and it has given to each form of life power to attract to itself whatever it needs for its perfect growth. The tree, the plant, and the animal—each one finds its need.

You are an intelligent, reasoning creature. Your mind is part of Universal Mind. And you have power to say what you require for perfect growth. Don't be a niggard with yourself. Don't sell yourself for a penny. Whatever price you set upon yourself, life will give. So aim high. Demand much! Make a clear, distinct mental image of what it is you want. Hold it in your thought. Visualize it, see it, and believe it! The ways and means of satisfying that desire will follow. For supply always comes on the heels of demand.

It is by doing this that you take your fate out of the hands of chance. It is in this way that you control the experiences you are to have in life. But be sure to visualize only what you want. The law works both ways. If you visualize your worries and your fears, you will make them real. Control your thought and you will control circumstances. Conditions will be what you make them.

Most of us are like factories where two-thirds of the machines are idle, where the workmen move around in a listless, dispirited sort of way, doing only the tenth part of what they could do if the head of the plant were watching and directing them. Instead of that, he is off idly dreaming or waiting for something to turn up. What he needs is someone to point out to him his listless workmen and idle machines, and show him how to put each one to working full time and overtime.

And that is what YOU need, too. You are working at only a tenth of your capacity. You are doing only a tenth of what you are capable of. The time you spend idly wishing or worrying can be used in so directing your subconscious mind that it will bring you anything of good you may desire.

Philip of Macedon, Alexander's father, perfected the "phalanx"—a triangular formation which enabled him to center the whole weight of his attack on one point in the opposing line. It drove through everything opposed to it. In that day and age it was invincible. And the idea is just as invincible today.

Keep the one thought in mind, SEE it being carried out step by step, and you can knit any group of workers into one homogeneous whole, all centered on the one idea. You can accomplish any one thing. You can put across any definite idea. Keep that mental picture ever in mind and you will make it as invincible as was Alexander's phalanx of old.

"It is not the guns or armament
Or the money they can pay,
It's the close cooperation
That makes them win the day.
It is not the individual
Or the army as a whole
But the everlasting team work
of every bloomin' soul."
—J. Mason Knox.

The error of the ages is the tendency mankind has always shown to limit the power of Mind, or its willingness to help in time of need.

"Know ye not," said Paul, "that ye are the temples of the Living God?"

No—most of us do not know it. Or at least, if we do, we are like the Indian family out on the Cherokee reservation. Oil had been found on their land and money poured in upon them. More money than they had ever known was in the world. Someone persuaded them to build a great house, to have it beautifully furnished, richly decorated. The house when finished was one of the show places of that locality. But the Indians, while very proud of their showy house, continued to *live in their old sod shack*!

So it is with many of us. We may know that we are "temples of the Living God." We may even be proud of that fact. But we never take advantage of it to dwell in that temple, to proclaim our dominion over things and conditions. We never avail ourselves of the power that is ours.

The great Prophets of old had the forward look. Theirs was the era of hope and expectation. They looked for the time when the revelation should come that was to make men "Sons of God." "They shall obtain joy and gladness, and sorrow and sighing shall flee away."

Jesus came to fulfill that revelation. "Ask and ye shall receive, that your joy may be full."

The world has turned in vain to matter and materialistic philosophy for deliverance from its woes. In the future the only march of actual progress will be in the mental realm, and this progress will not be in the way of human speculation and theorizing, but in the *actual demonstration* of the Universal, Infinite Mind.

The world stands today within the vestibule of the vast realm of divine intelligence, wherein is found the transcendent, practical power of Mind over all things.

"What eye never saw, nor ear ever heard,
What never entered the mind of man—
Even all that God has prepared for those who love Him."

STUDY GUIDE

VI *See Yourself Doing It*

1. This chapter opens with a poem by St. Clair Adams. What feelings does it create within you?

2. Do you work for a corporate or organization? If so, do you struggle doing so? What might you do to shift your focus from negativity to a more positive frame of mind?

3. Do you believe yourself to be a visionary? On a scale from one to ten (one being very little, and ten being very much so), rate your capacity as a visionary.

   1——2——3——4——5——6——7——8——9——10

4. When you have a vision, how often do you act upon it? Do you write out your inspiration somewhere, so that it is recorded and you can follow up on it? Why or why not?

5. Glenn Clark refers to the imagination is the most God-like. Do you believe this to be true? Why or why not?

6. Was your imagination encouraged and supported during your youth?

7. How much does your imagination excite you? Do you consciously try to stretch and work it as one would with a muscle? Why or why not?

8. Collier states that *"Imagination give you the picture the thing you desire. Vision gives you the impulse to make the picture your own"*. Provide an example of this in your own life.

9. The secret to visualization is to see things as you would have them, and not as they are. How often do you complain about how things currently are in your life? Next time

you catch yourself complaining, stop and allow yourself to visualize circumstances as you would like them to be. Write about your experience.

10. Do you find yourself daydreaming? If so, do you do so with a purpose? If not, practice doing so intentionally each day.

11. The trans-continental railway was made up of millions of little jobs. Do you currently have a task that you dread starting? Start by taking one small step into the project, and allow yourself to tackle it one step at a time.

12. Write about a task that you completed that at one time you believed to be daunting. Acknowledge yourself for your commitment and tenancy.

13. Relate Jessie B. Rittenhouse's poem to a specific situation in your life. When have you aimed low, only to find that purpose reflected in the outcome?

14. Is there anything that prevents you from aiming high? If so, what?

15. Collier encourages you not to sell yourself for a penny. How do you underestimate your talents? What is the outcome?

16. What percentage of your day do you spend idly wishing or worrying?

17. Choose one major task you need to act upon. List the steps it would take to complete it, and then visualize yourself successfully mastering each step. Then note the outcome as you actually complete the task. Did you find it easier or more difficult, once you broke it down into steps?

18. J. Mason Knox's poem focuses on the power of team work. Are you a leader? Are you a team player? Why or why not?

19. What evidence of your ability to be a team player do you see manifesting in your life?

20. Collier shares the example of the Indians who chose to live in a shack after acquiring riches and building a mansion. Do you suppose that their decision was because of their inability to see themselves as temples of the Living God, or might their priorities have been different that western man's?

21. Describe in as much detail was a joy-filled life would look, taste, smell and feel like to you.

22. The final paragraph of this chapter talks of *"What eye never saw, nor ear every heard"*. What innovation that has yet to be seen in this world would you like to see manifest?

VII

"As A Man Thinketh"

*"Our remedies in ourselves do lie
Which we ascribe to heaven."*
—SHAKESPEARE.

In our great-grandfather's day, when witches flew around by night and cast their spell upon all unlucky enough to cross them, men thought that the power of sickness or health, of good fortune or ill, resided outside himself or herself.

We laugh today at such benighted superstition. But even in this day and age there are few who realize that the things they *see* are but *effects*. Fewer still who have any idea of the *causes* by which those effects are brought about.

Every human experience is an effect. You laugh, you weep, you joy, you sorrow, you suffer or you are happy. Each of these is an effect, the cause of which can be easily traced.

But all the experiences of life are not so easily traceable to their primary causes. We save money for our old age. We put it into a bank or into safe bonds—and the bank breaks or the railroad or corporation goes into a receivership. We stay at home on a holiday to avoid risk of accident, and fall off a stepladder or down the stairs and break a limb. We drive slowly for fear of danger, and a speeding car comes from behind and knocks us into a ditch. A man goes over Niagara Falls in a barrel without harm, and then slips on a banana peel, breaks his leg, and dies of it.

What is the cause back of it all? If we can find it and control it, we can control the effect. We shall no longer then be the football of fate. We shall be able to rise above the conception of life in which matter is our master. There is but one answer. The world without is a reflection of the world within. We image thoughts of disaster upon our subconscious minds and the Genie-of-our Mind finds ways of bringing them into effect—even though we stay at home, even though we take every possible precaution. The mental image is what counts, be it for good or ill. It is a devastating or a beneficent force, just as we choose to make it. To paraphrase Thackeray—"The world is a looking-glass, and gives back to every man the reflection of his own thought."

For matter is not *real* substance. Material science today shows that matter has no natural eternal existence. Dr. Willis R. Whitney, in an address before the American Chemical Society on August 8th, 1925, discussing "Matter—Is There Anything In It?" stated, "the most we know about matter is that it is almost entirely *space*. It is as empty as the sky. It is almost as empty as a perfect vacuum, although it usually contains a lot of energy." Thought is the only force. Just as polarity controls the electron, gravitation the planets, tropism the plants and lower animals—just so thought controls the action and the environment of man. And thought is subject wholly to the control of mind. Its direction rests with us.

Walt Whitman had the right of it when he said—"Nothing external to me has any power over me."

The happenings that occur in the material world are in themselves neither cheerful nor sorrowful, just as outside of the eye that observes them colors are neither green nor red. It is our thoughts that make them so. And we can color those thoughts according to our own fancy. We can make the world without but a reflection of the world within. We can make matter a force subject entirely to the control of our mind. For matter is merely our wrong view of what Universal Mind sees rightly.

We cannot change the past experience, but we can determine what the new ones shall be like. We can make the coming day just what we want it to be. We can be tomorrow what we think today. For the thoughts are causes and the conditions are the effects.

What is the reason for most failures in life? The fact that they first thought failure; they allowed competition, hard times, fear and worry to undermine their confidence. Instead of working aggressively ahead, spending money to make more money, they stopped every possible outlay, tried to "play safe," but expected others to continue spending with them. War is not the only place where "The best defensive is a strong offensive."

The law of compensation is always at work. Man is not at the caprice of fate. He is his own fate. "As a man thinketh in his heart, so is he." We are our own past thoughts, with the things that these thoughts have attracted to us added on.

The successful man has no time to think of failure. He is too busy thinking up new ways to succeed. You can't pour water into a vessel already full.

All about you is energy—electronic energy, exactly like that which makes up the solid objects you possess. The only difference is that the loose energy round about is unappropriated. It is still virgin gold—undiscovered, unclaimed. You can think it into anything you wish—into gold or dross, into health or sickness, into strength or weakness, into success or failure. Which shall it be? "There is nothing either good or bad," said Shakespeare, "but thinking makes it so." The understanding of that law will enable you to control every other law that exists. In it is to be found the panacea for all ills, the satisfaction of all want, all desire. It is Creative Mind's own provision for man's freedom.

Have you ever read Basil King's "Conquest of Fear"? If you haven't, do so by all means. Here is the way he visions the future:

"Taking Him (Jesus) as our standard we shall work out, I venture to think, to the following points of progress:

"a. The control of matter in furnishing ourselves with food and drink by means more direct than at present employed, as He turned water into wine and fed the multitudes with the loaves and fishes.

"b. The control of matter by putting away from ourselves, by methods more sure and less roundabout than those of today, sickness, blindness, infirmity, and deformity.

"c. The control of matter by regulating our atmospheric conditions as He stilled the tempest.

"d. The control of matter by restoring to this phase of existence those who have passed out of it before their time, or who can ill be spared from it, as He 'raised' three young people from 'the dead' and Peter and Paul followed His example.

"e. The control of matter in putting it off and on at will, as He in His death and resurrection.

"f. The control of matter in passing altogether out of it, as He in what we call His Ascension into Heaven."

Mortals are healthy or unhealthy, happy or unhappy, strong or weak, alive or dead, in the proportion that they think thoughts of health or illness, strength or weakness. Your body, like all other material things, manifests only what your mind entertains in belief. In a general way you have often noticed this yourself. A man with an ugly disposition (which is a mental state) will have harsh, unlovely features. One with a gentle disposition will have a smiling and serene countenance. All the other organs of the human body are equally responsive to thought. Who has not seen the face become red with rage or white with fear? Who has not known of people who became desperately ill following an outburst of temper? Physicians declare that just as fear, irritability and hate distort the features; they likewise distort the heart, stomach and liver.

Experiments conducted on a cat shortly after a meal showed that when it was purring contentedly, its digestive organs functioned perfectly. But when a dog was brought into the room and the cat drew back in fear and anger, the X-ray showed that its digestive organs were so contorted as to be almost tied up in a knot!

Each of us makes his own world—and he makes it through mind. It is a commonplace fact that no two people see the same thing alike. "A primrose by a river's brim, a yellow primrose was to him, and it was nothing more."

Thoughts are the causes. Conditions are merely effects. We can mould our surroundings and ourselves by resolutely directing our thoughts towards the goal we have in mind.

Ordinary animal life is very definitely controlled by temperature, by climate, by seasonal conditions. Man alone can adjust himself to any reasonable temperature or condition. Man alone has been able to free himself to a great extent from the control of natural forces through his understanding of the relation of cause and effect. And now man is beginning to get a glimpse of the final freedom that shall be his from all material causes when he shall acquire the complete understanding that mind is the only cause and that effects are what he sees.

"We moderns are unaccustomed," says one talented writer, "to the mastery over our own inner thoughts and feelings. That a man should be a prey to any thought that chances to take possession of his mind, is commonly among us assumed as unavoidable. It may be a matter of regret that he should be kept awake all night from anxiety as to the issue of a lawsuit on the morrow, but that he should have the power of determining whether he be kept awake or not seems an extravagant demand. The image of an impending calamity is no doubt odious, but its very odiousness (we say) makes it haunt the mind all the more pertinaciously, and it is useless to expel it. Yet this is an absurd position for man, the heir of all the ages, to be in: Hag-ridden by the flimsy creatures of his own brain. If a pebble in our boot torments us, we expel it. We take off the boot and shake it out. And once the matter is fairly understood, it is just as easy to expel an intruding and obnoxious thought from the mind. About this there ought to be no mistake, no two opinions. The thing is obvious, clear and unmistakable. It should be as easy to expel an obnoxious thought from the mind as to shake a stone out of your shoe; and until a man can do that, it is just nonsense to talk about his ascendancy over nature, and all the rest of it. He is a mere slave, and a prey to the bat-winged phantoms that flit through the corridors of his own brain. Yet the weary and careworn faces that we meet by thousands, even among the affluent classes of civilization, testify only too clearly how seldom this mastery is obtained. How rare indeed to find a *man*! How common rather to discover a creature hounded on by tyrant thoughts (or cares, or desires), cowering, wincing under the lash.

"It is one of the prominent doctrines of some of the oriental schools of practical psychology that the power of expelling thoughts, or if need be, killing them dead on the spot, *must be* attained. Naturally the art requires practice, but like other arts, when once acquired there is no mystery or difficulty about it. It is worth practice. It may be fairly said that life only begins when this art has been acquired. For obviously when, instead of being ruled by individual thoughts, the whole flock of them in their immense multitude and variety and capacity is ours to direct and dispatch and employ where we list, life becomes a thing so vast and grand, compared to what it was before, that its former condition may well appear almost ante-natal. If you can kill a thought dead, for the time being, you can do anything else with it that you please. And therefore it is that this power is so valuable. And it not only frees a man from mental torment (which is nine-tenths at least of the torment of life), but it gives him a concentrated power of handling mental work absolutely unknown to him before. The two are co-relative to each other."

There is no intelligence in matter—whether that matter be electronic energy made up in the form of stone, or iron, or wood, or flesh. It all consists of Energy, the universal substance from which Mind forms all material things.

Mind is the only intelligence. It alone is eternal. It alone is supreme in the universe.

When we reach that understanding, we will no longer have cause for fear, because we will realize that Universal Mind is the creator of *life* only; that death is not an actuality—it is merely the *absence* of life—and life will be ever-present. Remember the old fairy story of how the Sun was listening to a lot of earthly creatures talking of a very dark place they had found? A place of Stygian blackness. Each told how terrifically dark it had seemed. The Sun went and looked for it. He went to the exact spot they had described. He searched everywhere. But he could find not even a tiny dark spot. And he came back and told the earth-creatures he did not believe there was any dark place.

When the sun of understanding shines on all the dark spots in our lives, we will realize that there is no cause, no creator, no power, except good; evil is not an entity—it is merely the *absence of good*. And there can be no ill effects without an evil cause. Since there is no evil cause, only good can have reality or power. There is no beginning or end to good. From it there can be nothing but blessing for the whole race. In it is found no trouble. If God (or Good—the two are synonymous) is the only cause, then the only effect must be like the cause. "All things were made by Him; and without Him was not anything made that was made."

Don't be content with passively reading this. Use it! Practice it! Exercise is far more necessary to mental development that it is to physical. Practice the "daily dozen" of right thinking. Stretch your mind to realize how infinitely far it can reach out, what boundless vision it can have. Breathe out all the old thoughts of sickness, discouragement, failure, worry and fear. Breathe in deep, long breaths (thoughts) of unlimited health and strength, unlimited happiness and success. Practice looking forward—always looking forward to something better—better health, finer physique, greater happiness, bigger success. Take these mental breathing exercises every day. See how easily you will control your thoughts. How quickly you will see the good effects. You've got to think all the time. Your mind will do that anyway. And the thoughts are constantly building—for good or ill. So be sure to exhale all the thoughts of fear and worry and disease and lack that have been troubling you, and inhale only those you want to see realized.

STUDY GUIDE

VII *"As a Man Thinketh"*

1. This chapter opens with a quote from Shakespeare. What does it mean?

2. Collier states that *"the world without is a reflection of the world within"*. He shares examples of how many seem to beat the odds, and then fall prey to apparent bad luck. Reflect on your life. Is there a specific challenge you face that came to mind as you read the situations he listed? Write about it.

3. Walt Whitman said, *"Nothing external to me ash any power over me."* If you are not familiar with Walt, research and write a short summary of what he was most renowned.

4. Collier reminds you that you cannot change the past. What percentage of your time do you focus on past grievances, sorrows or issues?

5. Do you allow competition to seep into your consciousness, and ultimately your subconscious?

6. List the ways in which you *"play it safe"* in your life.

7. Define the Law of Compensation in your own words.

8. It is said that a successful man has no time for failure. Do you busy your life with success-focused initiatives?

9. Shakespeare wrote, *"there is nothing either good or bad, but thinking makes it so."* Can you twist a situation which you previously deemed as bad into a positive? Re-write it from that perspective.

10. If you haven't already done so, read Basil King's "Conquest of Fear". Then write a short summary of the insights you gained from the book.

11. In the book, King lists six points of progress that are reflected in the New Testament of the Bible. Whether you believe in the bible or not, do you believe these points to be true?

12. Do you know of anyone who has distorted features, based on the way they act out rage or hatred? Do you know of someone whose features match their kind and gentle disposition? If so, whom.

13. Collier uses the example of the cat in the presence of a dog as an example of how stress affects the digestive system. Many in today's society suffer from growing stress. Do you? How well does your digestive system function?

14. The media is inundated with negative stories and images. On a scale from one to ten (one being very little, and ten being very much so), rate much you expose yourself to negative stories or images.

    1——2——3——4——5——6——7——8——9——10

15. Do you watch television or movies that are violent or tell fearful stories of horror and negativity? If so, why do you subject yourself to them? What benefits do you gain?

16. Do you believe it takes discipline to expel negative thoughts from your mind? If so, do you have it?

17. According to Collier, if you can free yourself from mental torment, you will gain concentration power—the two are correlated. How often does your mind wander into negativity? Sit quietly for at least 10 minutes and note how frequently negative thoughts appear in your head.

18. Collier asserts that goodness and Godliness and cyclical and infinite? Do you believe this to be true? If so, where do you see evidence of it in the world?

19. In the final paragraph of this chapter, Collier encourages you to breathe out all the old thoughts of sickness, dis-

couragement, failure, worry and fear. Then breathe in deep, long breathes (thoughts) of unlimited health and strength, unlimited happiness and success. Before you get out of bed each morning, do this exercise for at least 3 minutes. Do the same before going to sleep each night. Note and write down any shifts that arise.

VIII

The Law of Supply

"They do me wrong who say I come no more
When once I knock and fail to find you in;
For every day I stand outside your door,
And bid you wake, and rise to fight and win.

"Wail not for precious chances passed away,
Weep not for golden ages on the wane!
Each night I burn the records of the day—
At sunrise every soul is born again!"
—WALTER MALONE.*

Have you ever run a race, or worked at utmost capacity for a protracted period, or swum a great distance? Remember how, soon after starting, you began to feel tired? Remember how, before you had gone any great distance, you thought you had reached your limit? But remember, too, how, when you kept on going, you got your second wind, your tiredness vanished, your muscles throbbed with energy, you felt literally charged with speed and endurance?

---

* Courtesy of Mrs. Ella Malone Watson.

Stored in every human being are great reserves of energy of which the average individual knows nothing. Most people are like a man who drives a car in low gear, not knowing that by the simple shift of a lever he can set it in high and not merely speed up the car, but do it with far less expenditure of power.

The law of the universe is the law of supply. You see it on every hand. Nature is lavish in everything she does.

Look at the heavens at night. There are millions of stars there—millions of worlds—millions of suns among them. Surely there is no lack of wealth or profusion in the Mind that could image all of these; no place for limitation there! Look at the vegetation in the country round about you. Nature supplies all that the shrubs or trees may need for their growth and sustenance! Look at the lower forms of animal life—the birds and the wild animals, the reptiles and the insects, the fish in the sea.

Nature supplies them bountifully with everything they need. They have but to help themselves to what she holds out to them with such lavish hand. Look at all the natural resources of the world—coal and iron and oil and all metals. There is plenty for everyone. We hear a lot about the exhaustion of our resources of coal and oil, but there is available coal enough to last mankind for thousands of years. There are vast oil fields practically untouched, probably others bigger still yet to be discovered, and when all these are exhausted, the extraction of oil from shale will keep the world supplied for countless more years.

There is abundance for everyone. But just as you must strain and labor to reach the resources of your "second wind," just so you must strive before you can make manifest the law of supply in nature.

The World Belongs to You

It is your estate. It owes you not merely a living, but everything of good you may desire. You've got to *demand* these things of it, though. You've got to fear naught, dread naught, and stop at naught. You've got to have the faith of a Columbus, crossing an unknown sea, holding a mutinous crew to the task long after they had ceased to believe in themselves or in him—*and giving to the world a new hemisphere.* You've got to have the faith of a Washington—defeated, discredited, almost wholly deserted by his followers, yet holding steadfast in spite of all—*and giving to America a new liberty.* You've got to *dominate*—not to cringe. *You've* got to make the application of the law of supply.

"Consider the lilies how they grow." The flowers, the birds, all of creation, are incessantly active. The trees and flowers in their growth, the birds and wild creatures in building their nests and finding sustenance, are always working—*but never worrying.* "Your Father knoweth that ye have need of these things." "And all these things shall be added unto you."

If all would agree to give up worrying—to be industrious, but never anxious about the outcome it would mean the beginning of a new era in human progress, an age of liberty, of freedom from bondage. Jesus set forth the universal law of supply when he said—"Therefore I say unto you, be not anxious for the morrow, what ye shall eat, or wherewithal ye shall be clothed—but seek first the kingdom of God, *and all those things shall be added unto you.*"

What is this "Kingdom of God?"

Jesus tells us—"The Kingdom of God is within you." It is the "Father within you" to which He so frequently referred. It is Mind—your part of Universal Mind. "Seek first the Kingdom of God." Seek first an understanding of this Power within you—learn to contact with it—to use it—"and all those things shall be added unto you."

All riches have their origin in Mind. Wealth is in ideas—not money. Money is merely the material medium of exchange for ideas. The paper money in your pockets is in itself worth no more than so many Russian rubles. It is the idea behind it that gives it value. Factory buildings, machinery, materials, are in themselves worthless without a manufacturing or a selling idea behind them. How often you see a factory fall to pieces, the machinery rusts away, after the idea behind them gave out. Factories, machines, are simply the tools of trade. It is the idea behind them that makes them go.

So don't go out a-seeking of wealth. Look within you for ideas! "The Kingdom of God is within you." Use it—*purposefully*! Use it to THINK constructively. Don't say you are *thinking* when all you are doing is exercising your faculty of memory. As Dumont says in "The Master Mind"—"They are simply allowing the stream of memory to flow through their field of consciousness, while the Ego stands on the banks and idly watches the passing waters of memory flow by. They call this 'thinking', while in reality there is no process of thought under way."

They are like the old mountaineer sitting in the shade alongside his cabin. Asked what he did to pass the long hours away, he said—"Waal, sometimes I set and think; and sometimes I just set."

Dumont goes on to say, in quoting another writer: "When I use the word 'thinking,' I mean *thinking with a purpose, with an end in view, thinking to solve a problem*. I mean the kind of thinking that is forced on us when we are deciding on a course to pursue, on a life work to take up perhaps; the kind of thinking that was forced upon us in our younger days when we had to find a solution to a problem in mathematics; or when we tackled psychology in college. I do not mean 'thinking' in snatches, or holding petty opinions on this subject and on that. I mean thought on significant questions, which lie outside the bounds of your narrow personal welfare. This is the kind of thinking which is now so rare—so sadly needed!"

The Kingdom of God is the Kingdom of Thought, of Achievement, of Health, of Happiness and Prosperity. "I came that ye might have life and have it more abundantly."

But you have got to *seek* it. You have got to do more than ponder. You have got to *think*—to think constructively—to seek how you may discover new worlds, new methods, new needs. The greatest discoveries, you know, have arisen out of things, which everybody had *seen*, but only one man had NOTICED. The biggest fortunes have been made out of the opportunities, which many men had, but only one man GRASPED.

Why is it that so many millions of men and women go through life in poverty and misery, in sickness and despair? Why? Primarily because they make a reality of poverty through their fear of it. They visualize poverty, misery and disease, and thus bring them into being. And secondly, they cannot demonstrate the law of supply for the same reason that so many millions cannot solve the first problem in algebra. The solution is simple—but they have never been shown the method. They do not understand the law.

The essence of this law is that you must *think* abundance; *see* abundance *feel* abundance, *believe* abundance. Let no thought of limitation enter your mind. There is no lawful desire of yours for which, as far as mind is concerned, there is not abundant satisfaction. And if you can visualize it in mind, you can realize it in your daily world.

"Blessed is the man whose delight is in. the *law* of the Lord: And he shall be like a tree planted by the rivers of water, that bringeth forth his fruit in his season: his leaf also shall not wither; and whatsoever he doeth shall prosper."

Don't worry. Don't doubt. Don't dig up the seeds of prosperity and success to see whether they have sprouted. Have faith! Nourish your seeds with renewed desire. Keep before your mind's eye the picture of the thing you want. BELIEVE IN IT! No matter if you seem to be in the clutch of misfortune, no matter if the future looks black and dreary—FORGET YOUR FEARS! Realize that the future is of your own making. There is no power that can keep you down but yourself. Set your goal. Forget the obstacles between. Forget the difficulties in the way. Keep only the goal before your mind's eye—*and you'll win it*!

Judge Troward, in his Edinburgh Lectures on Mental Science, shows the way:

The initial step, then, consists in determining to picture the Universal Mind as the ideal of all we could wish it to be, both to ourselves and to b others, together with the endeavor to reproduce this ideal, however imperfectly, in our own life; and this step having been taken, we can then cheerfully look upon it as our ever-present Friend, providing all good, guarding from all danger, and guiding us with all counsel. Similarly if we think of it as a great power devoted to supplying all our needs, we shall impress this character also upon it, and by the law of subjective mind, it will proceed to enact the part of that special providence which we have credited it with being; and if, beyond general care of our concerns, we would draw to ourselves some particular benefit, the same rule holds good of impressing our desire upon the universal subjective mind. And thus the deepest problems of philosophy bring us back to the old statement of the law: 'Ask and ye shall receive; seek and ye shall find; knock and it shall be opened unto you.' This is the summing-up of the natural law of the relation between the Divine Mind and us. It is thus no vain boast that mental science can enable us to makes our lives what we will. And to this law there is no limit. What it can do for us today it can do tomorrow, and through all that procession of tomorrows that loses itself in the dim vistas of eternity. *Belief in limitation is the one and only thing that causes limitation*, because we thus impress limitation upon the creative principle; and in proportion as we lay that belief aside, our boundaries will expand, and increasing life and more abundant blessing will be ours."

You are not working for some firm merely for the pittance they pay you. You are part of the great scheme of things. And what you do has its bearing on the ultimate result. That being the case, you are working for Universal Mind, and Universal Mind is the most generous paymaster there is. Just remember that you can look to it for all good things. Supply is *where* you are and *what* you need.

Do you want a situation? Close your eyes and realize that somewhere is the position for which you of all people are best fitted, and which is best fitted to your ability. The position where you can do the utmost of good, and where life, in turn, offers the most to you. Realize that Universal Mind knows exactly where this position is, and that through your subconscious mind you, too, can know it. Realize that this is YOUR position, that it NEEDS you, that it belongs to you, that it is right for you to have it, that you are entitled to it. Hold this thought in mind every night for just a moment, then go to sleep knowing that your subconscious mind HAS the necessary information as to where this position is and how to get in touch with it. Mind you—not WILL have, but HAS. The earnest realization of this will bring that position to you, and you to it, as surely as the morrow will bring the sun. Make the law of supply operative and you find that the things you seek are seeking you.

Get firmly fixed in your own mind the definite conviction that you can do anything you greatly want to do. There is no such thing as lack of opportunity. There is no such thing as only one opportunity. You are subject to a law of boundless and perpetual opportunity, and you can enforce that law in your behalf just as widely as you need. Opportunity is infinite and ever present.

Berton Braley has it well expressed in his poem on "Opportunity"[*]:

"For the best verse hasn't been rhymed yet,
 The best house hasn't been planned,
The highest peak hasn't been climbed yet,
 The mightiest rivers aren't spanned;

Don't worry and fret, faint hearted,
 The chances have just begun,
For the Best jobs haven't been started,
 The Best work hasn't been done."

---

[*] From "A Banjo at Armageddon." Copyright 1917, George H. Doran Company.

Nothing stands in the way of a will, which wants—an intelligence, which knows. The great thing is to start. "Begin your work," says Ausonius. "To begin is to complete the first half. The second half remains. Begin again and the work is done." It matters not how small or unimportant your task may seem to be. It may loom bigger in Universal Mind than that of your neighbor, whose position is so much greater in the eyes of the world. Do it well—and Universal Mind will work with you.

But don't feel limited to any one job or any one line of work. Man was given dominion over all the earth. "And God said, Let us make man in our image, after our likeness: and let them have dominion over the fish of the sea, and over the fowl of the air, and over the cattle, and over all the earth, and over every creeping thing that creepeth upon the earth."

All of energy, all of power, all that can exercise any influence over your life, is in your hands through the power of thought. God—good—is the only power there is. Your mind is part of His mind. He is "the Father that is within you that doeth the works."

So don't put any limit upon His power by trying to limit your capabilities. You are not in bondage to anything. All your hopes and dreams can come true. Were you not given dominion over all the earth? And can anyone else take this dominion from you?

All the mysterious psychic powers about which you hear so much today are perfectly natural. I have them. You have them. They only await the time when they shall be allowed to assert their vigor and prove themselves your faithful servitors.

"Be not afraid!" Claim your inheritance. The Universal Mind that supplies all wisdom and power is your mind.

And to the extent that you are governed by your understanding of its infinite law of supply you will be able to demonstrate plenty. "According to your faith, be it unto you."

"Analyze most of the great American fortunes of the past generation," says *Advertising and Selling Fortnightly*, "and you will find that they were founded on great faiths. One man's faith was in oil, another's in land, and another's in minerals.

"The fortunes that are being built today are just as surely being built on great faiths, but there is this difference: the emphasis of the faith has been shifted. Today it takes faith in a product or an opportunity, as it always did, but it takes faith in the public, in addition. Those who have the greatest faith in the public—the kind of faith possessed by Henry Ford and H. J. Heinz—*and make that faith articulate*—build the biggest fortunes."

"Wanted"

There is one question that bothers many a man. Should he stick to the job he has, or cast about at once for a better one. The answer depends entirely upon what you are striving for. The first thing is to set your goal. What is it you want? A profession? A political appointment? An important executive position? A business of your own?

Every position should yield you three things:
1. Reasonable pay for the present.
2. Knowledge, training, or experience that will be worth money to you in the future.
3. Prestige or acquaintances that will be of assistance to you in attaining your goal.

Judge every opening by those three standards. But don't overlook chances for valuable training, merely because the pay is small. Though it is a pretty safe rule that the concern with up-to-the-minute methods that it would profit you to learn, also pays up-to-the-minute salaries.

Hold each job long enough to get from it every speck of information there is in it. Hold it long enough to learn the job ahead. Then if there seems no likelihood of a vacancy soon in that job ahead, find one that corresponds to it somewhere else.

Progress! Keep going ahead! Don't be satisfied merely because your salary is being boosted occasionally. Learn something every day. When you reach the point in your work that you are no longer adding to your store of knowledge or abilities, you are going backward, and it's time for you to move. Move upward in the organization you are with if you can—but MOVE!

Your actual salary is of slight importance compared with the knowledge and ability you add to your mind. Given a full storehouse there, the salary or the riches will speedily follow. But the biggest salary won't do you much good for long unless you've got the knowledge inside you to back it up.

It's like a girl picking her husband. She can pick one with a lot of money and no brains, or she can pick one with no money but a lot of ability. In the former case, she'll have a high time for a little while, ending in a divorce court or in her having a worthless young "rounder" on her hands and no money to pay the bills. In the other, the start will be hard, but she is likely to end up with a happy home she has helped to build, an earnest, hard working husband who has "arrived"—*and happiness.*

Money ought to be a consideration in marriage—but never *the* consideration. Of course it's an easy matter to pick a man with neither money nor brains. But when it's a choice of money or brains—take the brains every time. Possessions are of slight importance compared to mind.

Given the inquiring, alert type of mind—you can get any amount of possessions. But the possessions without the mind are nothing. Nine times out of ten the best thing that can happen to any young couple is to have to start out with little or nothing and work out their salvation together.

What is it *you* want most from life? Is it riches?

Picture yourself with all the riches you could use, with all the abundance that Nature holds out with such lavish hand everywhere. What would you do with it?

Daydream for a while. Believe that you *have* that abundance *now*. Practice being rich in your own mind. See yourself driving that expensive car you have always longed for, living in the sort of house you have often pictured, well-dressed, surrounded by everything to make life worthwhile. Picture yourself spending this money that is yours, lavishly, without a worry as to where more is coming from, knowing that there is no limit to the riches of Mind. Picture yourself doing all those things you would like to do, living the life you would like to live, providing for your loved ones as you would like to see them provided for. *See* all this in your mind's eye. *Believe* it to be true for the moment. *Know* that it will all be true in the not-very-distant future. Get from it all the pleasure and enjoyment you can.

It is the *first step* in making your dreams come true. You are creating the model in mind. And if you don't allow fear or worry to tear it down, Mind will re-create that model for you in your everyday life.

"All that the Father hath is yours," said Jesus. And a single glance at the heavens and the earth will show you that He has all riches in abundance. Reach out mentally and appropriate to yourself some of these good gifts. You've got to do it mentally before you can enjoy it physically. "'Tis mind that makes the body rich," as Shakespeare tells us.

See the things that you want as *already yours.* Know that they will come to you at need. Then LET them come. Don't fret and worry about them. Don't think about your LACK of them. Think of them as YOURS, as *belonging* to you, as already in your possession.

Look upon money as water that runs the mill of your mind. You are constantly grinding out ideas that the world needs. Your thoughts, your plans, are necessary to the great scheme of things. Money provides the power. But it needs YOU; it needs your ideas, before it can be of any use to the world. The Falls of Niagara would be of no use without the power plants that line the banks. The Falls need these plants to turn their power to account. In the same way, money needs your ideas to become of use to the world.

So instead of thinking that you need money, realize that money needs YOU. Money is just so much wasted energy without work to do. Your ideas provide the outlet for it, the means by which money can do things. Develop your ideas; secure in the knowledge that money is always looking for such an outlet. When the ideas are perfected, money will gravitate your way without conscious effort on your part, if only you don't dam up the channels with doubts and fears.

"First have something good—then advertise!" said Horace Greeley. First have something that the world needs, even if it be only faithful, interested service—then open up your channels of desire, and dollars will flow to you.

And remember that the more you have to offer—the more of riches will flow to you. Dollars are of no value except as they are used.

You have seen the rich attacked time and again in newspapers and magazines. You have read numberless articles and editorials against them. You have heard agitators declaim against them by the hour. But have you ever heard one of them say a single word against the richest man of them all—Henry Ford? I haven't. And why? Because Henry Ford's idea of money is that it is something to be *used*—something to provide more jobs, something to bring more comfort, more enjoyment, into an increasingly greater number of lives.

That is why money flows to him so freely. That is why he gets so much out of life. And that is how you, too, can get in touch with Infinite Supply. Realize that it is not money you have to seek, but a way to use money for the world's advantage. *Find the need!* Look at everything with the question—How could that be improved? To what new uses could this be put? Then set about supplying that need, in the absolute confidence that when you have found the way, money will flow freely to and through you. Do your part—and you can confidently look to Universal Mind to provide the means.

Get firmly in mind the definite conviction that YOU CAN DO ANYTHING RIGHT THAT YOU MAY WISH TO DO. Then set your goal and let everything you do, all your work, all your study, and all your associations, be a step towards that goal. To quote Berton Braley* again—

---

* From "Things As They Are." Copyright 1916, George H. Doran Company, New York.

"If you want a thing bad enough
To go out and fight for it,
Work day and night for it,
Give up your time and your peace and your sleep for it,
If only desire of it
Makes you quite mad enough
Never to tire of it,
Makes you hold all other things tawdry and cheap for it,
If life seems all empty and useless without it
And all that you scheme and you dream is about it,
If gladly you'll sweat for it,
Fret for it,

Plan for it,
Lose all your terror of God or man for it,
If you'll simply go after that thing that you want,
With all your capacity, strength and sagacity,
Faith, hope and confidence, stern pertinacity,
If neither cold poverty, famished and gaunt,
Nor sickness nor pain
Of body or brain
Can turn you away from the thing that you want,
If dogged and grim you besiege and beset it,
    You'll get it!"

STUDY GUIDE

VIII *The Law of Supply*

1. Who do you believe to be the speaker in Walter Malone's poem at the beginning of this chapter?

2. The final line of the poem states, *"At sunrise every soul is born again!"* If you believe you could re-invent yourself each new morning, who would you choose to be today? Would you make any changes to your current situation, beliefs or behaviors? If so, please describe them.

3. Have you ever experienced apparent exhaustion when physically exerting yourself, and then got a second wind? How did you feel when you were able to work through the fatigue and move further towards success?

4. Have there been times when you stopped with the initial feelings of exhaustion? Are you able to forgive yourself for doing so? Why or why not?

5. Collier speaks of an abundance of oil and natural resources. Since he wrote this book, we have created wind and solar energy sources. Do you believe resources to be infinite in nature, or could there be a time when we completely deplete such resources?

The World Belongs to You

6. Collier states, *"If all would agree to give up worrying – to be industrious, but never anxious about the outcome it would mean the beginning of a new era in human progress, an age of liberty, of freedom from bondage."* This sounds simple enough. Why do you believe humankind has such difficulty letting go of worry and negativity?

7. It is stated that wealth is in ideas, not money. Money is simply the material exchange for ideas. If you know this to be true, and you believe you have plenty of ideas, then what is stopping you from amassing huge wealth? Write the first thing that comes to mind after reading this statement.

8. Are you able to easily distinguish memory from thinking? If so, how?

9. Dumont speaks of the thinking that came from the pressure of others forcing upon us during our youth—a quest to find a solution to a problem. This kind of thinking is stress-inducing. Where you pressured in this way during your youth? Is the pressuring voice still perhaps within your mind?

10. Next time you find yourself feeling pressured to find a solution (either from within your own mind or by someone else, experiment with sitting quietly and just being. Note any feelings or thoughts that arise when doing so.

11. You have got to *seek* ways in which you can discover new worlds, find new and innovative ways of doing things. Do you believe yourself to be a passionate seeker? On a scale from one to ten (one being very little, and ten being very much so), rate how passionate a seeker you believe yourself to be.

    1——2——3——4——5——6——7——8——9——10

12. You make a reality of what you fear. Pinpoint your greatest fear. Then allow yourself to totally surrender into it, allowing all feelings to arise without repressing them. Completely submerge yourself and allow all that arises to do so. Just be a non-judgmental witness to the experience. Write any new insights, thoughts or feelings that arose after doing this exercise.

13. Now that you have allowed the fear to arise, hopefully in the allowing, it dissipated. Now make a commitment

to prevent yourself from re-experiencing it again. Put it behind you. Are you able to do so?

14. Now that you have experimented with exploring and experiencing your fear, do you believe it's better not to allow the fear into your consciousness, or better to go through it?

15. You are encouraged to see the Universal Mind as your ever-present friend. Do you believe that personifying it (giving it traits and a personality, like a friend) would better support your trust in it? Why or why not?

16. How can you best lay your belief in limitation aside? Are there tools and techniques that assist you? For example, have you found that distraction works (pulling your focus onto other things when negative thinking arises)?

17. Collier states that the Universal Mind is *"the most generous paymaster there is."* What sum would you ideally like to be receiving as your annual income?

18. You need to come to the realization that your position NEEDS you; that it is right for you to have it. Have you concerned that by not fulfilling your life's dreams, you are cheating the world of a gift?

19. What does true "opportunity" look like in your life?

20. Does Berton Braley poem rouse hopefulness or despair within you? Why?

21. It is important that you begin your work? Write a list of the procrastination techniques that you use to avoid beginning your work.

22. IF you are part of the Mind of God, then by setting limitations in your own belief in yourself, are you not seeing the divine as limited and flawed?

23. What does having faith in the public mean to you? Do you have it? Why or why not?

"Wanted"

24. According to Collier, whether you want to remain in your current job, or find something different, every position should yield you three things:
    1. Reasonable pay for the present.
    2. Knowledge, training, or experience that will be worth money to you in the future.
    3. Prestige or acquaintances that will be of assistance to you in attaining your goal.

    Do you have each of these criteria in your current position?

25. He continues by suggesting that you get "every speck" of information that you can from your current position. Do you believe that you have done so?

26. It is important that you continue to move forward and learn something every day. Do you believe that you are doing this? If not, is there something you can change so that you can? If so, what?

27. While dated in the example in which Collier suggests that a woman choose a husband that had brains over financial success, because the brains will take him further. Do you believe that brains over financial abundance is key to your success? Do you believe you have the brain power to succeed?

28. Write a list of the things that you would do when you acquire the riches that you desire. Be sure to be as detailed as you can.

29. How would you provide for your loved ones? Again, describe how in as much detail as possible.

30. It is important that, once you stipulate what you want, you do not worry and focus on the lack of them in your life. Do you tend to worry, or focus on lack? Whenever you catch yourself doing so, speak the opposite, more positive affirmation and take a moment to visualize your desire coming to fruition.

31. Collier suggests that you flip your perspective and realize that money needs you, otherwise it is wasted energy. Does contemplating this perspective support the manifestation of your dreams? How?

32. Collier sites Henry Ford as an example of an individual who is never criticized for his wealth, because he sees it as something to be used for the higher good of the world. What support would you provide in the world once you acquire the riches you desire? Be specific. Can you see money flowing to and through you to support that cause?

33. The author ends this chapter with a Berton Braley poem. Keeping in mind your one greatest desire, go through his list, and do an inventory. Put a check mark beside each task you are willing to do to acquire or achieve it. Note if there is anything you are not prepared to check off. This could be an indication of an emotional block you are holding in your subconscious mind.

VOLUME FOUR

IX

The Formula of Success

"One ship drives east, and another drives west,
With the self-same winds that blow.
'Tis the set of the sails, and not the gales
Which tells us the way they go.

"Like the waves of the sea are the ways of fate
As we voyage along thru life.
'Tis the set of the soul which decides its goal
And not the calm or the strife."
—Ella Wheeler Wilcox.

What is the eternal question, which stands up and looks you and every sincere man squarely in the eye every morning?

"How can I better my condition?" That is the real life question, which confronts you, and I will haunt you every day till you solve it.

Read this chapter carefully and I think you will find the answer to this important life question which you and every man must solve if he expects ever to have more each Monday morning, after pay day, than he had the week before.

To begin with, all wealth depends upon a clear understanding of the fact that mind—thought—is the only creator. The great business of life is thinking. Control your thoughts and you control circumstance.

Just as the first law of gain is desire, so the formula of success is BELIEF. Believe that you have it—see it as an existent fact—and anything you can rightly wish for is yours. Belief is "the substance of things hoped for, the evidence of things not seen."

You have seen men, inwardly no more capable than yourself accomplish the seemingly impossible. You have seen others, after years of hopeless struggle; suddenly win their most cherished dreams. And you've often wondered, "What is the power that gives new life to their dying ambitions, that supplies new impetus to their jaded desires, that gives them a new start on the road to success?"

That power is belief—faith. Someone, something, gave them a new belief in themselves and a new faith in their power to win—and they leaped ahead and wrested success from seemingly certain defeat.

Do you remember the picture Harold Lloyd was in two or three years ago, showing a country boy who was afraid of his shadow? Every boy in the countryside bedeviled him. Until one day his grandmother gave him a talisman that she assured him his grandfather had carried through the Civil War and which, so she said, had the property of making its owner invincible. Nothing could hurt him, she told him, while he wore this talisman. Nothing could stand up against him. He believed her. And the next time the bully of the town started to cuff him around, he wiped up the earth with him. And that was only the start. Before the year was out he had made a reputation as the most daring soul in the community.

Then, when his grandmother felt that he was thoroughly cured, she told him the truth—that the "talisman" was merely a piece of old junk she'd picked up by the roadside—that she knew all he needed was *faith in himself,* belief that he could do these things.

The Talisman of Napoleon

Stories like that are common. It is such a well-established truth that you can do only what you think you can, that the theme is a favorite one with authors. I remember reading a story years ago of an artist—a mediocre sort of artist—who was visiting the field of Waterloo and happened upon a curious lump of metal half buried in the dirt, which so attracted him that he picked it up and put it in his pocket. Soon thereafter he noticed a sudden increase in confidence, an absolute faith in himself, not only as to his own chosen line of work, but in his ability to handle any situation that might present itself. He painted a great picture—just to show that he *could* do it. Not content with that, he envisioned an empire with Mexico as its basis, actually led a revolt that carried all before it—until one day he lost his talisman. *And immediately his bubble burst.*

I instance this just to illustrate the point that it is *your own belief in yourself* that counts. It is the consciousness of dominant power within you that makes all things attainable. *You can do anything you think you can.* This knowledge is literally the gift of the gods, for through it you can solve every human problem. It should make of you an incurable optimist. It is the open door to welfare. *Keep it open*—by expecting to gain everything that is right.

You are entitled to every good thing. Therefore expect nothing but good. Defeat does not *need* to follow victory. You don't have to "knock wood" every time you congratulate yourself that things have been going well with you. Victory should follow victory—and it will if you "let this mind be in you which was also in Christ Jesus." it is the mind that means health and life and boundless opportunity and recompense. No limitation rests upon you. So don't let any enter your life. Remember that Mind will do every good thing for you. It will remove mountains for you.

"Bring ye all the tithes into the storehouse, and prove me now herewith, saith the Lord of hosts, if I will not open you the windows of heaven, and pour you out a blessing, that there shall not be room enough to receive it."

Bring all your thoughts, your desires, your aims, your talents, into the Storehouse—the Consciousness of Good, the Law of Infinite supply—and prove these blessings. There is every reason to know that you are entitled to adequate provision. Everything that is involved in supply is a thing of thought. Now reach out, stretch your mind, and try to comprehend *unlimited thought, unlimited supply.*

Do not think that supply must come through one or two channels. It is not for you to dictate to Universal Mind the means through which It shall send Its gifts to you. There are millions of channels through which It can reach you. Your part is to impress upon Mind your need, your earnest desire, your boundless belief in the resources and the willingness of Universal Mind to help you. Plant the seed of desire. Nourish it with a clear visualization of the ripened fruit. Water it with sincere faith. But leave the means to Universal Mind.

Open up your mind. Clear out the channels of thought. Keep yourself in a state of receptivity. Gain a mental attitude in which you are constantly *expecting good*. You have the fundamental right to all good, you know. "According to your faith, be it unto you."

The trouble with most of us is that we are mentally lazy. It is much easier to go along with the crowd than to break trail for ourselves. But the great discoverers, the great inventors, the great geniuses in all lines have been men who dared to break with tradition, who defied precedent, who believed that there is no limit to what Mind can do—and who stuck to that belief until their goal was won, in spite of all the sneers and ridicule of the wiseacres and the "It-can't-be-done'rs."

Not only that, but they were never satisfied with achieving just one success. They knew that the first success is like the first olive out of the bottle. All the others come out the more easily for it. They realized that they were a part of the Creative Intelligence of the Universe, and that the part shares all the properties of the whole. And that realization gave them the faith to strive for any right thing, the knowledge that the only limit upon their capabilities was the limit of their desires. Knowing that, they couldn't be satisfied with any ordinary success. They had to keep on and on and on.

Edison didn't sit down and fold his hands when he gave us the talking machine or the electric light. These great achievements merely opened the way to new fields of accomplishment.

Open up the channels between your mind and Universal Mind, and there is no limit to the riches that will come pouring in. Concentrate your thoughts on the particular thing you are most interested in, and ideas in abundance will come flooding down, opening up a dozen ways of winning the goal you are striving for.

But don't let one success—no matter how great—satisfy you. The Law of Creation, you know, is the Law of Growth. You can't stand still. You must go forward—or be passed by. Complacency—self-satisfaction—is the greatest enemy of achievement. You must keep looking forward. Like Alexander, you must be constantly seeking new worlds to conquer. Depend upon it, the power will come to meet the need. There is no such thing as failing powers, if we look to Mind for our source of supply. The only failure of mind comes from worry and fear—or from disuse.

William James, the famous psychologist, taught that "The more mind does, the more it can do." For ideas release energy. You can *do* more and better work than you have ever done. You can *know* more than you know now. You know from your own experience that under proper mental conditions of joy or enthusiasm, you can do three or four times the work without fatigue that you can ordinarily. Tiredness is more boredom than actual physical fatigue. You can work almost indefinitely when the work is a pleasure.

You've seen sickly persons, frail persons, who couldn't do an hour's light work without exhaustion, suddenly buckle down when heavy responsibilities were thrown upon them, and grow strong and rugged under the load. Crises not only draw upon the reserve power you have, but they help to create new power.

"It Couldn't Be Done"

It may be that you have been deluded by the thought of incompetence. It may be that you have been told so often that you cannot do certain things that you've come to believe you can't. Remember that success or failure is merely a state of mind. Believe you cannot do a thing—and you can't. Know that you *can* do it—and you *will*. You must *see yourself doing it.*

"If you think you are beaten, you are;
 If you think you dare not, you don't;
If you'd like to win, but you think you can't,
 It's almost a cinch you won't;
If you think you'll lose, you've lost,
 For out in the world you'll find
Success begins with a fellow's will—
 It's all in the state of mind.

"Full many a race is lost
 Ere even a race is run,
And many a coward fails
 Ere even his work's begun.
Think big, and your deeds will grow,
 Think small and you fall behind,
Think that you can, and you will;
 It's all in the state of mind.

"If you think you are outclassed, you are;
 You've got to think high to rise;
You've got to be sure of yourself before
 You can ever win a prize.

Life's battle doesn't always go
  To the stronger or faster man;
But sooner or later, the man who wins
  Is the fellow who thinks he can."

There's a vast difference between a proper understanding of one's own ability and a determination to make the best of it—and offensive egotism. It is absolutely necessary for every man to believe in himself, before he can make the most of himself. All of us have something to sell. It may be our goods, it may be our abilities, it may be our services. You've got to believe in yourself to make your buyer take stock in you at par and accrued interest. You've got to feel the same personal solicitude over a customer lost, as a revivalist over a backslider, and hold special services to bring him back into the fold. You've got to get up every morning with determination, if you're going to go to bed that night with satisfaction.

There's mighty sound sense in the saying that the entire world loves a booster. The one and only thing you have to win success with is MIND. For your mind to function at its highest capacity, you've got to be charged with good cheer and optimism. No one ever did a good piece of work while in a negative frame of mind. Your best work is always done when you are feeling, happy and optimistic.

And a happy disposition is the *result*—not the *cause*—of happy, cheery thinking. Health and prosperity are the *results* primarily of optimistic thoughts. You make the pattern. If the impress you have left on the world about you seems faint and weak, don't blame fate—blame your pattern! You will never cultivate a brave, courageous demeanor by thinking cowardly thoughts. You cannot gather figs from thistles. You will never make your dreams come true by choking them with doubts and fears. You've got to put foundations under your air castles, foundations of UNDERSTANDING and BELIEF. Your chances of success in any undertaking can always be measured by your BELIEF in yourself.

Are your surroundings discouraging? Do you feel that if you were in another's place success would be easier? Just bear in mind that your real environment is within you. All the factors of success or failure are in your inner world. *You* make that own inner world—and through it your outer world. You can choose the material from which to build it. If you've not chosen wisely in the past, you can choose again now the material you want to rebuild it. The richness of life is within you. No one has failed so long as he can begin again.

Start right in and *do* all those things you feel you have it in you to do. Ask permission of no man. Concentrating your thought upon any proper undertaking will make its achievement possible. Your belief that you *can* do the thing gives your thought forces their power. Fortune waits upon you. Seize her boldly, hold her—and she is yours. She belongs rightfully to you. But if you cringe to her, if you go up to her doubtfully, timidly, she will pass you by in scorn. For she is a fickle jade who must be mastered, who loves boldness, who admires confidence.

A Roman boasted that it was sufficient for him to strike the ground with his foot and legions would spring up. And his very boldness cowed his opponents. It is the same with your mind. Take the first step, and your mind will mobilize all its forces to your aid. But the first essential is that you *begin*. Once the battle is started, all that is within and without you will come to your assistance, if you attack in earnest and meet each obstacle with resolution. But *you* have got to start things.

"The Lord helps them that help themselves" is a truth as old as man.

It is, in fact, plain common sense. Your subconscious mind has all power, but your conscious mind is the watchman at the gate. *It* has got to open the door. *It* has got to press the spring that releases the infinite energy. No failure is possible in the accomplishment of any right object you may have in life, if you but understand your power and will perseveringly try to use it in the proper way.

The men who have made their mark in this world all had one trait in common—*they believed in themselves*! "But," you may say, "how can I believe in myself when I have never yet done anything worth while, when everything I put my hand to seems to fail?" You can't, of course. That is, you couldn't if you had to depend upon your conscious mind alone. But just remember what one far greater than you said—"I can of mine own self do nothing. The Father that is within me—He doeth the works."

That same "Father" is within you. And it is by knowing that He *is* in you, and that through Him you can do anything that is right, that you can acquire that belief in yourself which is so necessary. Certainly the Mind that imaged the heavens and the earth and all that they contain has all wisdom, all power, and all abundance. With this Mind to call upon, you know there is no problem too difficult for you to undertake. The *knowing* of this is the first step. *Faith*. But St. James tells us—"Faith without works is dead." So go on to the next step. Decide on the one thing you want most from life. No matter what it may be. There is no limit, you know, to Mind. Visualize this thing that you want. See it, feel it, BELIEVE in it. Make your mental blueprint, and *begin to build!*

Suppose some people DO laugh at your idea. Suppose Reason does say—"It can't be done!" People laughed at Galileo. They laughed at Henry Ford. Reason contended for countless ages that the earth was flat. Reason said—or so numerous automotive engineers argued—that the Ford motor wouldn't run. But the earth is round—and the twelfth or fifteenth million Ford is on the road.

Let us start right now putting into practice some of these truths that you have learned. What do you want most of life right now? Take that one desire, concentrate on it, and impress it upon your subconscious mind.

Psychologists have discovered that the best time to make suggestions to your subconscious mind is just before going to sleep, when the senses are quiet and the attention is lax. So let us take your desire and suggest it to your subconscious mind tonight. The two prerequisites are the earnest DESIRE, and an intelligent, understanding BELIEF. Someone has said, you know, that education is three-fourths encouragement, and the encouragement is the suggestion that the thing can be done.

You know that you can have what you want; if you want it badly enough and can believe in it earnestly enough. So tonight, just before you drop off to sleep, concentrate your thought on this thing that you most desire from life. BELIEVE that you have it. SEE YOURSELF possessing it. FEEL yourself using it.

Do that every night until you ACTUALLY DO BELIEVE that you have the thing you want. When you reach that point, YOU *WILL HAVE IT!*

STUDY GUIDE

IX *The Formula of Success*

1. This chapter opens with a wonderful poem from Ella Wheeler Wilcox. She uses the analogy of a boat at sea to express her sentiments. Give yourself permission to play, and write a short poem or narrative about your belief in the Secret of the Ages, using your own unique analogy.

2. Collier shares that the eternal question we each have as we awaken each morning as *"How can I better my condition?"* Have you ever experienced a time when you felt your condition was just perfect, and there was no need to better it? If so, when. If not, do you believe that such a day will come? Why or why not?

3. Collier asserts that if you control your thoughts, you will control your circumstances. On a scale from one to ten (one being very little, and ten being very much so), rate how much you believe you can control your mind.

    1——2——3——4——5——6——7——8——9——10

4. On a scale from one to ten (one being very little, and ten being very much so), rate how much you believe you control your circumstances.

    1——2——3——4——5——6——7——8——9——10

5. Belief is the *"evidence of things not seen"*. Something or someone gives you a belief in yourself and in your power to win. Reflect back on your life, and write a list of those individuals who raised your spirit and your confidence in yourself.

6. Have you ever thanked those that supported you in your life? If not, you make want to take some time to send them a letter or email of gratitude.

7. Collier shares the story of the insecure farm boy and the fake talisman his grandmother gave him. Do you ever carry a talisman to support you in your courageous journey? Do you think one might assist you Why or why not?

The Talisman of Napoleon

8. Do you knock on wood or follow any superstitions? If so, do you believe they support or lower your sense of well-being?

9. You are encouraged to bring your talents into the Storehouse—the Consciousness of Good. Write a comprehensive list of the talents that you possess.

10. Do you believe within your heart that there are a million channels through which goodness can come to you, or do you still struggle with a sense of lack? Write a list of at least ten means by which goodness could be delivered to you.

11. Have you ever noticed that the Universe often delivers our wishes in ways that we didn't expect? Write about at least one situation in which you experienced this.

12. Collier states that most of us are lazy and follow the status quo. On a scale from one to ten (one being very little, and ten being very much so), rate how lazy you believe yourself to be.

    1——2——3——4——5——6——7——8——9——10

13. The author asserts that like Edison, you need perseverance. Have you ever been in a situation where you felt you gave up too early on yourself? If so, write about it. If not, take a moment to congratulate yourself.

14. According to Collier, complacency and self-satisfaction are the enemies to achievement. Do you believe this to be true? Why or why not?

15. Ideas release energy, and according to William James, *"The more mind does, the more it can do."* Each day, try to do one small exercise that stretches your mind. This could be working on a crossword puzzle, studying the dictionary or doing automatic writing for 5 minutes each morning.

16. Collier asserts that you can work almost indefinitely if you enjoy the work that you do. Have you ever experienced this in some endeavor you were working on? If so, write about it.

"It Couldn't Be Done"

17. How do you believe your confidence has been lowered in your life?

18. Collier shares a poem that encourages a positive mindset. Copy and print this poem, then place it somewhere that you can read it often. Then be sure to take the time to both read and ingest it.

19. Define "offensive egoism" as you understand it.

20. Write a list of the goods, abilities and services that you have to sell the world.

21. Good cheer is necessary. Are there practices you do on a daily basis to support good cheer within you. If so, what? If not, take some time to research things that might enhance your mindset.

22. Some suggest that you have to "fake it until you make it". If there are times when you are not feeling optimistic, try pretending you are. Note any shifts practicing this creates within you.

23. Do you find your surroundings discouraging in any way? If so, remember that the real environment is within you. That being said, sometimes it's easier to remove yourself from negativity. Have you ever done so, or do you need to do so at this time?

24. You are encouraged to ask permission of no man. Is there anyone in your life (dead or alive) with whom you feel you need to ask permission or justify your actions?

25. Fortune *"loves boldness"*. Write at least one situation in which you were bold and unabashed in your actions.

26. Have you ever used your power improperly? Can you forgive yourself for doing so (holding onto the guilt maintains negative energy and will not support you)?

27. Psychologists have discovered that the best time to make suggestions to your subconscious mind is just before going to sleep. To do so, you need to have earnest desire and intelligent, understanding belief. Before going to sleep tonight and indefinitely, do this exercise, being sure to see and feel yourself possessing and using that which you most desire. Note any shifts in your thoughts and feelings.

28. When you do the evening subconscious suggestions exercise, do you do so with a sense of adventure and fun? If you do so, you will find that it is a joy, not a burden. With joy comes appreciation and ultimately results.

X

"This Freedom"

*"Ye shall know the truth
And the Truth shall make you free."*

I have heard that quotation ever since I was a little child. Most of us have. But to me it was never anything much but a quotation—until a few years ago. It is only in the past several years that I have begun to get an inkling of the real meaning of it—an understanding of the comfort back of it. Perhaps to you, too, it has been no more than a sonorous phrase. If so, you will be interested in what I have since gotten from it.

To begin with, what is the "truth" that is so often referred to in all our religious teaching? The truth about what? And what is it going to free us from?

The truth as I see it now is the underlying reality in everything we meet in life. There is, for instance, one right way to solve any given problem in mathematics. That one right way is the truth as far as that problem is concerned. To know it is to free yourself from all doubt and vain imagining and error. It is to free yourself from any trouble that might arise through solving the problem incorrectly.

In the same way, there is but one BEST way of solving every situation that confronts you. That BEST way is the truth. To know it is to make you free from all worry or trouble in connection with that situation. For if it is met in the RIGHT way, only good can come of it.

Then there is your body. There is only one RIGHT idea of every organism in your body. One CORRECT method of functioning for each of them. And Universal Mind holds that RIGHT idea, that CORRECT method. The functioning of your body, the rebuilding of each cell and tissue, is the work of your subconscious mind. If you will constantly hold before it the thought that its model is perfection, that weakness or sickness or deformity is merely ABSENCE of perfection—not a reality in itself—in short, if you will realize the *Truth* concerning your body, your subconscious mind will speedily make you free and keep you free from every ill.

It matters not what is troubling you today. If you will KNOW that whatever it may seem to be is merely the absence of the true idea, if you will realize that the only thing that counts is the truth that Universal Mind knows about your body, you can make that truth manifest.

Affirm the good, the true—and the evil will vanish. It is like turning on the light—the darkness immediately disappears. For there is no actual substance in darkness—it is merely absence of light. Nor is there any substance in sickness or evil—it is merely the absence of health or good.

That is the truth that was the mentality of Jesus—what Paul describes as "the mind, which was also in Christ Jesus."

Jesus declared that "we should know the truth, and the truth would make us free." That truth was the power, which He exercised. He had so perfect an understanding of truth that it gave Him absolute dominion over evil, enabled Him to heal diseases of every nature, even to raise the dead. The power that He exercised then was not confined to His time, nor limited to His own immediate followers. "Lo, I am with you always," He said, "even unto the end of the world." And He is just as available to us now as He was to His own disciples 1900 years ago.

"I have given you power to tread serpents and scorpions under foot and to trample on all the power of the enemy; and in no case shall anything do you harm."

That gift was never meant to be confined to His own disciples or to any other one group. God has never dealt in special or temporary gifts. He gives to *all*—to all who will accept—to all who have an understanding heart.

All sickness, all poverty, all sorrow, is the result of the incorrect use of some gift of God, which in itself is inherently good. It is just as though we took the numbers that were given us to work out a problem, and put them in the wrong places. The result would be incorrect, inharmonious. We would not be expressing the truth. The moment we rearrange those numbers properly, we get the correct answer—harmony—the *truth*! There was nothing wrong with the principle of mathematics before—the fault was all with us, with our incorrect arrangement of the figures.

What is true of the principle of mathematics is true of every principle. The principle is changeless, undying. It is only our expression of the principle that changes as our understanding of it becomes more thorough. Lightning held only terror for man until he made of electricity his servant. Steam was only so much waste until man learned to harness it. Fire and water are the most destructive forces known—until properly used, and then they are man's greatest helpers. There is nothing wrong with any gift of God—once we find the way to use it. The truth is always there if we can find the principle behind it. The figures in mathematics are never bad. It is merely our incorrect arrangement of them.

The great need is an open mind and the desire for understanding. How far in the science of mathematics would you get if you approached the study of it with the preconceived notion that two plus two makes five, and nothing you heard to the contrary was going to change that belief? "Except ye turn, and become as little children, ye shall not enter into the kingdom of heaven."

You must drop all your preconceived ideas, all your prejudices. You must never say—"Oh, that sounds like so-and-so. I don't want any of it." Just remember that any great movement must have at least a grain of truth back of it, else it could never grow to any size. Seek that grain of truth. Be open-minded. Keep your eyes and ears open for the truth. If you can do this, you will find that new wordings, different interpretations, are but the outer shell. You can still see the Truth beneath, the Christ that "before Abraham was, I am."

The Only Power

He who is looking for wisdom, power, or permanent success, will find it only within. Mind is the only cause. Your body is healthy or sick according to the images of thought you impress upon your subconscious mind. If you will hold thoughts of health instead of sickness, if you will banish all thoughts of disease and decay, you can build up a perfect body. Dr. William S. Patten of New York says, "To know and to understand the organization of mind and to recognize the action of mind is the first and the only requisite of a sound body." For all disease starts in the mind. It may be in your own conscious mind, from reading of an epidemic or from meeting with circumstances which education has taught you will bring about disease. It may be suggested to your subconscious mind, as so frequently happens with young children, by the fears and worries and thoughts of contagion of those around you.

But whichever it is, it is FEAR that starts it. You visualize, consciously or unconsciously, the disease that you fear, and because that is the image held before your thought, your body proceeds to build in accordance with that model. You believe that disease is necessary, that you have got to expect a certain amount of it. You hear of it every day, and subconsciously at least you are constantly in fear of it. And through that very fear you create it, when if you would spend that same amount of time thinking and believing in the necessity of HEALTH, you would never need to know disease.

God does not send disease. It is not a visitation of Providence. If it were, what would be the use of doctoring it? You couldn't fight against the power of God!

God never sent us anything but good. He never gave us disease. When we allow disease to take hold of us, it is because we have lost touch with God—lost the perfect model of us that He holds in mind. And what we have got to strive for is to get back the belief in that perfect model—to forget the diseased image we are holding in our thought.

Remember the story of Alexander and his famous horse, Bucephalus? No one could ride the horse because it was afraid of its shadow. But Alexander faced it towards the sun—and rode it without trouble. Face towards the sun and the shadows will fall behind you, too. Face towards the perfect image of every organ, and the shadows of disease will never touch you.

There is no germ in a draft capable of giving you a cold. There are no bacteria in exposure to the weather that can give you a fever or pneumonia. It is you that gives them to yourself. The draft doesn't reason this out. Neither does your body. They are both of them merely phases of matter. They are not intelligent. It is your conscious mind that has been educated to think that a cold must follow exposure to a draft. This it is that suggests it to your subconscious mind and brings the cold into being.

Before you decide again that you have a cold, ask yourself, who is it that is taking this cold? It cannot be my nose, for it has no intelligence. It does only what my subconscious mind directs. And anyway, how could my nose know that a draft of air has been playing on the back of my neck? If it wasn't my nose that decided it, what was it? The only thing it can have been is my mind. Well, if mind can tell me to have a cold, surely it can stop that cold, too. So let's reverse the process, and instead of holding before the subconscious mind images of colds and fevers, think only of health and life and strength. Instead of trying to think back to discover how we "caught" cold, and thus strengthening the conviction that we have one, let us deny its existence and so knock the props out from under the creative faculties that are originating the cold. Let us hold before our subconscious mind only the perfect idea of nose and head and throat that is in Universal Mind. Let us make it use the Truth for its pattern, instead of the illusory ideas of conscious mind.

Every form of disease or sickness is solely the result of wrong thinking. The primary law of being is the law of health and life. When you recognize this, when you hold before your mind's eye only a perfect body, perfect organisms functioning perfectly, you will "realize the truth that makes you free."

Farnsworth in his "Practical Psychology" tells of a physician who has lived on a very restricted diet for years while at home. But about once a year he comes to New York for a week. While here, he eats anything and everything that his fancy dictates, and never suffers the least inconvenience. As soon as he gets home he has to return to his diet. Unless he sticks to his diet, he expects to be ill—*and he is ill*. "As a man thinketh, so is he." What one expects to get he is apt to get, especially where health is concerned. For matter has no sensation of its own. The conscious mind is what produces pain, is what feels, acts or impedes action.

Functional disorders are caused by certain suggestions getting into the sub consciousness and remaining there. They are not due to physical, but to mental causes—due to wrong thinking. The basis of all functional disorders is in the mind, though the manifestation is dyspepsia, melancholia, palpitation of the heart, or any one of a hundred others. There is nothing organically wrong with the body. It is your mental image that is out of adjustment. Change the one and you cure the other.

In this day of the gymnasium and the daily dozen, it may sound impractical to suggest that it is the mind, not the body, which needs the care. But I am far from being the first to suggest it.

There is a very successful physician in London whose teaching is that gymnastic exercise does more harm than good. He contends that the only exercise necessary for the perfect development of the body is yawning and stretching.

I would go farther than that. I would say that no physical exercise is *essential* to the perfect development of the body. That since the only cause is mind, the principal good of exercise is that when we go through the motions we impress upon our subconscious mind the picture of the perfect figure that we would have. And that mental visualization is what brings the results.

You can get the same results without the physical exercise by visualizing in your mind's eye the figure of the man you want to be, by intensely desiring it, by BELIEVING that you have it.

You can win to perfect health by knowing that there is but one right idea in Universal Mind for every organism in your body—that this right idea is perfect and undying—that you have only to hold it before your subconscious mind to see it realized in your body. *This is the truth that makes you free.*

STUDY GUIDE

X *"This Freedom"*

1. *"Ye shall know the truth And the Truth shall make you free."* What did this quote mean to you prior to reading this book? Did it affect you in any way?

2. There is a Truth, a "RIGHT idea" for every organism in your body. Collier asserts that if you constantly hold the thought that its model is perfection, then sickness is not a reality because it is only the absence of that perfection. You would be free from illness. What about the aging process? How do you see it fitting into this equation?

3. If you realize that whatever is bothering you today, is merely an absence of truth, then you can give such thoughts little power. Do you believe this to be possible, perhaps even easy? Why or why not?

4. If you have an understanding heart, then Collier asserts that you have the powers that God gave Christ and His disciples. Is there anything that prevents you from seeing yourself in that light?

5. *"There is nothing wrong with any gift from God—once we find the way to use it."* Is there anything that you think is not a gift from God that could be used for the good of mankind? If so, what and why do you hold this belief?

6. You need to drop all of your preconceived ideas and prejudices. On a scale from one to ten (one being very little, and ten being very much so), rate how open-minded you believe yourself to be.

   1——2——3——4——5——6——7——8——9——10

The Only Power

7. Do you spend much time studying or researching ailments? If so, do you believe that focusing on them enhances your health or does not? Do you have a different perspective after reading this book?

8. There is a great deal of media focus on diseases like cancer. Do you fear getting it or other diseases? To add to the torment, do you fear your fear because you know of the power of your mind? What can you do to shift your focus?

9. Do you fear genetic transfer of illnesses within your lineage from your ancestors to you? Do some research on individuals who did not manifest genetic diseases during their lifetime. Write about your findings.

10. You are encouraged to face towards the perfect image of every organ in your body. Take one minute each day and scan your body, seeing all organs and systems functioning perfectly. Then thank your body for being so cooperative.

11. According to Collier, bacteria, viruses or germs do not give you a cold, your thoughts do. What do you believe weakens your immune system? What can you do to shift your perception of contractible illness?

12. What are your current beliefs around diet and weight gain? What suggestions do you hold in your mind about your metabolism? Visualize yourself at your ideal weight, and see your body metabolizing food in a healthy manner. Note how you feel after doing this exercise, and write about your findings.

13. The authors also claims that functional disorders like dyspepsia, melancholia, and palpitation of the heart are all mental images that are out of adjustment. He claims that if you change one, you cure the other. Could you fathom this to be true?

14. Working out is not necessary based on Collier's Secret of the Ages. You can get the same results by visualizing the perfect, fit body. Try visualizing your body the way you would like it to be every day for three months. Track your progress, and take note of any changes that you experience.

XI

The Law of Attraction

For life is the mirror of king and slave.
'Tis just what you are and do;
Then give to the world the best you have,
And the best will come back to you.
—MADELINE BRIDGES.

The old adage that "He profits most who serves best" is no mere altruism.

Look around you. What businesses are going ahead? What men are making the big successes? Are they the ones who grab the passing dollar, careless of what they offer in return? Or are they those who are striving always to give a little greater value, a little more work than they are paid for?

When scales are balanced evenly, a trifle of extra weight thrown into either side overbalances the other as effectively as a ton.

In the same way, a little better value, a little extra effort, makes the man or the business stand out from the great mass of mediocrity like a tall man among pigmies, and brings results out of all proportion to the additional effort involved.

It pays—not merely altruistically, but in good, hard, round dollars—to give a little more value than seems necessary, to work a bit harder than you are paid for. It's that extra ounce of value that counts.

For the law of attraction is service. We receive in proportion as we give out. In fact, we usually receive in far greater proportion. "Cast thy bread upon the waters and it will return to you an hundred-fold."

Back of everything is the immutable law of the Universe—that what you are but the effect. Your thoughts are the causes. The only way you can change the effect is by first changing the cause.

People live in poverty and want because they are so wrapped up in their sufferings that they give out thoughts only of lack and sorrow. They expect want. They open the door of their mind only to hardship and sickness and poverty. True—they hope for something better—but their hopes are so drowned by their fears that they never have a chance.

You cannot receive good while expecting evil. You cannot demonstrate plenty while looking for poverty. "Blessed is he that expecteth much, for verily his soul shall be filled." Solomon outlined the law when he said:

"There is that scattereth, and increaseth yet more;
And there is that withholdeth more than is meet,
   but it tendeth only to want.
The liberal soul shall be made fat;
And he that watereth shall be watered also himself."

The Universal Mind expresses itself largely through the individual. It is continually seeking an outlet. It is like a vast reservoir of water, constantly replenished by mountain springs. Cut a channel to it and the water will flow in ever-increasing volume. In the same way, if you once open up a channel of service by which the Universal Mind can express itself through you, its gifts will flow in ever increasing volume and YOU will be enriched in the process.

This is the idea through which great bankers are made. A foreign country needs millions for development. Its people are hard working, but lack the necessary implements to make their work productive. How are they to find the money?

They go to a banker—put their problem up to him. He has not the money himself, but he knows how and where to raise it. He sells the promise to pay of the foreign country (their bonds, in other words) to people who have money to invest. His is merely a service. But it is such an invaluable service that both sides are glad to pay him liberally for it.

In the same way, by opening up a channel between universal supply and human needs—by doing your neighbors or your friends or your customer's service—you are bound to profit yourself. And the wider you open your channel—the greater service you give or the better values you offer—the more things are bound to flow through your channel, the more you are going to profit thereby.

But you've got to *use* your talent if you want to profit from it. It matters not how small your service—using it will make it greater. You don't have to retire to a cell and pray. That is a selfish method—selfish concern for your own soul to the exclusion of all others. Mere self-denial or asceticism as such does no one good. You've got to DO something, to USE the talents God has given you to make the world better for your having been in it.

Remember the parable of the talents. You know what happened to the man who went off and hid his talent, whereas those who made use of theirs were given charge over many things.

That parable, it has always seemed to me, expresses the whole law of life. The only right is to use all the forces of good. The only wrong is to neglect or to abuse them.

"Thou shalt love the Lord thy God. This is the first and the greatest Commandment." Thou shalt show thy love by using to the best possible advantage the good things (the "talents" of the parable) that He has placed in your hands. "And the second is like unto it. Thou shalt love thy neighbor as thyself." Thou shalt not abuse the good things that have been provided you in such prodigality, by using them against your neighbor. Instead, thou shalt treat him (love him) as he would treat you. Thou shalt use the good about you for the advantage of all.

If you are a banker, you've got to use the money you have in order to make more money. If you are a merchant, you've got to sell the goods you have in order to buy more goods. If you are a doctor, you must help the patient you have in order to get more practice. If you are a clerk, you must do your work a little better than those around you if you want to earn more money than they. And if you want more of the universal supply, you must use that which you have in such a way as to make yourself of greater service to those around you.

"Whosoever shall be great among you," said Jesus, "shall be your minister, and whosoever of you will be the chiefest, shall be servant of all." In other words, if you would be great, you must serve. And he who serves most shall be greatest of all.

If you want to make more money, instead of seeking it for yourself, see how you can make more for others. In the process you will inevitably make more for yourself, too. We get as we give—but we must give first.

It matters not where you start—you may be a day laborer. But still you can give—give a bit more of energy, of work, of thought, than you are paid for. "Whosoever shall compel thee to go a mile," said Jesus, "go with him twain." Try to put a little extra skill into your work. Use your mind to find some better way of doing whatever task may be set for you. It won't be long before you are out of the common labor class.

There is no kind of work than cannot be bettered by thought. There is no method that cannot be improved by thought. So give generously of your thought to your work. Think every minute you are at it—"Isn't there some way in which this could be done easier, quicker, better?" Read in your spare time everything that relates to your own work or to the job ahead of you. In these days of magazines and books and libraries, few are the occupations that are not thoroughly covered in some good work.

Remember in Lorimer's "Letters of a Self-Made Merchant to His Son," the young fellow that old Gorgan Graham hired against his better judgment and put in the "barrel gang" just to get rid of him quickly? Before the month was out the young fellow had thought himself out of that job by persuading the boss to get a machine that did the work at half the cost and with a third of the gang. Graham just had to raise his pay and put him higher up. But he wouldn't stay put. No matter what the job, he always found some way it could be done better and with fewer people, until he reached the top of the ladder.

There are plenty of men like that in actual life. They won't stay down. They are as full of bounce as a cat with a small boy and a dog after it. Thrown to the dog from an upper window, it is using the time of falling to get set for the next jump. By the time the dog leaps for where it hit, the cat is up the tree across the street.

The true spirit of business is the spirit of that plucky old Danish sea captain, Peter Tordenskjold. Attacked by a Swedish frigate, after all his crew but one had been killed and his supply of cannon balls was exhausted, Peter boldly kept up the fight, firing pewter dinner-plates and mugs from his one remaining gun.

One of the pewter mugs hit the Swedish captain and killed him, and Peter sailed off triumphant!

Look around YOU now. How can YOU give greater value for what you get? How can you SERVE better? How can you make more money for your employers or save more for your customers? Keep that thought ever in the forefront of your mind and *you'll never need to worry about making more for yourself!*

A Blank Check

There was an article by Gardner Hunting in a recent issue of "Christian Business," that was so good that I reprint it here entire:

"All my life I have known in a vague way that getting money is the result of earning it; but I have never had a perfect vision of that truth till recently. Summed up now, the result of all my experience, pleasant and unpleasant, is that a man gets back exactly what he gives out, only multiplied.

"If I give to anybody service of a kind that he wants I shall get back the benefit myself. If I give more service I shall get more benefit. If I give a great deal more, I shall get a great deal more. But I shall get back more than I give. Exactly as when I plant a bushel of potatoes, I get back thirty or forty bushels, and more in proportion to the attention I give the growing crop. If I give more to my employer than he expects of me, he will give me a raise—and on no other condition. What is more, his giving me a raise does not depend on his fair-mindedness—he has to give it to me or lose me, because if he does not appreciate me somebody else will.

"But this is only part of it. If I give help to the man whose desk is next to mine, it will come back to me multiplied, even if he apparently is a rival. What I give to him, I give to the firm, and the firm will value it, because it is teamwork in the organization that the firm primarily wants, not brilliant individual performance. If I have an enemy in the organization, the same rule holds; if I give him, with the purpose of helping him, something that will genuinely help him, I am giving service to the organization. Great corporations appreciate the peacemaker, for a prime requisite in their success is harmony among employees. If my boss is unappreciative, the same rule holds; if I give him more, in advance of appreciation, he cannot withhold his appreciation and keep his own job.

"The more you think about this law, the deeper you will see it goes. It literally hands you a blank check, signed by the Maker of Universal Law, and leaves you to fill in the amount—and the kind—of payment you want! Mediocre successes are those that obey this law a little way—that fill in the check with a small amount—but that stop short of big vision in it. If every employee would only get the idea of this law firmly fixed in him as a principle, not subject to wavering with fluctuating moods, the success of the organization would be miraculous. One of my fears is apt to be that, by promoting the other fellow's success, I am sidetracking my own; but the exact opposite is the truth.

"Suppose every employee would look at his own case as an exact parallel to that of his firm. What does his firm give for the money it gets from the public? Service! Service in advance! The better the service that is given out, the more money comes back. What does the firm do to bring public attention to its service? It advertises; that is part of the service. Now, suppose that I, as an employee, begin giving my service to the firm in advance of all hoped for payment. Suppose I advertise my service. How do I do either? I cannot do anything constructive in that firm's office or store or plant or premises that is not service, from filing a letter correctly to mending the fence or pleasing a customer; from looking up a word for the stenographer, to encouraging her to look it up herself; demonstrating a machine to a customer or encouraging him to demonstrate it himself; from helping my immediate apparent rival to get a raise, to selling the whole season's output. As for advertising myself, I begin advertising myself the moment I walk into the office or the store or the shop in the morning; I cannot help it. Everybody who looks at me sees my advertisement. Everybody around me has my advertisement before his eyes all day long. So has the boss—my immediate chief and the head of the firm, no matter where they are. And if I live up to my advertising, nobody can stop me from selling my goods—my services! The more a man knocks me, the more he advertises me; because he calls attention to me; and ill am delivering something better than he says I am, the interested parties—my employers—will see it, and will not be otherwise influenced by what he says.

"More than that, I must give to every human being I come in contact with, from my wife to the bootblack who shines my shoes; from my brother to my sworn foe. Sometimes people will tell you to smile; but the smile I give has got to be a real smile that lives up to its advertising. If I go around grinning like a Cheshire cat, the Cheshire-cat grin will be what I get back—multiplied! If I give the real thing, I'll get back the real thing—multiplied! If anybody objects that this is a selfish view to take, I answer him that any law of salvation from anything by anybody that has ever been offered for any purpose, is a selfish view to take. The only unselfishness that has ever been truly taught is that of giving a lesser thing in hope of receiving a greater.

"Now, why am I so sure of this law? How can you be sure? I have watched it work; it works everywhere. You have only to try it, and keep on trying it and it will prove true for you. It is not true because I say so, nor because anybody else says so; it is just true. Theosophists call it the law of Karma; humanitarians call it the law of Service; businessmen call it the law of common sense; Jesus Christ called it the law of Love. It rules whether I know it or not, whether I believe it or not, whether I defy it or not. I *can't* break it! Jesus of Nazareth, without reference to any religious idea you may have about Him, without consideration as to whether He was or was not divine, was the greatest business Man that ever lived, and he said: 'Give and ye shall receive—good measure, pressed down, shaken together, running over!' And this happens to be so—not because He said it—but because it is the Truth, which we all, whether we admit it or not, worship *as* God.

No man can honestly say that he does not put the truth supreme.

"It is the truth—the principle of giving and receiving—only there are few men who go the limit on it. But going the limit is the way to unlimited returns!

"What shall I give? What I have, of course. Suppose you believe in this idea—and suppose you should start giving it out, the idea itself, tactfully, wisely, and living it yourself in your organization.

How long do you think it will be before you are a power in that organization, recognized as such and getting pay as such? It is more valuable than all the cleverness and special information you can possibly possess without it. What you have, give—to everybody. If you have an idea, do not save it for your own use only; give it. It is the best thing you have to give and therefore the thing best to give—and therefore the thing that will bring the best back to you. I believe that if a man would follow this principle, even to his trade secrets, he would profit steadily more and more; and more certainly than he will by holding on to anything for himself. He would never have to worry about his own affairs because he would be working on fundamental law. Law never fails—and it will be easy for you to discover what is or is not law. And if law is worth using part of the time, it is worth using all the time.

"Look around you first, with an eye to seeing the truth, and then put the thing to the test. Through both methods of investigation you will find a blank check waiting for you to fill in with 'whatsoever you desire,' and a new way to pray and to get what you pray for."

STUDY GUIDE

XI *The Law of Attraction*

1. Based on the wisdom of Madeline Bridges' poem, what examples of "the best" have come back to you in your life? List at least three examples of your life reflecting back your goodness to you.

2. *"He profits most who serves best"* is a powerful quote. However, serving others from an inauthentic place of "I should do it" rather than "I want to do it" can deplete your energy, rather than build it. Write a list of how you serve others. Then note which actions come from a place of "wanting to" and which come from the place of "I should". Then contemplate either removing the "should" activities from your life, or changing your perception of them. Note the shift in your physical energy once you complete this exercise.

3. How do you currently provide more value when you serve others?

4. How might you improve, so that you go the extra mile when serving others?

5. Perhaps more significantly, how do you feel when you give a little more value? Do you like yourself more? How much does that self-respect add to your physical, emotional and mental energy?

6. Your hopes can be so drowned by your fears that they never have a chance to be manifest. Ask yourself this question, "What is the worst thing that can happen if I give focusing on my greatest desire my total commitment?" Is it worth fighting for?

7. *"If you once open up a channel of service by which the Universal Mind can express itself through, its gifts will flow in every increasing volume and YOU will be enriched in the process."* Seeing yourself as a channel through which the Universal Mind can flow, takes you away from personal responsibility and ownership. Does this free you to apply your focus and commitment?

8. Have you ever considered how you are positively affecting the world in the work that you do? Take some time to list the ways in which you currently contribute to the world.

9. The larger your channel, the greater the opportunities come your way. How might you grow your channel?

10. Like the parable of the talents, are there talents you currently have that you are not using? If so, list them? Is there a way you can dig them up and start to use them?

11. Are there talents that you would like to develop, but have not? Write a list of them and set an intention and schedule to unearth them.

12. If you want to make more money, focus on how you can make it for others. What might you do with your talents to help others find abundance in their lives?

13. How might you improve upon the work that you are currently doing? Can you do further reading or research to enhance your knowledge and skills?

14. How might you make more money for your employers?

15. Is there any way you can save money for your customers?

A Blank Check

16. In Gardner Hunting's article, she emphasizes that we get back more than we give. One of her positions is *"The more a man knocks me, the more he advertises me; because he calls attention to me; and ill am delivering*

something better than he says I am, the interested parties—my employers—will see it, and will not be otherwise influenced by what he says" Do you believe this to be true? Is this always the case? Have you ever heard a rumor from a trusted friend, and because you trusted him or her, you believed the rumor to be true?

17. She further states in the article, *"Going the limit is the way to unlimited returns."* You may wish to add an interesting photo or graphic to this quote and hang it in your workplace as a reminder of this truth.

18. If you give of everything, including your trade secrets, according to Ms. Hunting's article, you will rise victorious. She suggests that you do not hold back and that the Law of Attraction will prove itself to you. Do you hold back on sharing your innovations with others in fear of them being stolen? Can you believe that your generosity would be protected by the Law? Why or why not?

XII

The Three Requisites

"Waste no tears
Upon the blotted record of lost years,
But turn the leaf, and smile, oh smile, to see
The fair white pages that remain for thee.

"Prate not of thy repentance. But believe
The spark divine dwells in thee: let it grow.
That which the up-reaching spirit can achieve
The grand and all creative forces know;
They will assist and strengthen as the light
Lifts up the acorn to the oak-tree's height.
Thou hast but to resolve, and lo! God's whole
Great universe shall fortify thy soul."
—Ella Wheeler Wilcox.

Sometime today or tomorrow or next month, in practically every commercial office and manufacturing plant in the United States, an important executive will sit back in his chair and study a list of names on a sheet of white paper before him.

Your name may be on it.

A position of responsibility is open and he is face to face with the old, old problem—"Where can I find the man?"

The faces, the words, the work, the impressions of various men will pass through his mind in quick review. What is the first question he will ask concerning each?

"Which man is strongest on initiative, which one can best assume responsibility?"

Other things being equal, THAT is the man who will get the job. For the first requisite in business as in social life is confidence in yourself—*knowledge of your power.* Given that, the second is easy—initiative or *the courage to start things.* Lots of men have ideas, but few have the confidence in themselves or the courage to start anything.

With belief and initiative, the third requisite follows almost as a matter of course—*the faith to go ahead* and do things in the face of all obstacles.

"Oh, God," said Leonardo da Vinci, "you sell us everything for the price of an effort."

Certainly no one had a better chance to know than he. An illegitimate son, brought up in the family of his father, the misfortune of his birth made him the source of constant derision. He had to do something to lift himself far above the crowd. And he did. "For the price of an effort" he became the greatest artist in Italy—probably the greatest in the world—in a day when Italy was famous for her artists. Kings and princes felt honored at being associated with this illegitimate boy. He made the name he had no right to famous for his work alone.

"Work out your own salvation," said Paul. And the first requisite in working it out is knowledge of your power. "Every man of us has all the centuries in him."—Morley. All the ages behind you have bequeathed you stores of abilities, which you are allowing to lie latent. Those abilities are stored up in your subconscious mind. Call upon them. Use them. As Whittier put it—

"All the good the past has had Remains to make our own time glad."

Are you an artist? The cunning of a da Vinci, the skill of a Rembrandt, the vision of a Reynolds, is behind those fingers of yours. Use the Genie-of-your-mind to call upon them.

Are you a surgeon, a lawyer, a minister, and an engineer, a businessman? Keep before your mind's eye the biggest men who have ever done the things you now are doing. Use them as your model and not as your model simply, but as your inspiration. Start in where they left off. Call upon the innermost recesses of your subconscious mind, for their skill, their judgment, their initiative. Realize that you have it in you to be as great as they. Realize that all that they did, all that they learned, all the skill they acquired is stored safely away in Universal Mind and that through your subconscious mind *you have ready access to it*.

The mind in you is the same mind that animated all the great conquerors of the past, all the great inventors, all the great artists, statesmen, leaders, business men. What they have done is but a tithe of what still remains to do—of what men in your day and your children's day will do. You can have a part in it. Stored away within you is every power that any man or woman ever possessed. It awaits only your call.

In "Thoughts on Business," we read: "It is a great day in a man's life when he truly begins to discover himself. The latent capacities of every man are greater than he realizes, and he may find them if he diligently seeks for them.

A man may own a tract of land for many years without knowing its value. He may think of it as merely a pasture. But one day he discovers evidences of coal and finds a rich vein beneath his land. While mining and prospecting for coal he discovers deposits of granite. In boring for water he strikes oil. Later he discovers a vein of copper ore, and after that silver and gold. These things were there all the time—even when he thought of his land merely as a pasture. But they have a value only when they are discovered and utilized.

"Not every pasture contains deposits of silver and gold, neither oil nor granite, nor even coal. But beneath the surface of every man there must be, in the nature of things, a latent capacity greater than has yet been discovered. And one discovery must lead to another until the man finds the deep wealth of his own possibilities. History is full of the acts of men who discovered somewhat of their own capacity; but history has yet to record the man who fully discovered all that be might have been."

Everything that has been done, thought, gained, or been is in Universal Mind. And you are a part of Universal Mind. You have access to it. You can call upon it for all you need in the same way you can go to your files or to a library for information. If you can realize this fact, you will find in it the key to the control of every circumstance, the solution of every problem, the satisfaction of every right desire.

But to use that key, you've got to bear in mind the three requisites of faith in your powers, initiative, and courage to start. "Who would stand before a blackboard," says "Science and Health," "and pray the principle of mathematics to solve the problem? The rule is already established, and it is our task to work out the solution." In the same way, all knowledge you can need is in Universal Mind, but it is up to *you* to tap that mind.

And without the three requisites you will never do it.

Never let discouragement hold you back. Discouragement is the most dangerous feeling there is, because it is the most insidious. Generally it is looked upon as harmless, and for that very reason it is the more sinister. For failure and success are oftentimes separated by only the distance of that one word—Discouragement.

There is an old-time fable that the devil once held a sale and offered all the tools of his trade to anyone who would pay their price. They were spread out on the table, each one labeled—hatred, and malice, and envy, and despair, and sickness, and sensuality—all the weapons that everyone knows so well.

But off on one side, apart from the rest, lay a harmless looking, wedge-shaped instrument marked "Discouragement." It was old and worn looking, but it was priced far above all the rest. When asked the reason why, the devil replied:

"Because I can use this one so much more easily than the others. No one knows that it belongs to me, so with it I can open doors that are tight bolted against the others. Once I get inside I can use any tool that suits me best."

No one ever knows how small is the margin between failure and success. Frequently the two are separated only by the width of that one word—*discouragement*. Ask Ford, ask Edison, ask any successful man and he will tell you how narrow is the chasm that separates failure from success, how surely it can be bridged by perseverance and faith.

Cultivate confidence in yourself. Cultivate the feeling that you ARE succeeding. Know that you have unlimited power to do every right thing. Know that with Universal Mind to draw upon, no position is too difficult, and no problem too hard. "He that believeth on me, the works that I do shall he do also; and greater works than these shall he do." When you put limitations upon yourself, when you doubt your ability to meet any situation, you are placing a limit upon Universal Mind, for "The Father that is within me, He doeth the works."

With that knowledge of your power, with that confidence in the unlimited resources of Universal Mind, it is easy enough to show initiative, it is easy enough to find the courage to start things.

You have a right to dominion over all things—over your body, your environment, your business, your health. Develop these three requisites and you will gain that dominion. Remember that you are a part of Universal Mind, and that the part shares every property of the whole. Remember that, as the spark of electricity to the thunderbolt, so is your mind to Universal Mind. Whatever of good you may desire of life, whatever qualification, whatever position, you have only to work for it whole heartedly, confidently, with singleness of purpose—*and you can get it.*

STUDY GUIDE

XII *The Three Requisites*

1. This chapter opens with a poem by Ella Wheeler Wilcox. List the images that your mind conjured as you read this poem.

2. Along with faith, initiative is key to becoming successful. On a scale from one to ten (one being very little, and ten being very much so), rate how much you have the courage to take initiative in your life.

   1——2——3——4——5——6——7——8——9——10

3. Collier uses Leonardo da Vinci as a prime example of initiative. He was a social outcast, yet he rose to the top of his trade, despite its competitive nature. Do you know of anyone who rose out of a rough childhood to great success? Write his or her story. If you do not, then research someone who has and write a short summary of your findings.

4. Research someone who has been a great success in the field of endeavor that you are pursuing. Write a summary of his or her rise to success.

5. Do you see yourself as equaling in his or her greatness?

6. Collier claims that *"beneath the surface of every man is a latent capacity greater than has yet been discovered."* You can call upon the Universal Mind to tap into any skill or expertise that you desire. Do you have a latent passion for some area of expertise that you have yet to pursue? Take some time to explore it, and see if you can take a small step towards delving into it.

7. According to the author, discouragement is the most dangerous feeling there is. Do you believe this to be true? Why or why not?

8. There is a narrow margin between success and failure. You have heard stories of authors, for example, that were rejected by publishers for years, but never gave up. Research one such individual and call their energy and perseverance into your life. Allow him or her to be an energetic muse. Try and develop a personal relationship. See him or her in your mind's eye, asking for support and encouragement when needed. Write about any wisdom or insights that arise in response to doing this exercise.

XIII

That Old Witch—Bad Luck

"How do you tackle your work each day?
Are you scared of the job you find?
Do you grapple the task that comes your way
With a confident, easy mind?
Do you stand right up to the work ahead
Or fearfully pause to view it?
Do you start to toil with a sense of dread
Or feel that you're going to do it?
"What is the thought that is in your mind?
Is fear ever running through it?
If so, just tackle the next you find
By thinking you're going to do it."
—Edgar A. Guest.*

Has that old witch—bad luck—ever camped on your doorstep? Have ill health, misfortune and worry ever seemed to dog your footsteps?

If so, you will be interested in knowing that YOU were the procuring cause of all that trouble. For fear is merely creative thought in negative form.

---

* From "A heap o' Livin'." The Reilly & Lee Co.

Remember back in 1920 how fine the business outlook seemed, how everything looked rosy and life flowed along like a song? We had crops worth ten billions of dollars. We had splendid utilities, great railways, almost unlimited factory capacity. Everyone was busy. The government had a billion dollars in actual money. The banks were sound. The people were well employed. Wages were good. Prosperity was general. *Then something happened.* A wave of fear swept over the country. The prosperity could not last. People wouldn't pay such high prices. There was too much inflation. What was the result?

As Job put it in the long ago, "The thing that I greatly feared has come upon me."

The prosperity vanished almost overnight. Failures became general. Hundreds of thousands were thrown out of work. And all because of panic, fear.

'Tis true that readjustments were necessary. 'Tis true that prices were too high, that inventories were too big, that values generally were inflated.

But it wasn't necessary to burst the balloon to let out the gas. There are orderly natural processes of readjustment that bring things to their proper level with the least harm to anyone.

But fear—panic—knows no reason. It brings into being overnight the things that it fears. It is the greatest torment of humanity. It is about all there is to Hell. *Fear is, in short, the devil.* It causes most of the sin, disaster, disease and misery of the world. It is the only thing you can put into business, which won't draw dividends in either fun or dollars. If you guess right, you don't get any satisfaction out of it.

The real cause of all sickness is fear. You image some disease in your thought, and your body proceeds to build upon this model that you hold before it. You have seen how fear makes the face pallid, how it first stops the beating of the heart, then sets it going at trip-hammer pace. Fear changes the secretions. Fear halts the digestion. Fear puts lines and wrinkles into the face. Fear turns the hair gray.

Mind controls every function of the human body. If the thought you hold before your subconscious mind is the fear of disease, of colds or catarrh, of fever or indigestion, those are the images your subconscious mind will work out in your body. For your body itself is merely so much matter—an aggregation of protons and electrons, just as the table in front of you is an aggregation of these same buttons of force, but with a different density. Take away your mind, and your body is just as inert, just as lifeless, and just as senseless, as the table. Every function of your body, from the beating of your heart to the secretions in your glands, is controlled by mind. The digestion of your food is just as much a function of your mind as the moving of your finger. So the all-important thing is not what food you put into your stomach, but what your mind decides shall be done with it. If your mind feels that certain food should make you sick, it will make you sick. If, on the other hand, your mind decides that though the food has no nutritive value, there is no reason why unintelligent matter should make you sick, mind will eliminate that food without harm or discomfort to you.

Your body is just like clay in the hands of a potter. Your mind can make of it what it will. The clay has nothing to say about what form it shall take. Neither have your head, your heart, your lungs, your digestive organs anything to say about how conditions shall affect them. They do not decide whether they shall be dizzy or diseased or lame. It is mind that makes this decision. They merely conform to it AFTER mind has decided it. Matter has undergone any and every condition without harm, when properly sustained by mind. And what it has done once, it can do again.

When you understand that your muscles, your nerves, your bones have no feeling or intelligence of their own, when you learn that they react to conditions only as mind directs that they shall react, you will never again think or speak of any organ as imperfect, as weak or ailing. You will never again complain of tired bodies, aching muscles, or frayed nerves. On the contrary, you will hold steadfast to thoughts of exhaustless strength, of super-abundant vitality, knowing that, as Shakespeare said—"There is nothing, either good or bad, but thinking makes it so."

Never fear disaster, for the fear of it is an invitation to disaster to come upon you. Fear being vivid, easily impresses itself upon the sub-conscious mind. And by so impressing itself, it brings into being the thing that is feared. It is the Frankenstein monster that we all create at times, and which, created, and turns to rend its creator. Fear that something you greatly prize will be lost and the fear you feel with creates the very means whereby you will lose it.

Fear is the Devil. It is the ravening lion roaming the earth seeking whom it may devour. The only safety from it is to deny it. The only refuge is in the knowledge that it has no power other than the power you give to it.

He Whom a Dream Hath Possessed

You fear debt. So your mind concentrates upon it and brings about greater debts. You fear loss. And by visualizing that loss you bring it about.

The only remedy for fear is to know that evil has no power—that it is a non-entity—merely a lack of something. You fear ill health, when if you would concentrate that same amount of thought upon good health you would insure the very condition you fear to lose. Functional disturbances are caused solely by the mind through wrong thinking. The remedy for them is a not drug, but right thinking, for the trouble is not in the organs but in the mind. Farnsworth in his "Practical Psychology" tells of a man who had conceived the idea when a boy that the eating of cherries and milk together had made him sick. He was very fond of both, but always had to be careful not to eat them together, for whenever he did he had been ill. Mr. Farnsworth explained to him that there was no reason for such illness, because all milk sours anyway just as soon as it reaches the stomach. As a matter of fact it cannot be digested until it does sour. He then treated the man mentally for this wrong association of ideas, and after the one treatment the man was never troubled in this way again, though he had been suffering from it for forty-five years.

If you had delirium tremens, and thought you saw pink elephants and green alligators and yellow snakes all about you, it would be a foolish physician that would try to cure you of snakes. Or that would prescribe glasses to improve your eyesight, when he knew that the animals round about you were merely distorted visions of your mind.

The indigestion that you suffer from, the colds that bother you—in short, each and every One of your ailments-is just as much a distorted idea of your mind as would be the snakes of delirium tremens. Banish the idea and you banish the manifestation.

The Bible contains one continuous entreaty to cast out fear. From beginning to end, the admonition "Fear not" is insistent. Fear is the primary cause of all bodily impairment.

Jesus understood this and He knew that it could be abolished. Hence His frequent entreaty, "Fear not, be not afraid."

Struggle there is. And struggle there will always be. But struggle is merely wrestling with trial. We need difficulties to overcome. But there is nothing to be afraid of. Everything is an effect of mind. Your thought forces, concentrated upon anything, will bring that thing into manifestation. Therefore concentrate them only upon good things, only upon those conditions you wish to see manifested. *Think* health, power, abundance, and happiness. Drive all thoughts of poverty and disease, of fear and worry, as far from your mind as you drive filth from your homes. For fear and worry is the filth of the mind that causes all trouble, that brings about all disease. Banish it! Banish from among your associates any man with a negative outlook on life. Shun him as you would the plague. Can you imagine a knocker winning anything? He is doomed before he starts. Don't let him pull you down with him. "Fret not thyself," says the Psalmist, "else shalt thou be moved to do evil."

That wise old Psalmist might have been writing for us today. For there is no surer way of doing the wrong thing in business or in social life than to fret yourself, to worry, to fume, to want action of some kind, regardless of what it may be. Remember the Lord's admonition to the Israelites, "*Be still*—and know that I am God."

Have you ever stood on the shore of a calm, peaceful lake and watched the reflections in it? The trees, the mountains, the clouds, the sky, all were mirrored there—just as perfectly, as beautifully, as the objects themselves. But try to get such a reflection from the ocean! It cannot be done, because the ocean is always restless, always stirred up by winds or waves or tides.

So it is with your mind. You cannot reflect the richness and plenty of Universal Mind, you cannot mirror peace and health and happiness, if you are constantly worried, continually stirred by waves of fear, winds of anger, tides of toil and striving. You must relax at times. You must give mind a chance. You must realize that, when you have done your best, you can confidently lean back and leave the outcome to Universal Mind.

Just as wrong thinking produces discord in the body, so it also brings on a diseased condition in the realm of commerce. Experience teaches that we need to be protected more from our fears and wrong thoughts, than from so-called evil influences external to ourselves. We need not suffer for another man's wrong, for another's greed, dishonesty, avarice or selfish ambition. But if we hug to ourselves the fear that we do have to so suffer, take it into our thought, allow it to disturb us, then we sentence ourselves. 'We are free to reject every suggestion of discord, and to be governed harmoniously, in spite of what anything or anybody may try to do to us.

Do you know why old army men would rather have soldiers of 18 or 20 than mature men of 30 or 40? Not because they can march farther. They can't! Not because they can carry more. They can't! But because when they go to sleep at night, they really sleep. *They wipe the slate clean!* When they awaken in the morning, they are ready for a new day and a new world.

But an older man carries the nervous strain of one day over to the next. He worries! With the result that at the end of a couple of month's' hard campaigning, the older man is a nervous wreck.

And that is the trouble with most men in business. *They never wipe the slate clean! They worry!* And they carry each day's worries over to the next, with the result that some day the burden becomes more than they can carry.

The Bars of Fate

Fear results from a belief that there are really two powers in this world—Good and Evil. Like light and darkness. When the fact is that Evil is no more real than darkness. True, we lose contact with Good at times. We let the clouds of fear and worry come between us and the sunlight of Good and then all seems dark. But the sun is still shining on the other side of those clouds, and when we drive them away, we again see its light.

Realizing this, realizing that Good is ever available if we will but turn to it confidently in our need, what is there to fear? "Fear not, little flock," said Jesus, "for it is the Father's good pleasure to give you the kingdom." And again—"Son, thou art ever with me, and all that I have is thine."

If this means anything, it means that the Father is ever available to all of us that we have but to call upon Him in the right way and our needs will be met. It doesn't matter what those needs may be.

If Universal Mind is the Creator of all, and if everything in the Universe belongs to It, then your business, your work, isn't really yours—but the "Father's." And He is just as much interested in its success, as long as you are working in accordance with His plan, as you can be.

Everyone will admit that Universal Mind can do anything good. Everyone will admit that It can bring to a successful conclusion any undertaking It may be interested in. If Mind created your business, if It inspired your work, then It is interested in its successful conclusion.

Why not, then, call upon Mind when you have done all you know how to do and yet success seems beyond your efforts. Why not put your problem up to Mind, secure in the belief that It CAN and WILL give you any right thing you may desire? I know that many people hesitate to pray for material things, but if Universal Mind made them, they must have been made for some good purpose, and as long as you intend to use them for good, by all means ask for them.

If you can feel that your business, your work, is a good work, if you can be sure that it is advancing the great Scheme of Things by ever so little, you will never again fear debt or lack or limitation. For "The earth is the Lord's and the fullness thereof." Universal Mind is never going to lack for means to carry on Its work. When Jesus needed fish and bread, fish and bread were provided in such abundance that a whole multitude was fed. When He needed gold, the gold coin appeared in the fish's mouth. Where you are, Mind is, and where Mind is, there is all the power, all the supply of the universe.

You are like the owner of a powerhouse that supplies electricity for light and heat and power to the homes and the factories around you. There is unlimited electricity everywhere about you, but you have got to set your dynamo going to draw the electricity out of the air and into your power lines, before it can be put to practical account.

Just so, there are unlimited riches all about you, but you have got to set the dynamo of your mind to work to bring them into such form as will make them of use to yourself and the world.

So don't worry about any present lack of money or other material things. Don't try to win from others what they have. Go where the money is! The material wealth that is in evidence is so small compared with the possible wealth available through the right use of mind, that it is negligible by comparison. The great rewards are for the pioneers. Look at Carnegie; at Woolworth; at Ford! Every year some new field of development is opened, some new world discovered. Steam, gas, electricity, telegraphy, wireless, the automobile, and the aeroplane—each opens up possibilities of new worlds yet to come.

A hundred years ago, people probably felt that everything had been discovered that could be discovered. That everything was already known that was likely ever to be known. Just as you may feel about things now, yet look at the tremendous strides mankind has taken in the past hundred years. And they are as nothing to what the future holds for us, once man has learned to harness the truly unlimited powers of his subconscious mind.

There are billions of dollars worth of treasure under every square mile of the earth's surface. There are millions of ways in which this old world of ours can be made a better place to live. Set your mind to work locating some of this treasure, finding some of those ways. Don't wait for someone else to blaze the trail.

No one remembers who else was on the *Santa Maria,* but Columbus' name will be known forever! Carnegie is said to have made a hundred millionaires, but he alone became almost a *billionaire!*

Have you ever read Kipling's "Explorer?"

"'There's no sense in going further—it's the edge of cultivation,
So they said, and I believed it—broke my land and sowed
my crop—

Built my barns and strung my fences in the little border station
  Tucked away below the foothills where the trails run out and stop.

"*Till a voice, as bad as Conscience, rang interminable changes*
  On one everlasting Whisper day and night repeated—so:
'Something hidden. Go and find it. Go and look behind the Ranges—
  Something lost behind the Ranges. Lost and waiting for you. Go!'"

Your mind is part and parcel of Universal Mind. You have the wisdom of all the ages to draw upon. Use it! Use it to do your work in a way it was never done before. Use it to find new outlets for your business, new methods of reaching people, new and better ways of serving them. Use it to uncover new riches, to learn ways to make the world a better place to live in.

Concentrate your thought upon these things, knowing that back of you is the vast reservoir of Universal Mind, that all these things are *already* known to It, and that you have but to make your contact for them to be known to you.

Optimism based on such a realization is never over-confidence. It is the joyous assurance of *absolute faith*. It is the assurance that made Wilson for a time the outstanding leader of the world. It is the assurance that heartened Lincoln during the black days of the Civil War. It is the assurance that carried Hannibal and Napoleon over the Alps, that left Alexander sighing for more worlds to conquer, that enabled Cortez and his little band to conquer a nation.

Grasp this idea of the availability of Universal Mind for your daily needs, and your vision will become enlarged, your capacity increased. You will realize that the only limits upon you are those you put upon yourself. There will be no such thing then as difficulties and opposition barring your way.

Exercise

You feed and nourish the body daily. But few people give any thought to nourishing that far more important part—the Mind. So let us try, each day, to set apart a few minutes time to give the Mind a repast.

To begin with, *relax*! Stretch out comfortably on a lounge or in an easy chair and let go of every muscle, loosen every bit of tension, forget every thought of fear or worry. Relax mentally and physically.

Few people know how to relax entirely. Most of us are on a continual strain, and it is this strain that brings on physical disturbances—not any real work we may do. Here is a little exercise that will help you to thoroughly relax:

Recline comfortably on a lounge or bed. Stretch luxuriously first, then when you are settled at your ease again, lift the right leg a foot or two. Let it drop limply. Repeat slowly twice. Do the same with the left leg. With the right arm. With the left arm. You will find then that all your muscles are relaxed. You can forget them and turn your thoughts to other things.

Try to realize the unlimited power that is yours. Think back to the dawn of time, when Mind first imaged from nothingness the heavens and the earth and all that in them is. Remember that, although your mind is to Universal Mind only as a drop of water to the ocean, this drop has all the properties of the great ocean; one in quality although not in quantity; your mind has all the creative power of Universal Mind.

"And God made man in His image, after His likeness." Certainly God never manifested anything but infinite abundance, infinite supply. If you are made in His image, there is no reason why you should ever lack for anything of good. You can manifest abundance, too.

Round about you are the same electronic energy from which Universal Mind formed the heavens and the earth. What do you wish to form from it? What do you want most from life? Hold it in your thought, visualize it, and SEE it! Make your model clear-cut and distinct.

1. Remember, the first thing necessary is a sincere desire, concentrating your thought on one thing with singleness of purpose.
2. The second is visualization—SEEING YOURSELF DOING IT—imaging the object in the same way that Universal Mind imaged all of creation.
3. Next is faith; BELIEVING that you HAVE this thing that you want. Not that you are GOING to have it, mind you—but that you HAVE it.
4. And the last is gratitude—gratitude for this thing that you have received, gratitude for the power that enabled you to create it, gratitude for all the gifts that Mind has laid at your feet.

"Trust in the Lord . . . and verily thou shalt be fed."
"Delight thyself also in the Lord, and He shall give thee the desires of thy heart."
"Commit thy way unto the Lord, and He Shall bring it to pass."

STUDY GUIDE

XIII *The Old Witch—Bad Luck*

1. In Edgar A. Guest's poem, he encourages you to stop thinking and take the first step. Do you have a tendency to procrastinate? On a scale from one to ten (one being very little, and ten being very much so), rate how much you tend to procrastinate.

   1——2——3——4——5——6——7——8——9——10

2. Do you often create stress and wait until the last minute when you have a task that is due? If so, why do you think you do this? If not, congratulations!

3. Fear is defined as "creative though in negative form". What do you think about this definition? Does it ring true for you?

4. Collier references the advent of the depression during his lifetime. He said that the root was panic and fear. Given our current state of affairs, and how the media perpetuates fear, do you see the potential for another depression to arise? If so, what can you personally do to help prevent it? If not, why not?

5. *"Fear is, in short, the devil".* It causes most of the sin, disaster, misery and sickness in the world. Do you believe this to be true? How has fear sabotaged your life?

6. If you believe your food has no nutritive value, then, as unintelligent matter, it should not make you sick. Your mind would eliminate it from your body without any harm. Do you have reactions to certain types of foods? Do you believe that your mind somehow created the reaction? Why or why not?

7. You are encouraged to never fear disaster, for the fear of it is an invitation for it to manifest in your life. Do you spend a great deal of time watch news footage of disasters, repeated and repeated in the media? Do you believe that it can infect your mind? For a month, see if you can abstain from news reports, whether on the television, radio or other social media avenues. Note how much better you feel when you do not subject yourself to the negativity. Write about your experience.

He Whom a Dream Hath Possessed

8. Collier writes, *"You fear debt. So your mind concentrates upon it and brings about greater debt. You fear loss. And by visualizing that loss you bring it about."* Have you experienced either in your life? If so, do you feel responsible for creating it? Why or why not?

9. The story of how Dr. Farnsworth treated his patient for his allergic reaction to cherries and milk is a powerful example of the power of the mind. In a similar vein, The Secret author, Rhonda Byrnes claims that she cured herself of vision issues. Do you wear eyeglasses. Do you believe your vision challenges to be rooted in your mind? Is this something you are willing to further explore? If you do not wear glasses, do you believe your excellent eyesight is a result of your mind's focus?

10. The quiet stillness of a lake cannot be found in the restless ocean. Like the ocean, your mind can be stirred with the waves of fear and anger. For at least 2 minutes each day, please gentle music and either close your eyes with the intention to quiet your mind, or watch a peaceful natural scene on your computer. How do you feel after spending time quieting and calming your mind? Do you feel more energized?

11. The author claims that the older solider is less preferred because he carries worry and nervous strain into his sleep. Are you able to wipe your slate clean and sleep

well at night, or is unrest an issue for you? Reflect back to your youth? Did you sleep better then?

The Bars of Fate

12. Like the clouds that exist behind the sunshine, there is no evil entity, just the covering of the light. If you have been raised on the belief in the devil, then what means do you use to shift that belief? Have you been successful at doing so?

13. If you believe that darkness is the absence of light, then focus on someone whom you are concerned casts evil your way. Practice shining the light of goodness upon him, and note how your feelings and perceptions shift after doing so.

14. Do you feel any guilt towards praying for material things? If so, where do you think the guilt originated and how can you erase it from your psyche?

15. Do you call upon the Universal Mind to assist you when you have done all you can and success still doesn't seem within your reach? If not, do so and trust that your prayers will be answered. Note any shifts as you practice prayer.

16. You are encouraged not to let anyone else blaze the trail before you. Who are the trail blazers in history that you most admired and why?

17. In Kipling's "Explore" he speaks of a voice that repeated day and night. Have you ever experienced a voice as such? If so, did you follow it? What did it uncover? If not, do you believe you missed out on an opportunity by refusing to follow its lead?

18. Optimism based on faith in your access to the Universal Mind is not overconfidence, but an assurance. Do you ever fear being or appearing to be overconfident? Why do you see it as a negative trait?

Exercise

19. The first exercise that Collier prescribes relaxes your body and mind. Practice this exercise daily at a time when you believe you most need it. Note any shifts in your energy or mindset after doing it.

20. To review, desire, visualizing your wish as manifest, having faith and expressing gratitude are the four steps to manifesting your heart's desire in your life. Before proceeding, take a moment to go through these steps with your one greatest desire.

VOLUME FIVE

XIV

Your Needs Are Met

"Arise, O Soul, and gird thee up anew,
Though the black camel Death kneel at this gate;
No beggar thou that thou for alms shouldst sue;
Be the proud captain still of thine own fate."
—KENYON.

You've heard the story of the old man who called his children to his bedside to give them a few parting words of advice. And this was the burden of it.

"My children," he said, "I have had a great deal of trouble in my life—a great deal of trouble—*but most of it never happened.*"

We are all of us like that old man. Our troubles weigh us down—in prospect—but we usually find that when the actual need arrives, Providence has devised some way of meeting it.

Dr. Jacques Loeb, a member of the Rockefeller Institute, conducted a series of tests with parasites found on plants, which show that even the lowest order of creatures have the power to call upon Universal Supply for the resources to meet any unusual need.

"In order to obtain the material," reads the report of the tests, "potted rose bushes are brought into a room and placed in front of a closed window. If the plants are allowed to dry out, the aphides (parasites), previously wingless, change to winged insects. After the metamorphosis, the animals leave the plants, fly to the window and then creep upward on the glass.

"It is evident that these tiny insects found that the plants on which they had been thriving were dead, and that they could therefore secure nothing more to eat and drink from this source. The only method by which they could save themselves from starvation was to grow temporary wings and fly, which they did."

In short, when their source of sustenance was shut off and they had to find the means of migrating or perish, Universal Supply furnished the means for migration.

If Universal Mind can thus provide for the meanest of its creatures, is it not logical to suppose that It will do even more for us—the highest product of creation—if we will but call upon It, if we will but have a little faith? Viewed in the light of Mind's response to the need of those tiny parasites, does it seem so unbelievable that a sea should roll back while a people marched across it dry-shod? That a pillar of fire should lead them through the wilderness by night? That manna should fall from heaven, or water gush forth from a rock?

In moments of great peril, in times of extremity, when the brave soul has staked its all—those are the times when miracles are wrought, if we will but have faith.

That doesn't mean that you should rest supinely at your ease and let the Lord provide. When you have done all that is in you to do—when you have given of your best—

don't worry or fret as to the outcome. Know that if more is needed, your need will be met. You can sit back with the confident assurance that having done your part; you can depend upon the Genie-of-your-Mind to do the rest.

When the little state of Palestine was in danger of being overrun by Egypt on the one hand, or gobbled up by Assyria on the other, its people were frantically trying to decide which horn of the dilemma to embrace, with which enemy they should ally themselves to stave off the other. "With neither," the Prophet Isaiah told them, "in calmly resting your safety lieth; in quiet trust shall be your strength."

So it is with most of the great calamities that afflict us. If we would only "calmly rest, quietly trust," how much better off we should be. But no—we must fret and worry, and nine times out of ten do the wrong thing. And the more we worry and fret, the more likely we are to go wrong.

All of Universal Mind that is necessary to solve any given problem, to meet any need, is wherever that need may be. Supply is always *where* you are and *what* you need. It matters not whether it be sickness or trouble, poverty or danger, the remedy is there, waiting for your call. Go at your difficulty boldly, knowing that you have infinite resources behind you, and you will find these forces closing around you and coming to your aid.

It's like an author writing a book. For a long time he works in a kind of mental fog, but let him persevere, and there flashes suddenly a light that clarifies his ideas and shows him the way to shape them logically. At the moment of despair, you feel a source of unknown energy arising in your soul.

That doesn't mean that you will never have difficulties. Difficulties are good for you. They are the exercise of your mind. You are the stronger for having overcome them. But look upon them as mere exercise. As "stunts" that are given you in order that you may the better learn how to use your mind, how to draw upon Universal Supply. Like Jacob wrestling with the Angel, don't let them go until they have blessed you—until, in other words, you have learned something from having encountered them.

Remember this: No matter how great a catastrophe may befall mankind, no matter how general the loss, you and yours can be free from it. There is always a way of safety. There is always an "ark" by which the understanding few can be saved from the flood. The name of that ark is understanding—understanding of your inner powers. When the children of Israel were being led into the Promised Land, and Joshua had given them their directions, they answered him: "All that thou commandest us we will do, and whithersoever thou sendest us, we will go . . . Only the Lord thy God be with thee, as He was with Moses."

They came to the river Jordan, and it seemed an insurmountable barrier in their path, but Joshua commanded them to take the Ark of the Covenant, representing God's understanding with them, before them into the Jordan. They did it, and "the waters which came down from above stood and rose up upon an heap. . . . And the priests that bare the Ark of the Covenant of the Lord stood firm on dry ground in the midst of Jordan, and all the Israelites passed over on dry ground, until all the people were passed clean over Jordan."

The Ark of the Covenant

All through the Old Testament, when war and pestilence, fire and flood, were the common lot of mankind, there is constant assurance of safety for those who have this understanding, this "Covenant" with the Lord. "Because thou hast made the Lord which is my refuge—even the Most High—thy habitation, there shall no evil befall thee, neither shall any plague come nigh thy dwelling. For He shall give His angels charge over thee to keep thee in all thy ways."

That is His agreement with us—an agreement that gives us the superiority to circumstances, which men have sought from time immemorial. All that is necessary on our side of the agreement is for us to remember the infinite powers that reside within us, to remember that our mind is part of Universal Mind and as such it can foresee, it can guard against and it can protect us from harm of any kind. We need not run away from trials or try to become stoical towards them. All we need is to bring our understanding to bear upon them—to know that no situation has ever yet arisen with which Universal Mind—and through it our own mind—was not fully competent to deal. To know that the right solution of every problem is in Universal Mind. We have but to seek that solution and our trial is overcome.

"But where shall Wisdom be found? And where is the place of understanding? Acquaint now thyself with God, and be at peace."

If evil threatens us, if failure, sickness or accident seems imminent, we have only to decide that these evils do not come from Universal Mind, therefore they are unreal and have no power over us. They are simply the absence of the right condition, which Universal Mind knows. Refuse, therefore, to see them, to acknowledge them—and seek through Mind for the right condition, which shall nullify them.

If you will do this, you will find that you can appropriate from Mind whatever you require for your needs, *when* you require it. The greater your need, the more surely it will be met, if you can but realize this truth. "Fear not, little flock," said Jesus, "for it is your Father's good pleasure to give you the Kingdom."

Remember that your thought is all-powerful. That it is creative. That there is no limitation upon it of time or space. And that it is ever available.

Forget your worries. Forget your fears. In place of them, visualize the conditions you would like to see. Realize their availability. Declare to yourself that you already *have* all these things that you desire, that your needs *have* been met. Say to yourself: "How thankful I am that Mind has made all these good things available to me. I have everything that heart could desire to be grateful for."

Every time you do this, you impress the thought upon your subconscious mind. And the moment you can convince your subconscious mind of the truth of it—*that moment* your mind will proceed to *make* it true. This is the way to put into practice the Master's advice—"Believe that ye RECEIVE it, and ye SHALL HAVE it."

There is no condition so hopeless, no cause so far gone, that this truth will not save it. Time and again patients given over by their doctors as doomed have made miraculous recoveries through the faith of some loved one.

"I hope that everyone who reads this Book may gain as much from their first reading as I did," writes a happy subscriber from New York City. "I got such a clear understanding from that one reading that I was able to break the mental chain holding a friend to a hospital bed, and she left the hospital in three days, to the very great astonishment of the doctors handling the case."

In the same way, there are innumerable instances where threatened calamity has been warded off and good come instead. The great trouble with most of us is, we do not *believe*. We insist upon looking for trouble. We feel that the "rainy day" is bound to come, and we do our utmost to make it a surety by keeping it in our thoughts, preparing for it, fearing it. "Cowards die many times before their deaths; the valiant never taste of death but once." We cross our bridges a dozen times before we come to them. We doubt ourselves, we doubt our ability, we doubt everyone and everything around us, and our doubts sap our energy; kill our enthusiasm; rob us of success. We arc like the old lady who "enjoys poor health." We always place that little word "but" after our wishes and desires, feeling deep down that there are some things too good to be true. We think there is a power apart from Good, which can withhold blessings that should be ours. We doubt because we cannot see the way by which our desires can be fulfilled. We put a limit upon the good that can come to us.

"Prove me now herewith, saith the Lord of Hosts," cried the Prophet Malachi, "if I will not open you the windows of heaven and pour you out a blessing that there shall not be room enough to receive it . . . And all nations shall call you blessed, for ye shall be a delightsome land."

Your mind is part of Universal Mind. And Universal Mind has all supply. You are entitled to, and you can have, just as much of that supply as you are able to appropriate. To expect less is to get less, for it dwarfs your power of receiving.

It doesn't matter what your longings may be, provided they are right longings. If your little son has his heart set on a train and you feel perfectly able to get him a train, you are not going to hand him a picture book instead. It may be that the picture book would have greater educational value, but the love you have for your son is going to make you try to satisfy his longings as long as those longings are not harmful ones.

In the same way, Universal Mind will satisfy your longings, no matter how trivial they may seem, as long as they are not harmful ones. "Delight thyself also in the Lord, and He shall give thee the desires of thine heart."

If we would only try to realize that God is not some far-off Deity, not some stern Judge, but the beneficent force that we recognize as Nature—the life Principle that makes the flowers bud, and the plants grow, that spreads abundance about us with lavish band. If we could realize that He is the Universal Mind that holds all supply, that will give us the toy of our childhood or the needs of maturity, that all we need to obtain from Him our Heart's Desire is a right understanding of His availability—then we would lose all our fears, all our worries, all our sense of limitation.

For Universal Mind is an infinite, unlimited source of good. Not only the source of general good, but the specific good things you desire of life. To It there is no big or little problem. The removal of mountains is no more difficult than the feeding of a sparrow.

And to one—like the Master—with a perfect understanding, the "miracle" of raising Lazarus from the dead required no more effort than the turning of the water into wine. He knew that Universal Mind is all power—and there cannot be more than ALL. He knew that "To know

God aright is life eternal." And Jesus knew God aright, so was able to demonstrate this knowledge of life eternal in overcoming sin, disease and death. For it is one and the same law that heals sin, sickness, poverty, heartaches, or death itself. That law is the right understanding of Divine Principle.

But what does this ability to perform "miracles" consist of? What is the power or force by which we can prove this ability? Perhaps the simplest way is to begin with the realization that Universal Mind is man's working power.

The Science of Thought

Can you stretch your mind a bit and try to comprehend this wonderful fact—that the ALL POWERFUL, ALL-KNOWING, EVERLASTING CREATOR and Governor of the infinite universe, "Who hath measured the waters in the hollow of his hand, and meted out heaven with the span, and comprehended the dust of the earth in a measure, and weighed the mountains in scales, and the hills in a balance," is your working power? In proportion as we understand this fact, and make use of it, in that same proportion are we able to perform our miracles.

Your work is inspired to the extent that you realize the presence of Universal Mind in your work. When you rely entirely on your own conscious mind, your work suffers accordingly. "I can of mine own self do nothing; for the works which the Father hath given me to finish, the same works that I do bear witness of me." The miracles of Jesus bear witness of the complete recognition of God the Father as his working power.

And mind you, this inspiration, this working of Universal Mind with you, is available for all of your undertakings.

Mind could not show Itself in one part of your life and withhold Itself from another, since It is all in all. Every rightly directed task, no matter how insignificant or menial it may appear to you, carries with it the inspiration of Universal Mind, since by the very nature of omnipotence, Its love and bestowals must be universal and impartial, "and whatsoever ye do, do it heartily as to the Lord."

Too many of us are like the maiden in the old Eastern legend. A Genii sent her into a field of grain, promising her a rare gift if she would pick for him the largest and ripest ear she could find; His gift to be in proportion to the size and perfection of the ear.

But he made this condition—she must pluck but one ear, and she must walk straight through the field without stopping, going back or wandering hither and thither.

Joyously she started. As she walked through the grain, she saw many large ears, many perfect ones. She passed them by in scorn, thinking to find an extra-large, super-perfect one farther along. Presently, however, the soil became less fertile, the ears small and sparse. She couldn't pick one of these! Would now that she had been content with an ordinary-sized ear farther back. But it was too late for that. Surely they would grow better again farther on!

She walked on—and on—and always they became worse—'till presently she found herself at the end of the field—*empty handed as when she set out!*

So it is with life. Every day has its worthwhile rewards for work well done. Every day offers its chance for happiness. But those rewards seem so small, those chances so petty, compared with the big things we see ahead. So we pass them by, never recognizing that the great position we look forward to, the shining prize we see in the distance, is just the sum of all the little tasks, the heaped up result of all the little prizes that we must win as we go along.

You are not commanded to pick out certain occupations as being more entitled to the Lord's consideration than others, but "Whatsoever ye do." Whether it be in the exalted and idealistic realms of poetry, music and art, whether in the cause of religion or philanthropy, whether in government, in business, in science, or simply in household cares, "whatsoever ye do" you are entitled to and *have* all of inspiration at your beck and call. If you seem to have less than all, it is because you do not utilize your gift.

"Now he that planteth and he that watereth are one; and every man shall receive his own reward according to his own labour. For we are labourer's together with God." "All things are yours; and ye are Christ's and Christ's is God's."

How shall you take advantage of this Universal Supply? When next any need confronts you, when next you are in difficulties, close your eyes for a moment and realize that Universal Mind knows how that need can best be met, knows the solution of your difficulties. Your sub-conscious mind, being part of the Universal Mind, can know this, too. So put your problem up to your subconscious mind with the sublime confidence that it will find the solution. Then forget it for a while. When the time comes, the need will be met.

Dr. Winbigler corroborates the working out of this idea in the following:

"Suggestions lodged in the mind can effect a complete change, morally and physically, if mankind would become in spirit 'as a little child,' trusting in God implicitly, the greatest power would be utilized in the establishment of health and equilibrium, and the results would be untold in comfort, sanity, and blessing. For instance, here is one who is suffering from worry, fear, and the vexations of life. How can he get rid of these things and relieve this suffering? Let him go to a quiet room or place, twice a day, lie down and relax every muscle, assume complete indifference to those things which worry him and the functions of the body, and quietly accept what God, through this law of demand and supply, can give. In a few days he will find a great change in his feelings, and the sufferings will pass away and life will look bright and promising. Infinite wisdom has established that law; and its utilization by those who are worried and fearful will secure amazing results in a short time.

"The real reason for the change is found in the possibility of recovery by using the laws that God has placed within our reach, and thus securing the coveted health and power for all that we want and ought to do. The subliminal life is the connecting link between man and God, and by obeying His laws, one's life is put in contact with infinite resources and all that God is able and willing to give. Here is the secret of all the cures of disease, and the foundation for the possibility of a joyful existence, happiness and eternal life. Suggestion is the method of securing what God gives, and the mind is the agent through which these gifts are received. This is not a matter of theory, but a fact. If any one who is sick or who desires to he kept well will have stated periods of relaxation, open-mindedness, and faith, he can prove the beneficial and unvarying result of this method."

STUDY GUIDE

XIV *Your Needs Are Met*

1. Collier opens this chapter with the science of the aphides and their ability to grow wings when they can no longer get nutrients from dying rose bushes. The argument is that if the God or the Universal Mind can create wings for the smallest of creatures, then it can support you in seeming miraculous ways. What would you see as a miracle in your life right now?

2. You must not rest, expecting miracles, but take all actions you can, and then rest and have faith. At times do you rest before your work is done?

3. You are urged to "calmly rest, quietly trust". The more you worry, the more likely things are to go wrong. Do you think that worrying is a habit or pattern? If so, what can you do to shift the pattern?

4. You are encouraged to look upon difficulties as learning tools, exercises of your mind that will build strength within you when overcome. Do not let them go until you have learned from them. The next time you find yourself challenged, stop and ask the Universal Mind *"What is the lesson I am meant to learn from this?"* Note any insights you gain.

The Ark of the Covenant
5. As part of the Universal Mind, your mind has the capacity to foresee. Next time you find yourself in fear of a future event, ask the Universal Mind to assist you in tapping into premonition and foresight. Write about your findings.

6. If evil threatens, you are encouraged not to acknowledge it. Next time you find yourself feeling fear, write that fear on a piece of page, and burn it as a symbolic representation of its powerlessness over you. Write about your feelings and thoughts after practicing this exercise.

7. Do you have a loved one who is caught up in the mental chain of negativity, sickness and despair? Practice seeing them in perfect health and wellbeing, and encourage them to do the same. Have faith and note any changes that occur.

8. Your doubts drain your energy. When do you find yourself most drained during your day? Are there circumstances that you face at that time that discourage you? Take note and write about any insights.

9. You might want to practice chanting the mantra, *"I allow . . ."* into your mindset. This informs the Universal Mind that you are open and ready to receive the goodness that is your birthright. Practice this technique and note any changes that arise.

10. There is no difference in difficulty when performing so-called miracles. It took Christ no more effort to raise Lazarus from the dead, than to turn water into wine. If the same source can manifest a parking space for you, then what prevents it from manifesting a comfortable income?

The Science of Thought

11. Can you stretch your mind to comprehend that the all-powerful, all-knowing, everlasting creator is your working power? When you rely entirely upon your own conscious mind, your work suffers. Before staring the next task in your day, ask for assistance from the Universal Mind and note the ease that befalls you.

12. Collier shares the story of the maiden and her search for the largest ear of corn as an analogy of our own over-

sights in the current rewards in our lives, when constantly looking for greater in the future. Do you find yourself constantly seeking for greater happiness in the future, missing out on the abundance and joy of the present? Take a moment and list all that you are grateful for within the last 24 hours. Then allow yourself to feel that gratitude whole—heartedly.

13. Dr. Winbigler suggests relaxing at least twice a day, with open-mindedness and faith will relieve your suffering and quell your fears. Try this and note any physical, mental or spiritual shifts you experience in doing so.

XV

The Master of Your Fate

"A craven hung along the battle's edge,
And thought, 'Had I a sword of keener steel—
That blue blade that the king's son bears,—but this blunt thing—!'
And lowering crept away and left the field.
Then came the king's son, wounded, sore bestead
And weaponless, and saw the broken sword,
And ran and snatched it, and with battle-shout
Lifted afresh he hewed his enemy down,
And saved a great cause that heroic day."
—Edward Rowland Sill.*

Where will you be at 65? Five men in six at the age of 65 are living on charity. Just one in twenty is able to live without working at 65.

That is what the American Bankers Association found when it took one hundred healthy men at 25 and traced them to 65.

These hundred were healthy to start with. They all had the same chance for success. The difference lay in the way

---

* From 'Poems,' Houghton, Muffin Co.

they used their MINDS. Ninety-five out of one hundred just do the tasks that are set them. They have no faith in themselves—no initiative—none of the courage that starts things. They are always directed or controlled by someone else.

At 65, where will you be? Dependent or independent? Struggling for a living—accepting charity from someone else—or at the top of the heap?

"I am the Master of my fate."

Until you have learned that, you will never attain life's full success. Your fate is in your own hands. *You* have the making of it. What you are going to be six months or a year from now depends upon what you think today.

So make your choice now:

Are you going to bow down to matter as the only power? Are you going to look upon your environment as something that has been wished upon you and for which you are in no way responsible?

Or are you going to try to realize in your daily life that matter is merely an aggregation of protons and electrons subject entirely to the control of Mind, that your environment, your success, your happiness, are all of your own making, and that if you are not satisfied with conditions as they you have but to visualize them as you would have them be in order to change them?

The former is the easier way right now—the easy way that leads to the hell of poverty and fear and old age.

But the latter is the way that brings you to your Heart's Desire.

And merely because this Power of Universal Mind is invisible, is that any reason to doubt it? The greatest powers of Nature are invisible. Love is invisible, but what greater power is there in life? Joy is invisible, happiness, peace, and contentment. The radio is invisible—yet you hear it. It is a product of the law governing sound waves. Law is invisible, yet you see the manifestation of different laws every day. To run a locomotive, you study the law of applying power, and you apply that law when you make the locomotive go.

These things are not the result of invention. The law has existed from the beginning. It merely waited for man to learn how to apply it. If man had known how to call upon Universal Mind to the right extent, he could have applied the law of sound waves, the law of steam, ages ago. Invention is merely a revelation and an unfoldment of Universal Wisdom.

That same Universal Wisdom knows millions of other laws of which man has not even a glimmering. You can call upon It. You can use that Wisdom as your own. By thinking of things as they might be instead of as they are you will eventually find some great Need. And to find a need is the first step towards finding the supply to satisfy that need. You've got to know what you are after, before you can send the Genie-of-your Mind a-seeking of it in Universal Mind.

The Acre of Diamonds

You remember the story of the poor Boer farmer who struggled for years to glean a livelihood out of his rocky soil, only to give it up in despair and go off to seek his fortune elsewhere. Years later, coming back to his old farm, he found it swarming with machinery and life—more wealth being dug out of it every day than he had ever dreamed existed. It was the great Kimberley Diamond Mine!

Most of us are like that poor Boer farmer. We struggle along under our surface power, never dreaming of the giant power that could be ours if we would but dig a little deeper—rouse that great Inner Self who can give us more even than any acre of diamonds.

As Orison Swett Marden put it:

"The majority of failures in life are simply the victims of their mental defeats. Their conviction that they cannot succeed as others do, rob them of that vigor and determination which self-confidence imparts, and they don't even half try to succeed.

"There is no philosophy by which a man can do a thing when he thinks he can't. The reason why millions of men are plodding along in mediocrity today, many of them barely making a living, when they have the ability to do something infinitely bigger, is because they lack confidence in themselves. They don't believe they can do the bigger thing that would lift them out of their rut of mediocrity and poverty; they are not winners mentally.

"The way always opens for the determined soul, the man of faith and courage.

"It is the victorious mental attitude, the consciousness of power, the sense of mastership, that does the big things in this world. If you haven't this attitude, if you lack self-confidence, begin now to cultivate it.

"A highly magnetized piece of steel will attract and lift a piece of unmagnetized steel ten times its own weight. Demagnetize that same piece of steel and it will be powerless to attract or lift even a feather's weight.

"Now, my friends, there is the same difference between the man who is highly magnetized by a sublime faith in himself, and the man who is de-magnetized by his lack of faith, his doubts, his fears, that there is between the magnetized and the de-magnetized pieces of steel. If two men of equal ability, one *magnetized by a divine self-confidence*, the other demagnetized by fear and doubt, are given similar tasks, one will succeed and the other will fail. The self-confidence of the one *multiplies his powers a hundredfold;* the lack of it subtracts a hundredfold from the power of the other."

Have you ever thought how much of your time is spent in choosing what you shall do, which task you will try, which way you shall go? Every day is a day of decision. We are constantly at crossroads, in our business dealings, our social relations, in our homes; there is always the necessity of a choice. How important then that we have faith in ourselves and in that Infinite intelligence within. "Commit thy works unto the Lord, and thy thoughts shall be established." "In all thy ways acknowledge him, and he shall direct thy paths."

In this ever-changing material age, with seemingly complex forces all about us, we sometimes cry out that we are driven by force of circumstances. Yet the fact remains that we do those things, which we choose to do. For even though we may not wish to go a certain way, we allow ourselves to pursue it because it offers the least resistance.

"To every man there openeth
A way, and ways, and a way.
And the high soul climbs the high way,
And the low soul gropes the low:
And in between, on the misty flats,
The rest drift to and fro.
But to every man there openeth
A high way and a low,
And every man decideth
The way his soul shall go."
—JOHN OXENHAM.

Now, how about you? Are you taking active control of your own thought? Are you imaging upon your subconscious mind only such things, as you want to see realized? Are you thinking healthy thoughts, happy thoughts, and successful thoughts?

The difference between the successful man and the unsuccessful one is not so much a matter of training or equipment. It is not a question of opportunity or luck. It is just in the way they each of them look at things.

The successful man sees an opportunity, seizes upon it, and moves upward another rung on the ladder of success. It never occurs to him that he may fail. He sees only the opportunity, he visions what he can do with it, and all the forces within and without him combine to help him win.

The unsuccessful man sees the same opportunity, he wishes that he could take advantage of it, but he is fearful that his ability or his money or his credit may not be equal to the task. He is like a timid bather, putting in one foot and then drawing it swiftly back again—and while he hesitates some bolder spirit dashes in and beats him to the goal.

Nearly every man can look back—and not so far back either with most of us—and say, "If I had taken that chance, I would be much better off now."

You will never need to say it again, once you realize that the future is entirely within your own control. It is not subject to the whims of fortune or the capriciousness of luck. There is but one Universal Mind and that mind contains naught but good. In it is no images of Evil. From it comes no lack of supply. Its ideas are as numberless as the grains of sand on the seashore. And those ideas comprise all wealth, all power, and all happiness.

You have only to image vividly enough on your subconscious mind the thing you wish, to draw from Universal Mind, the necessary ideas to bring it into being. You have only to keep in mind the experiences you wish to meet, in order to control your own future.

When Frank A. Vanderlip, former President of the National City Bank, was a struggling youngster, he asked a successful friend what one thing he would urge a young man to do who was anxious to make his way in the world. "Look as though you have already succeeded," his friend told him. Shakespeare expresses the same thought in another way—"Assume a virtue if you have it not." Look the part. Dress the part. Act the part. Be successful in your own thought first. It won't be long before you will be successful before the world as well.

David V. Bush, in his book "Applied Psychology and Scientific Living," says:

"Man is like the wireless operator. Man is subject to miscellaneous wrong thought currents if his mind is not in tune with the Infinite, or if he is not keyed up to higher vibrations than those of negation.

"A man who thinks courageous thoughts sends these courageous thought waves through the universal ether until they lodge in the consciousness of someone who is tuned to the same courageous key. Think a strong thought, a courageous thought, a prosperity thought, and these thoughts will be received by someone who is strong, courageous and prosperous.

"It is just as easy to think in terms of abundance as to think in terms of poverty. If we think poverty thoughts we become the sending and receiving stations for poverty thoughts. We send out a 'poverty' mental wireless and it reaches the consciousness of some poverty-stricken 'receiver.' We get what we think.

"It is just as easy to think in terms of abundance, opulence and prosperity as it is to think in terms of lack, limitation and poverty.

"If a man will raise his rate of vibration by faith currents or hope currents, these vibrations go through the Universal Mind and lodge in the consciousness of people who are keyed to the same tune. Whatever you think is sometime, somewhere, received by a person who is tuned to your thought key.

"If a man is out of work and he thinks thoughts of success, prosperity, harmony, position and growth, just as surely as his thoughts are things—as Shakespeare says—someone will receive his vibrations of success, prosperity, harmony, position and growth.

"If we are going to be timid, selfish, penurious and picayunish in our thinking, these thought waves which we have started in the universal ether will go forth until they come to a mental receiving station of the same caliber. 'Birds of a feather flock together,' and minds of like thinking are attracted one to the other.

"If you need money, all you have to do is to send up your vibrations to a strong, courageous receiving station, and someone who can meet your needs will be attracted to you or you to him."

When you learn that you are entitled to win—in any right undertaking in which you may be engaged—*you will win*. When you learn that you have a right to a legitimate dominion over your own affairs, *you will have dominion over them*. The promise is that we can do all things through the Mind that was in Christ.

Universal Mind plays no favorites. No one human being has any more power than any other. It is simply that few of us use the power that is in our hands. The great men of the world are in no wise SUPER Beings. They are ordinary creatures like you and me, who have stumbled upon the way of drawing upon their subconscious mind—and through it upon the Universal Mind. Speaking of Henry Ford's phenomenal success, his friend Thomas A. Edison said of him—"He draws upon his subconscious mind."

The secret of being what you have it in you to be is simply this: Decide now what it is you want of life, exactly what you wish your future to be. Plan it out in detail. Vision it from start to finish. See yourself as you are now, doing those things you have always wanted to do. Make them REAL in your mind's eye—feel them, live them, believe them, especially at the moment of going to sleep, when it is easiest to reach your subconscious mind—and you will soon be seeing them in real life.

It matters not whether you are young or old, rich or poor. The time to begin is NOW. It is never too late. Remember those lines of Appleton's:*

"I knew his face the moment that he passed
Triumphant in the thoughtless, cruel throng—
I gently touched his arm—he smiled at me—
He was the Man that Once I Meant to Be!

"Where I had failed, he'd won from life, Success;
Where I had stumbled, with sure feet he stood;

---

* From "The Quiet Courage." D. Appleton & Co., New York.

Alike—yet unalike—we faced the world,
And through the stress he found that life was good.
And I? The bitter wormwood in the glass,
The shadowed way along which failures pass!
Yet as I saw him thus, joy came to me—
He was the Man that Once I Meant to Be!

"We did not speak. But in his sapient eyes
I saw the spirit that had urged him on,
The courage that had held him through the fight
Had once been mine. I thought, 'Can it be gone?'
He felt that unasked question—felt it so
His pale lips formed the one-word answer, 'No!'

"Too late to win? No! Not too late for me—
He is the Man that Still I Mean to Be!"

STUDY GUIDE

XV *The Master of Your Fate*

1. How does Edward Rowland Sill's poem apply to your life? What broken swords have you left unused for others to utilize?

2. Collier asks where you will be at age 65? Do you believe you will be struggling or thriving? If you are already 65, would you consider yourself living your success dream?

3. Joy, happiness, peace and contentment are all invisible, and yet you know they exist. What other invisible forces exist on the earth? List at least five.

4. *"By thinking of things as they might be instead of as they are, you will eventually find some great Need. And to find a need is the first step towards finding the supply to satisfy that need. You have to know what you are after . . ."* What comes to mind when you read this quote? What needs arise? List anything that comes to mind.

The Acre of Diamonds

5. You are encouraged to dig a little deeper into your Inner Self to uncover the acres of diamond within you. How might you cultivate greater confidence in yourself? If you do not have an answer, dig deeper into your Inner Self and ask for an answer. Then trust the first thing that comes to mind.

6. The analogy of a magnetized piece of steel is used to describe a man who has faith in himself and is magnetized with divine self-confidence, compared to a demagnetized piece of steel and one overwhelmed with fear and doubt. Note how Collier references it as "divine"

self-confidence. If you do not have it, then ask your divine or the Universal Mind to grace you with it. Then trust that it will experience it.

7. You are inundated with choices throughout your day. Having faith in yourself and the Infinite Intelligence within you makes these tasks less daunting. For a day, consciously focus on each decision as it arises. Before making it, consciously call upon your Infinite Intelligence to make it for you. Do you find the choices you have to make easier after doing so?

8. When do you find yourself taking the path of least resistance in your life? Are there certain patterns that you tend to follow?

9. Failure never occurs to the successful man. The unsuccessful man hesitates and questions his ability, and a bolder spirit seizes the opportunity. Have you ever experienced having an ideal that you did not follow with action, only to find someone else had the same idea and took the necessary action on it? Can you make a commitment to act on your impulse next time an innovative idea arises in your mind?

10. Frank A. Vanderlip's friend encouraged him to look as though he had already succeeded. Do you currently dress for success? If not, be sure to start doing so.

11. When you think a strong, courageous, prosperous thought, it will be received by someone who is strong, courage and prosperous. Reflect on your life and write about a situation in which you attracted someone of like mind.

12. *"If you need money, all you have to do is to send up your vibrations to a strong, courageous receiving station, and someone who can meet your needs will be attracted to you or you to him."* If you need money, then do this exercise now, with the expectation that your vibration will be received.

13. No human being has any more power than you do. They just know, trust and use the power of the Universal Mind. Write a list of individuals you believed to be more powerful than you. Then state aloud, their name and that you have an equal amount of power within you. Note how you feel after doing this exercise.

14. You are encouraged to plan your future in detail. Plan exactly what you want, how much you want, when and where you want it with as much detail as possible. Then each night as you go to sleep, read your plan and see it happening in the present. Journal about your progress.

15. You do not wish to be the man in Appleton's poem, and Collier insists that it is never too late. Make a point of focusing on the joys of your present and future. When you focus on the past, cancel that thought and envision that which you desire. Find the joy in the anticipation.

XVI

Unappropriated Millions

"Somebody said that t couldn't be done,
But he with a chuckle replied
That 'maybe it couldn't,' but he would be one
Who wouldn't say so till he'd tried.
So he buckled right in with the trace of a grin
On his face. If he worried he hid it.
He started to sing as he tackled the thing
That couldn't be done, and he did it."
—Edgar A. Guest.*

The main difference between the mind of today and that of our great-great-grandfathers was that in their day conditions were comparatively static, whereas today they are dynamic. Civilization ran along for centuries with comparatively little change. Most people lived and died in the places where they were born. They followed their fathers' avocations. Seldom, indeed, did one of them break out of the class into which he had been born. Almost as

---

* From "The Path to Home." The Reilly & Lee Co.

seldom did they even *think* of trying to. No wonder, then, that civilization made little progress.

Today we are in the presence of continual change. Men are imbued with that divine unrest which is never satisfied with conditions as they are, which is always striving for improvement. And *thought* is the vital force behind all this change.

Your ability to think is your connecting link with Universal Mind, that enables you to draw upon It for inspiration, for energy, for power. Mind is the energy in *static* form. Thought is the energy in *dynamic* form.

And because life is dynamic—not static; because it is ever moving forward—not standing still; your success or failure depends entirely upon the *quality* of your thought.

For thought is creative energy. It brings into being the things that you think. Think the things you would see manifested, see them, *believe* them, and you can leave it to your subconscious mind to bring them into being.

Your mind is a marvelous storage battery of power on which you can draw for whatever things you need to make your life what you would have it be. It has within it all power, all resource, all energy—but YOU are the one that must use it. All that power is static unless you make it dynamic. In the moment of creative thinking your conscious mind becomes a Creator—it partakes of the power of Universal Mind. And there is nothing static about one who shares that All-power. The resistless Life Energy within him pushes him on to new growth, new aspirations. Just as the sap flowing through the branches of the trees pushes off the old dead leaves to make way for the new life, just so you must push away the old dead thoughts of poverty and lack and disease, before you can bring on the new life of health and happiness and unlimited supply.

This life is in all of us, constantly struggling for an outlet. Repress it—and you die. Doctors will tell you that the only reason people grow old is because their systems get clogged. The tiny pores in your arteries get stopped up. You don't throw off the old. You don't struggle hard enough, and the result is you fall an easy victim to failure and sickness and death.

Remember the story of Sinbad the Sailor, and the Old Man of the Sea? The Old Man's weight was as nothing when Sinbad first took him on his shoulders, but he clung there and clung there, slowly but surely sapping Sinbad's strength, and he would finally have killed him as he had killed so many others if Sinbad, by calling to his aid all his mental as well as his physical resources, had not succeeded in shaking him off.

Most of us have some Old Man of the Sea riding us, and because he clings tightly and refuses to be easily shaken off, we let him stay there, sapping our energies, using up our vitality, when to rid us of him it is only necessary to call to our aid ALL our resources, mental as well as physical, for one supreme effort.

When a storm arises, the hardy mariner doesn't turn off steam and drift helplessly before the wind. That might be the easy way, but that way danger lies. He turns on more steam and fights against the gale. And so should you. There is a something within you that thrives on difficulties. You prize that more which costs an effort to win. You need to blaze new trails, to encounter unusual hardships, in order to reach your hidden mental resources, just as the athlete needs to exert himself to the utmost to reach his "second wind."

Have you ever seen a turtle thrown on its back? For a while it threshes around wildly, reaching for something outside to take hold of that shall put it on its feet. Just as we humans always look for help outside ourselves first, but presently he draws all his forces within his shell, rests a bit to regain his strength, and then throws his whole force to one side—legs, head, tail, and all—*and over he goes!*

So it is with us. When we realize that the power to meet any emergency is within ourselves, when we stop looking outside for help and intelligently call upon Mind in our need, we shall find that we are tapping Infinite Resource. We shall find that we have but to center all those resources on the one thing we want most—to get anything from life that it has.

As Emerson put it, when we once find the way to get in touch with Universal Mind we are—

". . . owner of the sphere,
Of the Seven stars and the solar year,
Of Caesar's hand and Plato's brain,
Of the Lord Christ's heart and Shakespeare's strain."

STUDY GUIDE

XVI *Unappropriated Millions*

1. The poem by Edgar A. Guest is both joyful and encouraging. Have you ever sought to do what others said was impossible? If so, what was the outcome? Are you glad that you made the effort?

2. The poem has a sense of humor and a lightness to it. Do you approach new project with a sense of fun and adventure? Is your progress reflected by your joyful disposition?

3. The author compares his time to his great-great grandfathers time as being much more dynamic. Fast-forward another century to the present day and the dynamic has exponentially grown. We see it especially in technology. Things are changing so quickly. What do you believe is responsible for the growing dynamic?

4. If your mind is a storage battery of power and Resistless Life Energy, then how do you plan on using it today?

5. What is the "Old Man of the Sea" that is riding your back (taking your energy away from moving forward in your life)? In other words, what is the main emotional block that keeps your energy static and prevents you from manifesting your desires?

6. How have you been reaching outside of yourself for help? Has it been working?

7. Using Emerson's poem as a resource, consciously call in the hand of Caesar, Plato's brain, Christ's heart and Shakespeare's strain. Write a short request to each of them, asking that they be your guiding muses.

XVII

The Secret of Power

"The great were once as you.
They whom men magnify today
Once groped and blundered on life's way
Were fearful of themselves, and thought
By magic was men's greatness wrought.
They feared to try what they could do;
Yet Fame hath crowned with her success
The selfsame gifts that you possess.
—Edgar A. Guest*

There is a woman in one of the big Eastern cities whose husband died a year or two ago and left her nearly $100,000,000. She has unlimited power in her hands—yet she uses none of it. She has unlimited wealth—yet she gets no more from it than if it were in the thousands instead of millions. She knows nothing of her power, of her wealth. She is insane.

---

* Published by permission of The International Magazine Co. (Cosmopolitan Magazine) Copyright, 1921.

You have just as great power in your hands—without this poor woman's excuse for not using it.

You have access to unlimited ideas, unlimited energy, and unlimited wealth. The "Open, Sesame!" is through your subconscious mind. So long as you limit yourself to superficial conditions, so long as you are a mere "hewer of wood or carrier of water" for those around you who *do* use their minds, you are in no better position than the beasts of burden.

The secret of power is in understanding the infinite resources of your own mind. When you begin to realize that the power to do anything, to be anything, to have anything, is within yourself, then *and then only* will you take your proper place in the world.

As Bruce Barton has it in "The Man Whom Nobody Knows"—"Somewhere, at some unforgettable hour, the daring filled

His (Jesus) heart. He knew that He was bigger than Nazareth."

Again in speaking of Abraham Lincoln, Barton says—"Inside himself he felt his power, but where and when would opportunity come?" And later in the book—

"But to every man of vision the clear voice speaks. Nothing splendid has ever been achieved except by those who dared believe that *something inside them was superior to circumstance.*"

No doubt Jesus' friends and neighbors all ridiculed the idea of any such power within Him. Just as most people today laugh at the thought of a power such as that within themselves.

So they go on with their daily grind, with the gaunt specters of sickness and need ever by their side, until death comes as a welcome relief. Are you going to be one of those? Or will you listen to that inner consciousness of power and find the "Kingdom of Heaven that is within you." For whatever you become conscious of, will be quickly brought forth into tangible form.

Don't judge your ability by what you have done in the past. Your work heretofore has been done with the help of your conscious mind alone. Add to that the infinite knowledge at the disposal of your subconscious mind, and what you have done is as nothing to what you will do in the future.

For knowledge does not apply itself. It is merely so much static energy. You must convert it into dynamic energy by the power of your thought. The difference between the $25-a-week clerk and the $25,000-a-year executive is solely one of thought. The clerk may have more brains than the executive—frequently *has* in actual weight of gray matter. He may even have a far better education. But he doesn't know how to apply his thought to get the greatest good from it.

If you have brains, *use* them. If you have skill, *apply* it. The world must profit by it, and therefore you.

We all have inspired moments when we see clearly how we may do great things, how we may accomplish wonderful undertakings. But we do not believe in them enough to make them come true. An imagination, which begins and ends in daydreaming, is weakening to character.

Make the daydreams come true. Make them so clear and distinct that they impress themselves upon your subconscious mind. There's nothing wrong with daydreaming, except that most of us stop there. We don't try to make the dreams come true. The great inventor, Tesla, "dreams" every new machine complete and perfect in every particular before ever he begins his model for it. Mozart "dreamed" each of his wonderful symphonies complete before ever he put a note on paper. But they didn't stop with the dreaming. They visualized those dreams, *and then brought them into actuality.*

We lose our capacity to have visions if we do not take steps to realize them.

Power implies service, so concentrate all your thought on making your visions of great deeds come true. Thinking is the current that runs the dynamo of power. To connect up this current so that you can draw upon universal supply through your subconscious mind is to become a Super-man. Do this, and you will have found the key to the solution of every problem of life.

STUDY GUIDE

XVII *The Secret Power*

1. In Edgar A. Guest's poem, the great once groped and blundered. As a child, when you first learned to read and write, did you judge yourself or move forward, committed to learn? Do you judge a toddler who is learning to walk? Similarly, do you judge yourself when you make mistakes? Could you see yourself with greater compassion, and allow mistakes as part of the growing process? Would this help you keep a more positive, optimistic frame of mind?

2. If you were the woman who was left with $100,000,000, what would you do with the money. Create a breakdown of how you would spend it. Then see yourself having that much money and enjoying it.

3. If you could announce "Open Sesame", what would you immediate have manifested in your life? Why?

4. Like Lincoln, do you believe that something inside you is superior to circumstances?

5. Do you fear ridicule from friends and family? On a scale from one to ten (one being very little, and ten being very much so), rate how much you believe you are influenced by fear of ridicule by others.

   1——2——3——4——5——6——7——8——9——10

6. Do you make good use of your imagination? Do you ever take time to embark on creative endeavors? If so, how do you feel after doing so? Do you have a greater sense of calm and optimism?

7. Study Tesla and Mozart. Note how they took action on their daydreams. Take one small action step on a daydream you have today, then note how you feel in doing so.

XVIII

This One Thing I Do

"How do you tackle your work each day?
Do you grapple the task that comes your way
With a confident, easy mind?
Do you start to toil with a sense of dread
Or feel that you're going to do it?
"You can do as much as you think you can,
But you'll never accomplish more;
If you're afraid of yourself, young man,
There's little for you in store.
For failure comes from the inside first,
It's there, if we only knew it,
And you can win, though you face the worst,
If you feel that you're going to do it."
—Edgar A. Guest.*

How did the Salvation Army get so much favorable publicity out of the War? They were a comparatively small part of the "Services" that catered to the boys "over

---

* From "A Heap o' Livin'." The Reilly & Lee Co.

there," yet they carried off the lion's share of the glory. Do you know how they did it?

By concentrating on just one thing—DOUGHNUTS!

They served doughnuts to the boys—and they did it well. And that is the basis of all success in business—to focus on one thing and do that thing well. Better far to do one thing pre-eminently well than to dabble in forty.

Two thousand years ago, Porcius Marcus Cato became convinced, from a visit to the rich and flourishing city of Carthage, that Rome had in her a rival who must be destroyed. His countrymen laughed at him. He was practically alone in his belief. But he persisted. He concentrated all his thought, all his faculties, to that one end. At the end of every speech, at the end of every talk, he centered his hearers' thought on what he was trying to put over by epitomizing his whole idea in a single sentence—"Carthage must be destroyed!" *And Carthage was destroyed.*

If one man's concentration on a single idea could destroy a great nation, what can you not do when you apply that same principle to the *building* of a business?

I remember when I was first learning horsemanship, my instructor impressed this fact upon me: "Remember that a horse is an animal of one idea. You can teach him only one thing at a time." Looking back, I'd say the only thing wrong with his instruction was that he took in too little territory. He need not have confined himself to the horse. Most humans are the same way.

In fact, you can put ALL humans into that class if you want a thing done well. For you cannot divide your thought and do justice to any one of the different subjects you are thinking of. You've got to do one thing at a time. The greatest success rule I know in business—the one that should be printed over every man's desk, is—"This One Thing I Do." Take one piece of work at a time. Concentrate on it to the exclusion of all else. *Then finish it!* Don't half-do it, and leave it around to clutter up your desk and interfere with the next job. Dispose of it completely. Pass it along wherever it is to go. Be through with it *and forget it!* Then your mind will be clear to consider the next matter.

"The man who is Perpetually hesitating which of two things he will do first," says William Wirt, "will do neither. The man who resolves, but suffers his resolution to be changed by the first counter-suggestion of a friend—who fluctuates from plan to plan and veers like a weathercock to every point of the compass with every breath of caprice that blows—can never accomplish anything real or useful. It is only the man who first consults wisely, then resolves firmly, and then executes his purpose with inflexible perseverance, undismayed by those petty difficulties that daunt a weaker spirit, that can advance to eminence in any line."

Everything in the world, even a great business, can be resolved into atoms. And the basic principles behind the biggest business will be found to be the same as those behind the successful running of the corner newsstand. The whole practice of commerce is founded upon them. Any man can learn them, but only the alert and energetic can apply them. The trouble with most men is that they think they have done all that is required of them when they have earned their salary.

Why, that's only the beginning. Up to that point, you are working for someone else. From then on, you begin to work for yourself. Remember, you must *give to get* and it is when you give that *extra* bit of time and attention and thought to your work that you begin to stand out above the crowd around you.

Norval Hawkins, for many years General Manager of Sales for the Ford Motor Company, wrote, "the greatest hunt in the Ford business right now is the MAN hunt." And big men in every industrial line echo his words. 'When it comes to a job that needs real ability, they are not looking for relatives or friends or men with "pull." They want a MAN—and they will pay any price for the right man.

Not only that, but they always have a weather eye open for promising material. And the thing they value most of all is INITIATIVE.

But don't try to improve the whole works at once. Concentrate on one thing at a time. Pick some one department or some one process or some one thing and focus all your thought upon it. Bring to bear upon it the limitless resources of your subconscious mind. Then prepare a definite plan for the development of that department or the improvement of that process. Verify your facts carefully to make sure they are workable. *Then*—and not till then—present your plan.

In "Thoughts on Business," you read: "Men often think of a position as being just about so big and no bigger, when, as a matter of fact, a position is often what one makes it. A man was making about $1,500 a year out of a certain position and thought he was doing all that could be done to advance the business. The employer thought otherwise, and gave the place to another man who soon made the position worth $8,000 a year—at exactly the same commission.

"The difference was in the man—in other words, in what the two men thought about the work. One had a little conception of what the work should be, and the other had a big conception of it. One thought little thoughts, and the other thought big thoughts.

"The standards of two men may differ, not especially because one is naturally more capable than the other, but because one is familiar with big things and the other is not. The time was when the former worked in a smaller scope himself, but when he saw a wider view of what his work might be he rose to the occasion and became a bigger man. It is just as easy to think of a mountain as to think of a hill—when you turn your mind to contemplate it. The mind is like a rubber band—you can stretch it to fit almost anything, but it draws in to a smaller scope when you let go.

"Make it your business to know what is the best that might be in your line of work, and stretch your mind to conceive it, and then devise some way to attain it.

"Big things are only little things put together. I was greatly impressed with this fact one morning as I stood watching the workmen erecting the steel framework for a tall office building. A shrill whistle rang out as a signal, a man over at the engine pulled a lever, a chain from the derrick was lowered, and the whistle rang out again. A man stooped down and fastened the chain around the center of a steel beam, stepped back and blew the whistle once more. Again the lever was moved at the engine, and the steel beam soared into the air up to the sixteenth story, where it was made fast by little bolts.

"The entire structure, great as it was, towering far above all the neighboring buildings, was made up of pieces of steel and stone and wood, put together according to a plan. The plan was first imagined, then penciled, then carefully drawn, and then followed by the workmen. It was all a combination of little things.

"It is encouraging to think of this when you are confronted by a big task. *Remember that it is only a group of little tasks, any of which you can easily do.* It is ignorance of this fact that makes men afraid to try."

One of the most essential requisites in the accomplishment of any important work is patience. Not the patience that sits and folds its hands and waits—Micawber like—for something to turn up. But the patience that never jeopardizes or upsets a plan by forcing it too soon. The man who possesses that kind of patience can always find plenty to do in the meantime.

Make your plan—then wait for the opportune moment to submit it. You'd be surprised to know how carefully big men go over suggestions from subordinates, which show the least promise. One of the signs of a really big man, you know, is his eagerness to learn from everyone and anything. There is none of that "know it all" about him that characterized the German general who was given a book containing the strategy by which Napoleon had for fifteen years kept all the armies of Europe at bay. "I've no time to read about bygone battles," he growled, thrusting the book away, "I have my own campaign to plan."

There is priceless wisdom to be found in books. As Carlyle put it—"All that mankind has done, thought, gained or been—it is lying in matchless preservation in the pages of books."

The truths which mankind has been laboriously learning through countless ages, at who knows what price of sweat and toil and starvation and blood—all are yours for the effort of reading them.

And in business, knowledge was never so priceless or so easily acquired. Books and magazines are filled with the hows and whys, the rights and wrongs of buying and selling, of manufacturing and shipping, of finance and management. They are within the reach of anyone with the desire to KNOW.

Nothing pays better interest than judicious reading. The man who invests in more knowledge of his business than he needs to hold his job, is acquiring capital with which to get a better job.

As old Gorgon Graham puts it in "The Letters of a Self-Made Merchant To His Son"—

"I ain't one of those who believe that a half knowledge of a subject is useless, but it has been my experience that when a fellow has that half knowledge, he finds it's the other half which would really come in handy.

"What you know is a club for yourself, and what you don't know is a meat-ax for the other fellow. That is why you want to be on the look-out all the time for information about the business and to nail a fact just as a sensible man nails a mosquito—the first time it settles near him."

The demands made upon men in business today are far greater than in any previous generation. To meet them, you've got to use your talents to the utmost. You've got to find in every situation that confronts you, the best, the easiest and the quickest way of working it out. And the first essential in doing this is to plan your work ahead.

You'd be surprised at how much more work you can get through by carefully planning it, and then taking each bit in order and disposing of it before starting on the next.

Another thing—once started at work, don't let down. Keep on going until it is time to quit. You know how much power it takes to start an auto that is standing motionless. But when you get it going, you can run along in high at a fraction of the expenditure of gas. It is the same way with your mind. We are all mentally lazy. We hate to start using our minds. Once started, though, it is easy to keep along on high, if only we won't let down. For the moment we let down, we have that starting to do all over again. You can accomplish ten times as much, with far less effort or fatigue, if you will keep right on steadily instead of starting and stopping, and starting and stopping again.

Volumes have been written about personal efficiency, and general efficiency, and every other kind of efficiency in business. But boiled down, it all comes to this:

1—Know what you want.
2—Analyze the thing you've got to do to get it.
3—Plan your work ahead.
4—Do one thing at a time.
5—Finish that one thing and send it on its way before starting the next.
6—Once started, KEEP GOING!

And when you come to some problem that "stumps" you, give your subconscious mind a chance.

Frederick Pierce, in "Our Unconscious Mind," gives an excellent method for solving business problems through the aid of the subconscious:

"Several years ago, I heard a successful executive tell a group of young men how he did his work, and included in the talk was the advice to prepare at the close of each day's business, a list of the ten most important things for the next day. To this I would add: Run them over in the mind just before going to sleep, not thoughtfully, or with elaboration of detail, but with the sure knowledge that the deeper centers of the mind are capable of viewing them constructively even though conscious attention is surrendered in sleep.

"Then, if there is a particular problem which seems difficult of solution, review its features lightly as a last game for the imaginative unconscious to play at during the night. Do not be discouraged if no immediate results are apparent. Remember that fiction, poetry, musical composition, inventions, innumerable ideas, spring from the unconscious, often in forms that give evidence of the highest constructive elaboration.

"Give your unconscious a chance. Give it the material, and stimulate it with keenly dwelt-on wishes along frank Ego Maximation lines. It is a habit which, if persisted in, will sooner or later present you with some very valuable ideas when you least expect them."

I remember reading of another man—a genius at certain kinds of work—who, whenever an especially difficult problem confronted him, "slept on it." He had learned the trick as a child. Unable to learn his lessons one evening, he had kept repeating the words to himself until he dozed in his chair, the book still in his hands. What was his surprise, on being awakened by his father a few minutes later to find that he knew them perfectly! He tried it again and again on succeeding evenings, and almost invariably it worked. Now, whenever a problem comes up that he cannot solve, he simply stretches out on a lounge in his office, thoroughly relaxes, *and lets his subconscious mind solve the problem!*

STUDY GUIDE

XVIII *This One Thing I Do*

1. How do you tackle your work each day? If with dread, today tackle it with a sense of enthusiasm and adventure. Note how changing your mindset makes you feel.

2. Do you have difficulty focusing your energy and intentions on one desire? If so, chose only one now, and commit only to it.

3. Are you a multi-tasker? If so, today focus on only doing one task at a time. Practice being single-minded and note what feelings arise when you do? Do you have a greater sense of urgency? If so, then channel that energy to your commitment and ambition towards your one great goal.

4. Print the quote *"This one thing I do"* in the place where you do your work. Find a great graphic to go along with it, and then be sure to read it frequently throughout your day.

5. Do you have a cluttered work environment? Is that clutter an extension of your unfocused brain? If so, take some time to organize your desk. If not, congratulate yourself on creating a healthy, productive work environment.

6. If you have a day job, do you follow your own career aspirations after work? If you haven't done so, then start by taking a small step today. Write the step that you have taken once you start.

7. Is there a department that you note needs improvement in your workplace? If so, write out an implementation plan for its improvement. Once completed, take the plan to management and offer it as an option. Note how you feel in completing this task. Whether it is responded to or not, is not your problem or issue. The fact is that you relied on the Infinite Mind within you and took action.

8. Are you a visionary, a "big picture" thinker? If not, try to think big when tackling the business world. What major shift do you believe would enhance your company's bottom line? Work on it, and then take action on it.

9. *"Nothing pays better interest than judicious reading",* Clearly you are a reader because you are reading this book. Research and find another book that will assist and inspire you to have greater faith in the Infinite Mind within you. Perhaps a biography of someone who beat the odds and achieved greatness in his or her life. Then find the book and read it. Write about any insights you gain.

10. How does Gorgon Graham's letter to his son apply in your life? What is the mosquito that you need to nail? Have you done so?

11. Planning ahead is essential to getting more done. If you do not already do so, get a scheduler and take the time to do a daily, weekly and monthly work plan. Stephen Covey has a powerful time management system. Use his or another to plan and prioritize.

12. Steady and continued focus on the work that you are doing is also key to your success. Constantly starting and stopping takes much greater effort. On a scale from one to ten (one being very little, and ten being very much so), rate how effective you are at starting and following through on your efforts.

    1——2——3——4——5——6——7——8——9——10

13. To be most efficient, you need to do the following:
    1. Know what you want.
    2. Analyze the thing you've got to do to get it.
    3. Plan your work ahead.
    4. Do one thing at a time.
    5. Finish that one thing and send it on its way before starting the next.
    6. Once started, KEEP GOING!

Go through this list and note if there is any step that you have yet to master. Then focus on following the steps and note your productivity when you do.

14. Have you ever dreamed a solution to a problem? If so, please write about your experience. If not, perhaps you want to set a strong intention to experience this phenomenon.

15. Frederick Pierce ended each work day with a list of the ten most important things to get done the next day. He would then run them over in his mind before going to sleep, allowing his subconscious mind to problem solve while he was sleeping. Practice this technique, being sure you allow your subconscious mind time to digest and come up with solutions. Track your progress, and when you get answered, be sure to express gratitude. Doing so will invite more solutions.

VOLUME SIX

XIX

The Master Mind

*"One who never turned his back
but marched breast forward,
Never doubted clouds would break,
Never dreamed though right were worsted
Wrong would triumph,
Held we fall to rise, are baffled to fight better,
Sleep to wake."*
—BROWNING.

Among your friends there is one of those men who doesn't have much use for the word "can't."

You marvel at his capacity for work.

You'll admire him the more the longer you know him. You'll always respect him.

For he not only has made good, but he always will make good. He has found and appropriated to himself the "Talisman of Napoleon"—*absolute confidence in himself.*

The world loves a leader. All over the world, in every walk of life, people are eagerly seeking for some one to follow. They want some one else to do their thinking for them; they need some one to hearten them to action; they like to have some one else on whom to lay the blame when things go wrong; they want some one big enough to share the glory with them when success crowns his efforts.

But to instill confidence in them, that leader must have utter confidence in himself. A Roosevelt or a Mussolini who did not believe in himself would be inconceivable. It is that which makes men invincible—the Consciousness of their own Power. They put no limit upon their own capacities—therefore they have no limit. For Universal Mind sees all, knows all, and can do all, and we share in this absolute power to the exact extent to which we permit ourselves. Our mental attitude is the magnet that attracts from Universal Mind everything we may need to bring our desires into being. We make that magnet strong or weak as we have confidence in or doubt of our abilities. We draw to ourselves unlimited power or limit ourselves to humble positions according to our own beliefs.

A long time ago Emerson wrote: "There is one mind common to all individual men. Every man is an inlet to the same *and to all* of the same. He that is once admitted to the right of reason is made a freeman of the whole estate. What Plato has thought, he may think; what a saint has felt, he may feel; what at any time has befallen any man, he can understand. Who hath access to this Universal Mind, *is a party to all that is or can be done*, for this is the only and sovereign agent."

The great German physicist, Nernst, found that the longer an electric current was made to flow through a filament of oxide of magnesium, the greater became the conductivity of the filament.

In the same way, the more you call upon and use your subconscious mind, the greater becomes its conductivity in passing along to you the infinite resources of Universal Mind. The wisdom of a Solomon, the skill of a Michael Angelo, the genius of an Edison, the daring of a Napoleon, all may be yours. It rests with you only to form the contact with Universal Mind in order to draw from it what you will.

Think of this power as something that you can connect with any time. It has the answer to all of your problems. It offers you freedom from fear, from worry, from sickness, from accident. No man and no thing can interfere with your use of this power or diminish your share of it. No one, that is, but yourself.

Don Carlos Musser expresses it well in "You Are": "Because of the law of gravitation the apple falls to the ground. Because of the law of growth the acorn becomes a mighty oak. Because of the law of causation, a man is 'as he thinketh in his heart.' Nothing can happen without its adequate cause."

Success does not come to you by accident. It comes as the logical result of the operation of law. Mind, working through your brain and your body, makes your world. That it is not a better world and a bigger one is due to your limited thoughts and beliefs. They dam back the flood of ideas that Mind is constantly striving to manifest through you. God never made a failure or a nobody. He offers to the highest and the lowest alike, all that is necessary to happiness and success. The difference is entirely in the extent to which each of us AVAILS himself of that generosity.

There is no reason why you should hesitate to aspire to any position, any honor, any goal, for the Mind within you is fully able to meet any need. It is no more difficult for it to handle a great problem than a small one. Mind is just as much present in your little everyday affairs as in those of a big business or a great nation. Don't set it doing trifling sums in arithmetic when it might just as well be solving problems of moment to yourself and the world.

Start something! Use your initiative. Give your mind something to work upon. The greatest of all success secrets is initiative. It is the one quality which more than any other has put men in high places.

Conceive something. Conceive it first in your own mind. Make the pattern there and your subconscious mind will draw upon the plastic substance or energy all about you to make that model real.

Drive yourself. Force yourself. It is the dreamer, the man with imagination, who has made the world move. Without him, we would still be in the Stone Age.

Galileo looked at the moon and dreamed of how he might reach it. The telescope was the fruition of that dream. Watt dreamed of what might be done with steam—and our great locomotives and engines of today are the result. Franklin dreamed of harnessing the lightning—and today we have man-made thunderbolts.

Initiative, plus imagination, will take you anywhere. Imagination opens the eyes of the mind, and there is nothing good you can imagine there that is not possible of fulfillment in your daily life.

Imagination is the connecting link between the human and the Divine, between the formed universe and formless energy. It is, of all things human, the most God-like. It is our part of Divinity. Through it we share in the creative power of Universal Mind. Through it we can turn the drabbest existence into a thing of life and beauty. It is the means by which we avail ourselves of all the good, which Universal Mind is constantly offering to us in such profusion. It is the means by which we can reach any goal; win any prize.

What was it gave us the submarine, the aeroplane, wireless, electricity? Imagination. What was it that enabled man to build the Simplon Tunnel, the Panama Canal, the Hell Gate span? Imagination. What is it that makes us successful and happy, or poor and friendless? Imagination—or the lack of it.

It was imagination that sent Spanish and English and French adventurers to this new world. It was imagination that urged the early settlers westward—ever westward. It was imagination that built our railroads, our towns, and our great cities.

Parents foolishly try to discourage imagination in their children, when all it needs is proper guidance. For imagination forms the world from which their future will take its shape. Restrain the one and you constrict the other. Develop the one in the right way, and there is no limit to the other. Uncontrolled, the imagination is like a rudderless ship. Or even, at times, like the lightning. But properly controlled, it is like the ship that carries riches from port to port. Or like the electric current, carrying unlimited power for industry and progress.

Do you want happiness? Do you want success? Do you want position, power, and riches? *Image them!* How did God first make man? "In his image created He him." He "imaged" man in His Mind.

And that is the way everything has been made since time began. It was first imaged in Mind. That is the way everything you want must start—with a mental image.

So use your imagination! Picture in it your Heart's Desire. Imagine it—daydream it so vividly, so clearly, that you will actually BELIEVE you HAVE it. In the moment that you carry this conviction to your subconscious mind—in that moment your dream will become a reality. It may be a while before you realize it, but the important part is done. You have created the model. You can safely leave it to your subconscious mind to do the rest.

When Jesus adjured His disciples—"Whatsoever ye desire, when ye pray, believe that ye RECEIVE it," He was not only telling them a great truth, but he was teaching what we moderns would call excellent psychology as well. For this "belief" is what acts upon the subconscious mind. It is through this "belief" that formless energy is compressed into material form.

Every man wants to get out of the rut, to grow, to develop into something better. Here is the open road—open to you whether you have schooling, training, position, wealth, or not. Remember this: Your subconscious mind knew more from the time you were a baby than is in all the books in all the colleges and libraries of the world.

So don't let lack of training, lack of education, hold you back. Your mind can meet every need—and will do so if you give it the chance. The Apostles were almost all poor men, uneducated men, yet they did a work that is unequalled in historical annals. Joan of Arc was a poor peasant girl, unable to read or write—*yet she saved France!* The pages of history are dotted with poor men, uneducated men, who thought great thoughts, who used their imaginations to master circumstances and became rulers of men. Most great dynasties started with some poor, obscure man. Napoleon came of a poor, humble family. He got his appointment to the Military Academy only through very hard work and the pulling of many political strings. Even as a Captain of Artillery he was so poverty-stricken that he was unable to buy his equipment when offered an appointment to India. Business today is full of successful men who have scarcely the rudiments of ordinary education. It was only after he had made his millions that Andrew Carnegie hired a tutor to give him the essentials of an education.

So it isn't training and it isn't education that makes you successful. These help, but the thing that really counts is that gift of the Gods—*Creative Imagination!*

You have that gift. Use *it*! Make every thought, every fact, that comes into your mind *pay you a profit*. Make it work and produce for you. Think of things—not as they are but as they MIGHT be. Make them real, live and interesting. Don't merely dream—but *CREATE*! Then use your imagination to make that CREATION of advantage to mankind—and, incidentally, yourself.

STUDY GUIDE

XIX *The Master Mind*

1. Write a short summary of what Browning's poem meant to you, and how you could apply it to your life.

2. Collier states that the world loves a leader. Which leader do you have the highest respect for and why?

3. Do you believe yourself to be a leader or a follower?

4. What leadership skills and traits to you possess? Which do you need to further cultivate?

5. Emerson was aware of the Universal Mind and its infinite power. What other prolific pioneer or leader in history was also conscious of it?

6. Collier states that the more you call upon and use your subconscious mind, the greater is conductivity. All you need do is avail yourself of the generosity of the Universal Mind. Start tracking how often you call upon the Universal Mind throughout each day and make a point of calling upon it more frequently.

7. *"Initiative plus imagination will take you anywhere"*. Have you ever wanted to go to outer space? Do you believe this to be possible? If so, allow yourself to imagine doing so, knowing that you have planted the seed.

8. Of all your traits and talents, how much respect do you have for your imagination?

9. Was your imagination encouraged during your childhood? On a scale from one to ten (one being very little, and ten being very much so), rate how much your imagination was encouraged and flourished during your childhood.

1——2——3——4——5——6——7——8——9——10

10. Do you enjoy daydreaming?

11. Do you feel held back by lack of training? According to Collier, your *"Creative Imagination"* is more valuable. Could you shift this perception, or start to take training that you are interested in?

12. Research a world leader, or someone who had a great impact on the world who did not have a higher education. Write a short summary of their story. If they can achieve what they have without a degree, can you give yourself permission to do the same?

XX

What Do You Lack?

"I read the papers every day, and oft encounter tales which show there's hope for every jay who in life's battle fails. I've just been reading of a gent who joined the has-been ranks, at fifty years without a cent, or credit at the banks. But undismayed he buckled down, refusing to be beat, and captured fortune and renown; he's now on Easy Street. Men say that fellows down and out ne'er leave the rocky track, but facts will show, beyond a doubt, that has-beens do come back. I know, for I who write this rhyme, when forty-odd years old, was down and out, without a dime, my whiskers full of mold. By black disaster I was trounced until it jarred my spine; I was a failure so pronounced I didn't need a sign. And after I had soaked my coat, I said (at forty-three), 'I'll see if I can catch the goat that has escaped from me.' I labored hard; I strained my dome, to do my daily grind, until in triumph I came home, my billy goat behind. And any man who still has health may with the winners stack, and have a chance at fame and wealth—for has-beens do come back."

—Walt Mason.*

---

* From "Walt Mason—His Book." Barse & Hopkins, Newark, N. J.

Do you know why it is that the Bolsheviki are so opposed to religion?

Because religion, as it is commonly accepted, teaches man resignation to conditions as they are—teaches, in effect, that God created some men poor and some rich. That this unequal distribution is a perfectly natural thing. And that we must not rail against it because it will all be made right in the next world.

Napoleon, in his early Jacobin days, denounced religion for that very reason. But when he had won to power, when he planned to make himself Emperor, then he found he had need for that religion, and re-established the Church in France.

For, he reasoned, how can people be satisfied without religion? If one man is starving, near another who is making himself sick by eating too much, how can you expect to keep the starving one resigned to his fate unless you teach him it will all be made right in some indefinite future state?

Organized society could not exist, as he planned it, without some being rich and some poor, and to keep the poor satisfied, there must be an authority to declare—"God wills it thus. But just be patient. In the hereafter all this will be different. YOU will be the ones then to occupy the places of honor."

Religion, in other words—as it is ordinarily taught—*is a fine thing to keep the common people satisfied!*

But Christianity was never meant for a weapon to keep the rich wealthy and secure, the poor satisfied and in their proper place. On the contrary, Christianity as taught by Jesus opened the way to all Good. And Christianity as it was practiced in its early years was an idealized form of Socialism that benefited each and all. No one was wealthier than his neighbors, it is true—but neither was any poverty-stricken. Theirs was the creed of the Three Musketeers—"All for one, and one for all!"

"Ask and ye shall receive," said Jesus. "Seek and ye shall find." That was not directed to the rich alone. That was to ALL men.

Providence has never made a practice of picking out certain families or certain individuals and favoring them to the detriment of other people—much as some of our "leading families" would have us believe it. It is only man that has arrogated to himself that privilege. We laugh now at the "divine right of Kings." It is just as ridiculous to think that a few have the right to all the good things of life, while the many have to toil and sweat to do them service.

To quote Rumbold's last words from the scaffold—"I never could believe that Providence had sent a few men into the world ready booted and spurred to ride, and millions ready saddled and bridled to be ridden."

There is nothing right in poverty. Not only that, but there is nothing meritorious in poverty. The mere fact that you are poor and ground down by fear and worry is not going to get you any forwarder in the hereafter. On the contrary, your soul is likely to be too pinched by want, too starved and shriveled to be able to expand.

"The Kingdom of Heaven is within you" to me that means that Heaven is here and now. That if we want any happiness from it we've got to get it as we go along. I've never been much of a believer in accepting these promissory notes for happiness. Every time one of them falls due, you find you just have to renew it for another six months or a year, until one of these days you wake up and find that the bank has busted and all your notes are not worth the paper they are written on.

The Cumaean Sibyl is said to have offered Tarquin the Proud nine books for what he thought an exorbitant sum. So he refused. She burned three of the books, and placed the same price on the six as on the original nine. Again he refused. She burned three more books, and offered the remainder for the sum she had first asked. This time Tarquin accepted. The books were found to contain prophecies and invaluable directions regarding Roman policy, but alas, they were no longer complete.

So it is with happiness. If you take it as you go along, you get it in its entirety. But if you keep putting off the day when you shall enjoy it—if you keep taking promissory notes for happiness—every day will mean one day less of it that you will have. Yet the cost is just the same.

The purpose of existence is GROWTH. You can't grow spiritually or mentally without happiness. And by Happiness I don't mean a timid resignation to the "Will of God." That so-called "Will of God" is more often than not either pure laziness on the part of the resigned one or pure cussedness on the part of the one that is "putting something over" on him. It is the most sanctimonious expression yet devised to excuse some condition that no one has the energy or the ability to rectify.

No—by Happiness I mean the everyday enjoyment of everyday people. I mean love and laughter and honest amusement. Every one of us is entitled to it. Every one of us can have it—if he has the WILL and the ENERGY to get out and get it for himself.

Joyless work, small pay, no future, nothing to look forward to—God never planned such an existence. It is man-made—and you can be man enough to unmake it as far as you and yours are concerned.

God never made any man poor any more than He made any man sick. Look around you. All of Nature is bountiful. On every hand you see profusion—in the trees, in the flowers, in everything that He planned. The only Law of Nature is the law of Supply. Poverty is unnatural. It is man-made, through the limits man puts upon himself. God never put them there any more than He showed partiality by giving to some of His children gifts and blessings, which He withheld from others. His gifts are just as available to you as to any man on earth. The difference is all in your understanding of how to avail yourself of the infinite supply all about you.

Take the worry clamps off your mentality and you will make the poverty clamps loosen up from your finances. Your affairs are so closely related to your consciousness that they too will relax into peace, order, and plenty. Divine ideas in your spiritual consciousness will become active in your business, and will work out as your abundant prosperity.

As David V. Bush says in "Applied Psychology and Scientific Living"—"Thoughts are things; thoughts are energy; thoughts are magnets which attract to us the very things which we think.

Therefore, if a man is in debt, he will, by continually thinking about debt, bring more debts to him. For thoughts are causes, and he fastens more debts on to himself and actually creates more obligations by thinking about debts.

"Concentrate and think upon things that you want; not on things which you ought not to have. Think of abundance, of opulence, of plenty, of position, harmony and growth, and if you do not see them manifested today, they will be realized tomorrow. If you must pass through straits of life where you do not outwardly see abundance, know that you have it within, and that in time it will manifest itself.

"I say, if you concentrate on debt, debt is what you will have; if you think about poverty, poverty is what you will receive. It is just as easy, when once the mind becomes trained, to think prosperity and abundance and plenty, as it is to think lack, limitation and poverty."

Prosperity is not limited to time or to place. It manifests when and where there is consciousness to establish it. It is attracted to the consciousness that is free from worry, strain, and tension.

So never allow yourself to worry about poverty. Be careful; take ordinary business precautions of course. But don't center your thought on your *troubles*. The more you think of them, the more tightly you fasten them upon yourself. Think of the *results* you are after—not of the difficulties in the way. Mind will find the way. It is merely up to you to choose the goal, and then keep your thought steadfast until that goal is won.

The greatest short cut to prosperity is to *LIVE IT!* Prosperity attracts. Poverty repels. To quote Orison Swett Marden—"To be ambitious for wealth and yet always expecting to be poor, to be always doubting your ability to get what you long for, is like trying to reach East by traveling West. There is no philosophy which will help a man to succeed when he is always doubting his ability to do so, and thus attracting failure."

Again: "No matter how hard you may work for success, if your thought is saturated with the fear of failure it will kill your efforts, neutralize your endeavors, and make success impossible."

The secret of Prosperity lies in so vividly imaging it in your own mind that you literally exude prosperity. You feel prosperous, you look prosperous, and the result is that before long you ARE prosperous.

I remember seeing a play a number of years ago that was based on this thought. A young fellow—a chronic failure—was persuaded by a friend to carry a roll of $1,000 counterfeit bills in his pocket, and to show them, unostentatiously, when the occasion offered. Of course, everyone thought he had come into some legacy.

The natural inference was that anyone who carried fifty or a hundred thousand dollar bills in his pockets must have a lot more in the bank. Opportunities flocked to him. Opportunities to make good. Opportunities to make money. He made good! Without having to spend any of this spurious money of his. For most business today is done on credit. I know many wealthy men who seldom carry anything but a little change in their pockets for tips. Everything they do, everything they buy, is "Charged." And big deals are put through in the same way. If a man is believed to have plenty of money, if he has a reputation for honesty and fair dealing, he may put through a transaction running into six or seven figures without paying one cent down. The thing that counts is not the amount of your balance at the Bank, but what others THINK of you, the IMAGE you have created in your own and in others minds.

What do you lack? What thing do you want most? Realize that before it or any other thing can be, it must first be imaged in Mind. Realize, too, that when you can close your eyes and actually SEE that thing, *you have brought it into being*—you have drawn upon that invisible substance all about you—you have *created something*. Hold it in your thought, focus your mind upon it, "BELIEVE THAT YOU HAVE IT"—and you can safely leave its material manifestation to the Genie-of-your-Mind.

God is but another name for the invisible, everywhere present, and Source-of-things. Out of the air the seed gathers the essences which are necessary to its bountiful growth; out of the invisible ether our minds gather the rich ideas that stimulate us to undertake and to carry out enterprises that bring prosperity to us. Let us see with the eye of the mind a bountiful harvest; then our minds will be quickened with ideas of abundance, and plenty will appear, not only in our world, but also everywhere.

"As the rain cometh down and the snow from heaven, and returneth not thither, but watereth the earth, and maketh it bring forth and bud, and giveth seed to the sower and bread to the eater; so shall my word be that goeth forth out of my mouth: it shall not return unto me void, but it shall accomplish that which I please, and it shall prosper in the thing whereto I sent it."—Isaiah.

STUDY GUIDE

XX *What Do You Lack?*

1. Following Walt Mason's witty piece, in a similar way, write your story, with yourself as the hero who has overcome the mundane, unsuccessful life.

2. What thoughts and feelings arise within you when you hear the statement, *"God willed it"*?

3. If you experience financial poverty, what do you believe you gain by being in this state? There must be some kind of emotional payoff, otherwise you would choose differently. Do you agree? Why or why not?

4. Collier states that if you take happiness as you go along, you will get it in its entirety. Do you seek out joyful experiences throughout your day? Set an intention today to experience as much joy as you can. At the end of the day, write about your experiences.

5. It is said that if you take the worry clamp off your mentality, you will loosen the poverty clamps from your finances. Each time you start to worry, imagine literally loosening that clamp in your mind's eye. See yourself releasing the tension of the clamp. Then see more money in your bank account each time you do. Record any shifts that arise.

6. Who experiences the kind of prosperity you wish for? Research them and then see yourself living in the opulence and abundance that they do. Note how you feel when you allow yourself to do so. Then express gratitude to your imagination for taking you there.

7. Collier references a play he saw in which the lead character carried a great deal of money in his wallet and "acted" rich. In response, his prosperity grew and grew. Experiment with always keeping at least $1,000 in your wallet. Imagine yourself spending $100 each day on something you love; something that is not a need, but a desire. Note how doing this exercise makes you feel.

XXI

The Sculptor and the Clay

> *"Eternal mind the Potter is,*
> *And thought the eternal clay.*
> *The hand that fashions is divine;*
> *His works pass not away.*
> *God could not make imperfect man*
> *His model Infinite, Unhallowed thought*
> *He could not plan—Love's work and*
> *Love must fit."*
> —Alice Dayton.

When you step into your office on Monday morning, no doubt you have dreams of wonderful achievement. Your step is firm, your brain is clear and you have carefully thought out just WHAT you will do and HOW you will accomplish big things in your business. Perhaps the very plans you have in mind will influence your whole business career, and you have visions of the dollars that will be yours rolling into your bank account.

But do these dreams come true?

Are you always able to put through what you had planned to do—does your day's work have the snap and power you imagined it would have? Are you ever forced to admit that your dreams of big accomplishment are often shattered because of "fagged nerves" and lack of energy, because you have not the "pep"?

How easy it is to think back and see how success was in your grasp if only you had felt equal to that extra bit of effort, if only you had had the "pep," the energy to reach out and take it. The great men of the world have been well men, strong men. Sickness and hesitancy go hand in hand. Sickness means weakness, querulousness, lack of faith, and lack of confidence in oneself and in others.

But there is no real reason for sickness or weakness, and there is no reason why you should remain weak or sick if you are so afflicted now.

Remember the story of the sculptor Pygmalion? How he made a statue of marble so beautiful that every woman who saw it envied it? So perfect was it that he fell in love with it himself, hung it with flowers and jewels, spent day after day in rapt admiration of it, until finally the gods took pity upon him and breathed into it the breath of life.

There is more than Pagan mythology to that story. There is this much truth in it—that any man can set before his mind's eye the image of the figure he himself would like to be, and then breathe the breath of life into it merely by keeping that image before his subconscious mind as the model on which to do its daily building.

For health and strength are natural. It is ill health and weakness that are unnatural. Your body was meant to be lithe, supple, muscular, and full of red-blooded energy and vitality. A clear brain, a powerful heart, a massive chest, wrists and arms of steel—all these were meant for you—all these you can have if you will but *know*, and *feel*, and *think aright*.

Just take stock of yourself for a moment. Are your muscles tough, springy and full of vim? Do they do all you ask of them—and then beg for more? Can you eat a good meal—and forget it?

If you can't, it's your own fault. You can have a body alive with vitality, a skin smooth and fine of texture, muscles supple and virile. You can be the man you have always dreamed of being, without arduous dieting, without tiresome series of exercises, merely by following the simple rules herein laid down.

For what is it that builds up the muscles, puts energy and vitality into your system, gives you the pep and vigor of youth? *Is it exercise?* Then why is it that so many day laborers are poor, weak, anemic creatures, forced to lay off from one to three months every year on account of sickness? They get plenty of exercise and fresh air. Why is it that so many athletes die of tuberculosis or of weak hearts? They get the most scientific exercise year in and year out.

Just the other day I read of the sudden death of Martin A. Delaney, the famous trainer, known all over the country as a physical director. He taught thousands how to be strong, but "Athletic Heart" killed him at 55. Passersby saw him running for a car, then suddenly topple over dead.

"Exercise as a panacea for all human ills is dangerously overrated," Dr. Charles M. Wharton, in charge of health and physical education at the University of Pennsylvania, said today (March 20, 1926), according to an Associated Press dispatch.

Dr. Wharton, who has been a trainer of men for thirty years and was an all-American guard on the Pennsylvania football team in 1895 and 1896, declared the search for the fountain of youth by exercise and diet has been commercialized to a point of hysteria.

"Some one should cry a halt against this wild scramble for health by Unnatural means," said Dr. Wharton. "This indiscriminate adoption of severe physical training destroys the health of more people than it improves."

Dr. Wharton said he was appalled by the amount of physical defects and weaknesses developed by overindulgence in athletics by students in preparatory schools.

"I know I am presenting an unpopular viewpoint, and it may sound strange coming from a physical director.

"In gymnasium work at the University of Pennsylvania we try to place our young men in sports *which they will enjoy*, and thus get a physical stimulation from *relaxed play.*"

Is it diet? Then why is it that so many people you know, who have been dieting for years, are still such poor, flabby creatures? Doesn't it always work, or is it merely a matter of guess-work-and those were the cases where no one happened to guess right? Why is it that doctors disagree so on what is the correct diet? For years we have been taught to forswear too much meat. For years we have been told that it causes rheumatism and gout and hardening of the arteries—and a dozen or more other ailments.

Now comes Dr. Woods Hutchinson—a noted authority, quoted the world over—and says: "All the silly old prejudice against meat, that it heated the blood (whatever that means) and produced uric acid to excess, hardened the arteries, inflamed the kidneys, caused rheumatism, etc., has now been proved to be pure fairy tales, utterly without foundation in scientific fact.

"Red meats have nothing whatever to do with causing gout and rheumatism, because neither of these diseases is due to foods or drinks of any sort, but solely to what we call local infections. Little pockets of pus (matter) full of robber germs—mostly streptococci—around the roots of our teeth, in the pouches of our tonsils, in the nasal passages and sinuses of our foreheads and faces opening into them; . . . Our belief now is: 'No pockets of pus, no rheumatism or gout.' Food of any kind has absolutely nothing to do with the case.

"On the other hand, the very worst cases on record in all medical history of hardening and turning to lime (calcification) of the arteries all over the body, and in the kidneys and intestines particularly, have been found in Trappist and certain orders of Oriental monks who live almost exclusively upon starch and—that is, peas, beans, and lentils, and abstain from meat entirely."

Then what is right? *Is it the combination of diet and exercise?* But surely the patients in sanitariums and similar institutions would have every chance to get just the right combination, yet how often you see them come out little, if any, better off than when they went in.

No. None of these is the answer. As a matter of fact, the principal good of either diet or exercise is that it keeps before the patient's mind the RESULT he is working for, and in that way tends to impress it upon his subconscious mind. That is why physical culturists always urge you to exercise in front of a mirror. If results are achieved, it is MIND that achieves them—not the movements you go through or the particular kind of food you eat.

Understand, I don't ask you to stop exercising. A reasonable amount of light, pleasant exercise is good for you mentally and physically. It develops your will power. It helps to impress upon your subconscious mind the image you want to see realized in your body. And it takes your mind off your troubles and worries, centering your thoughts instead upon your desires; just where your thoughts should always be.

Outdoor exercise, tennis, horseback, swimming—any sort of active *game*—is the best rest there is for a tired mind. For mental tiredness comes from a too steady contemplation of ones problems. And anything that will take ones mind completely off them, and give the subconscious time to work out the solution, is good. That is why it so often happens that you go back to your work after a day of play—not merely refreshed, but with so clear a mind that the problems, which before seemed insurmountable are but as child's play to you.

You who envy the rosy cheek and sparkling eye of youth, who awake in the morning weary and un-refreshed, who go to your daily tasks with fagged brain and heavy tread—just remember that Perfect Youth or Perfect Health is merely a state of mind.

There is only one thing that puts muscles on your bones. There is only one thing that keeps your organs functioning with precision and regularity. There is only one thing that builds for you a perfect body. That one thing is your subconscious mind.

Every cell and tissue, every bone and sinew, every organ and muscle in your entire body is subject to the control of your subconscious mind. As it directs, so they build or function.

True, that subconscious mind accepts suggestions from your conscious mind. Hold before it the thought that the exercise you are taking is building muscle upon your arms or shoulders, and your subconscious mind will fall in readily with the suggestion and strengthen those muscles. Hold before it the thought that some particular food gives you unusual energy and "pep," and the subconscious mind will be entirely agreeable to producing the added vigor.

But have you ever noticed how some sudden joy (which is entirely a mental state) energizes and revitalizes you—*more than all the exercise or all the tonics you can take?* Have you ever noticed how martial music will relieve the fatigue of marching men? Have you ever noticed how sorrow (which is entirely a mental state) will depress and devitalize you, *regardless of any amount of exercise or health foods you may take?*

Each of us has within him all the essentials that go to the making of a Super-Man. But so has every acorn the essentials for making a great oak tree, yet the Japanese show us that even an oak may be stunted by continual pruning of its shoots. Negative and weak thoughts, thoughts of self-doubt, of mistrust, continually prune back the vigorous life ever seeking so valiantly to show forth the, splendor and strength of the radiant inner self.

Choose what you will be! Your responsibility is to think, speak, act the true inner self. Your privilege is to show forth in this self, the fullness of peace and plenty. Keep steadfastly in mind the idea of yourself that you want to see realized. Your daily, hourly, and continual idea of yourself, your life, your affairs, your world, and your associates, determines the harvest, the showing forth. Look steadfastly to your highest ideal of self, and your steadfast and lofty ideal will draw forth blessing and prosperity not only upon you, but also upon all who know you.

For mind is the only creator, and thought is the only energy. All that counts is the image of your body that you are holding in your thought. If heretofore that image has been one of weakness, of ill health, change it *now*—TODAY. Repeat to yourself, the first thing upon awakening in the morning and the last thing before going to sleep at night—"My body was made in the image and likeness of God. God first imagined it in its entirety, therefore every cell and bone and tissue is perfect, every organ and muscle performing its proper function. That is the only model of me in Universal Mind. That is the only model of me that my Subconscious Mind knows. Therefore, since Mind—God—is the only creator, that is the only model of me that I can have!"

STUDY GUIDE

XXI *The Sculptor and the Clay*

1. What does Alice Dayton's poem mean to you?

2. On a scale from one to ten (one being very little, and ten being very much so), rate how much "pep" you have.

   1——2——3——4——5——6——7——8——9——10

3. Like the sculptor, Pygmalion, imagine a figure of yourself as you would like to be. Then imagine God or the Universal Mind breathing life into it. Then imagine yourself embodying that "new" self. Write about any insights you gain when doing this exercise.

4. Are your muscles currently feeling tough, springy and full of vim?

5. Is your skin smooth and supple?

6. According to Dr. Charles M. Wharton, *"Exercise as a panacea for all human ills is dangerously overrated".* Do you believe this to be so? Do you exercise on a regular basis? Do you do it because you enjoy it or because you think you should? Knowing what you know now, what is your belief around exercise?

7. Do you believe you eat a healthy diet? Do you enjoy your food, or eat it because you think you should? Experiment with enjoying your food (either change your diet to food that you enjoy, or make a choice to enjoy the food you eat). Note any shifts in your energy or mindset.

8. Mental fatigue comes from a steady contemplation on one's problems. Take note of how many times each day you say the words, "I can't afford . . ." Do you believe

such statements undermine your ability to experience abundance? Might you re-phrase your statement to "I choose not to purchase this at this time"?

9. On a scale from one to ten (one being very little, and ten being very much so), rate how satisfied you are with the recreation time you spend relaxing and out in nature.

1——2——3——4——5——6——7——8——9——10

10. If you are dissatisfied with a lack of recreation time, can you commit to at least stepping outside and taking a couple of deep breaths at least 3 times a day?

11. See your ideal-self experiencing a really peaceful, tranquil day. Perhaps you are getting a massage, sitting in the sun, or swimming in a crystal-clear lake. Take at least five minutes to visualize yourself in a peaceful, tranquil place. Once you are finished notice how your body feels.

12. Collier ends this chapter with the following suggestion: *"Repeat to yourself, the first thing upon awakening in the morning and the last thing before going to sleep at night—"My body was made in the image and likeness of God. God first imagined it in its entirety, therefore every cell and bone and tissue is perfect, every organ and muscle performing its proper function. That is the only model of me in Universal Mind. That is the only model of me that my Subconscious Mind knows. Therefore, since Mind—God—is the only creator, that is the only model of me that I can have!"* Practice this for at least a month and record any shifts in your energy and overall sense of wellbeing.

XXII

Why Grow Old?

"And Moses was an hundred and twenty years old when he died: his eye was not dim, nor his natural force abated."

Remember how you used to plough through great masses of work day after day and month after month, cheerily, enthusiastically, with never a sign of tiring or nervous strain? Remember how you used to enjoy those evenings, starting out as fresh from your office or shop as if you hadn't just put a hard day's work behind you?

No doubt you've often wondered why you can't work and enjoy yourself like that now, but solaced yourself with the moth-eaten fallacy that "As a man grows older he shouldn't expect to get the same fun out of life that he did in his earlier years."

Poor old exploded idea!

Youth is not a matter of time. It is a mental state. You can be just as brisk, just as active, just as light-hearted now as you were ten or twenty years ago. Genuine youth is just a perfect state of health. You can have that health, and the boundless energy and capacity for work or enjoyment that go with it. You can cheat time of ten, twenty or fifty years—not by taking thought of what you shall eat or what you shall drink, not by diet or exercise, but solely through a right understanding of what you should expect of your body.

"If only I had my life to live over again!" How often you have heard it said. How often you have thought it.

But the fact is that you CAN have it. You can start right now and live again as many years as you have already experienced. Health, physical freedom and full vigor need not end for you at 35 or 40—nor at 60 or 70. Age is not a matter of years. It is a state of mind.

In an address before the American Sociological Society a few months ago Dr. Hornell Hart of Bryn Mawr predicted that—"Babies born in the year 2000 will have something like 200 years of life ahead of them, and men and women of 100 years will be quite the normal thing. But instead of being wrinkled and crippled, these centenarians will be in their vigorous prime."

Thomas Parr, an Englishman, lived to be 152 years old, and was sufficiently hale and hearty at the age of 120 to take unto himself a second wife. Even at 152, his death was not due to old age, but to a sudden and drastic change in his manner of life. All his days he had lived upon simple fare, but his fame reaching the King, he was invited to London and there feasted so lavishly that he died of it.

In a dispatch to the New York Times on February 14th last, I read of an Arab now in Palestine, one Salah Mustapha Salah Abu Musa, who at the age of 105 *is growing his third set of teeth!*

There is an ancient city in Italy, which can be approached by sea only through a long stretch of shallow water full of rocks and cross currents. There is one safe channel, and it is marked by posts. In the days of the Sea Rovers the city used to protect itself by pulling up the posts whenever a rover hove in sight.

Mankind has taken to planting posts along its way to mark the flight of time. Every year we put in a new one, heedless of the fact that we are thus marking a clear channel for our Archenemy, Age, to enter in from the sea of human belief.

But the fact is that there is no natural reason for man to grow old as soon as he does, *no biological reason for him to grow old at all!*

Why is it that the animals live eight to ten times their maturity, when man lives only about twice his? Why? Because man hastens decrepitude and decay by holding the thought of old age always before him.

Dr. Alexis Carrel, Noble Prize winner and member of the Rockefeller Institute, has demonstrated that living cells taken from a body, properly protected and fed, can be kept alive indefinitely. Not only that, but they grow! In 1912 he took Sonic tissue from the heart of an embryo chick and placed it in a Culture medium. It is living and growing yet.

Recently Dr. Carrel showed a moving picture of these living cells before the American Institute of Electrical Engineers. They grow so fast that they double in size every twenty-four hours, and have to be trimmed daily!

The cells of your being can be made to live indefinitely when placed outside your body. Single-celled animals never die a natural death. They live on and on until something kills them. Now scientists are beginning to wonder if multi-cellular animals like man really need to die.

Under the title, "Immortality and Rejuvenation in Modern Biology," M. Metalnikov, of the Pasteur Institute, has just published a volume that should be read by all those who have decided that it is necessary to grow old and die.

Here is the first sentence of the concluding chapter of the book: "What we have just written forces us to maintain our conviction that immortality is the fundamental property of living organisms."

And further on:

"Old age and death are not a stage of earthly existence . . .

And that, mind you, is set forth under the aegis of a scientific establishment that has no equal in the world, and of a scholar universally respected.

As the *Journal of Paris* says in reviewing the article:

"Most religious and philosophic systems assert the immortality of the soul. But the positive sciences have shown themselves more skeptical on this point. This idea seems to them quite contradictory to all that we know, or think we know, of animal life. Animal life originates as a tiny germ, which becomes an embryo, developing into an adult organism, which grows old and finally dies. This means the disappearance of all the faculties of life that so clearly distinguish it from an inanimate object. There is no scientific evidence to show that at this moment the 'soul' does not disappear with the body, and that it continues its existence separately. Biologists cannot even conceive the possibility of separation of soul and body, so strong and indissoluble are the bonds that unite all our psychic manifestations with our bodily life. For them an immortal soul only can exist in an immortal body. What if it were so? What if our organism is really indestructible? It is this that M. Metalnikoy attempts scientifically to prove.

"Death is a permanent and tangible phenomenon only in the case of man and the higher animals. It is not so for plants and for the simpler forms of animal life, the protozoans. These last, composed often of a single cell, just observable under the microscope, are however without the chief faculties that characterizes the higher animals. They move about by means of vibratory hair-like processes, sustain themselves, seek their food, hunt animals still smaller than themselves, react to irritations of different kinds, and multiply. But this multiplication is not effected by means of special organs, as among the higher animals, but by the division of the whole organism into two equal parts. The common infusorians, which abound in fresh water, thus divide once or twice every twenty-four hours. Each daughter cell continues to live like the mother cell, of which it is the issue; it feeds, grows, and divides in its turn. And never, in this constantly renewed cycle in their lives, do we find the phenomenon of natural death, so characteristic and so universal in the higher animals. The infusorium is subject only to accidental death, such as we can cause by the addition of some poisonous element to the water in which it lives, or by heat.

"Experiments along this line were made long ago. The first were by de Saussure, in 1679. Having put an infusorium in a drop of water, he saw it divide under his eye. Four days later it was impossible to count the number of creatures. However, some authors thought that this reproductive facility was not unlimited. Maupas himself, who made a minute study of it forty years ago and succeeded in observing 700 successive generations of a single species, thought that it was finally subject to old age and to death.

"But the more recent works of Joukovsky at Heidelberg, of Koulaghine at Petrograd, of Calkins in England, of Weissmann, and still others, lead to an opposite opinion. The degeneration observed by these workers was due to autointoxication, caused by not renewing the culture medium.

"Decisive experiments were made in Russia, 'dating from 1907, by Woodruff and by M. Metalnikoy himself. Begun at Tsarskoe Selo, they continued until the tragic hours of the 1917 revolution, and were renewed at the University of Crimea. These investigators took an infusorium found in an aquarium, the Paramoecium caudatum, whose characteristics are well determined, and in thirteen years, in 1920, they had obtained 5,000 successive generations. . . .

"Thus we are bound to say that a unicellular body possesses within itself the power of immortality.

"And we ourselves are made up only by the juxtaposition of simple cells."

The Fountain of Youth

Four hundred years ago Ponce de Leon set sail into the mysteries of an unknown world in search of the Fountain of Youth, when all the time the secret of that fountain was right within himself.

For the fact is, that no matter how many years have passed since you were born, *you are only eleven months old today!* Your body is constantly renewing itself. The one thing about it you can be surest of is CHANGE. Every one of the millions of cells of which it is composed is constantly being renewed. Even your bones are daily renewing themselves in this way.

These cells are building—building—building. Every day they tear down old tissue and rebuild it with new. There is not a cell in your body, not a muscle or tissue, not a bone, that is more than eleven months old! Why then should you feel age? Why should you be any less spry, any less cheerful, than these youngsters around you that you have been envying?

The answer is that you *need not*—if you will but realize your YOUTHFULNESS. Every organ, every muscle, tissue and cell of your body is subject to your subconscious mind. They rebuild exactly as that mind directs them. What is the model you are holding before your mind's eye? Is it one of age, of decrepitude? That is the model that most men use, because they know no better. That is the result that you see imaged upon their bodies.

But you need not follow their outworn models. You can hold before your mind's eye only the vision of youth, of manly vigor, of energy and strength and beauty *and that is the model that your cells will use to build upon.*

Do you know what is responsible for the whole difference between Youth and Age? Just one thing. Youth looks *forward* always to something better. Age looks backward and sighs over its "lost" youth.

In youth we are constantly growing. We KNOW we have not yet reached our prime. We know we can expect to continually IMPROVE. We look forward to ever-increasing physical powers. We look forward to a finer, more perfect physique. We look forward to greater mental alertness. We have been educated to expect these things. Therefore we BELIEVE we shall get them—and we GET them!

But what happens after we get to be thirty or forty years of age? We think we have reached our prime. We have been taught that we can no longer look forward to greater growth—that all we can hope for is to "hold our own" for a little while, and then start swiftly downward to old age and decay. History shows that no nation, no institution and no individual can continue for any length of time to merely "hold his own." You must go forward—or back. You must move—or life will pass you by. Yours is the choice if you will realize that there is never any end to GROWTH—that your body is constantly being rebuilt—that perfection is still so far ahead of you that you can continue GROWING towards it indefinitely—you need never know age. You can keep on growing more perfect, mentally and physically, every day. Every minute you live is a minute of Conception and rebirth.

You may be weak and anemic. You may be crippled or bent. No matter! You can start today to rebuild along new lines. In eleven months at the most, every one of those weak and devitalized cells, every one of those bent and crippled bones, will be replaced by new, strong, vigorous tissue.

Look at Annette Kellerman—crippled and deformed as a child—yet she grew up into the world's most perfectly formed woman. Look at Roosevelt—weak and anemic as a young man—yet he made himself the envy of the world for boundless vigor and energy. And they are but two cases out of thousands I could quote. Many of the world's strongest men were weaklings in their childhood. It matters not what your age, what your condition—you can start now renewing your youth, growing daily nearer the model of YOU that is imaged in Universal Mind.

Arthur Brisbane says that at the age of 85 George F. Baker is doing the work of ten men.

That is what every man of 85 ought to be doing, for he should have not only the physical vigor and strength and enthusiasm of 21, but combined with them he should have the skill and experience, the ripened judgment of 85.

There is no more despairing pronouncement than the belief of the average man that he matures only to begin at once to deteriorate and decay. When the actual fact is, as stated in a recent utterance by the eminent Dr. Hammond, *there is no physiological reason* why a man should die. He asserted—and the statement is corroborated by scientists and physiologists—that the human body possesses inherent capacity to renew and continue itself and its functions, indefinitely!

Your body wears out? Of course it does—just as all material things do. But with this difference your body is being renewed just as fast as it wears out! Have you damaged some part of it? Don't worry. Down inside you is a chemical laboratory, which can make new parts just as good or better than the old. Up in your subconscious mind is a Master Chemist with all the formulas of Universal Mind to draw upon, who can keep that chemical laboratory of yours making new parts just as fast as you can wear out the old.

But that Master Chemist is like all of us—like you. He is inclined to lazy a bit on the job—if you let him. Try to relieve him of some of his functions—and he won't bother about them further. Take to the regular use of drugs or other methods of eliminating the waste matter from the body, and your Master Chemist will figure that your conscious mind has taken over this duty from him—and he will leave it thereafter to your conscious mind. Lead him to believe that you no longer expect him to rebuild your body along such perfect lines as in youth—and he will slow down in his work of removing the old, worn-out tissues, and of replacing them with new, better material. The result? Arteries clogged with worn-out cells. Tissues dried and shrunken. Joints stiff and creaky. In short—Old Age.

The fault is not with the Master Chemist. It is with you. You didn't hold him to the job. When a business or an enterprise or an expedition fails, it is not the rank and file who are to blame—it is the directing head. He didn't give his men the right plans to work on. He didn't supply the proper leadership. He didn't keep them keyed up to their best work.

What would you think of an engineer who, with the best plans in the world, the best material with which to build, threw away his plans when he was half through with the job and let his men do as they pleased, ruining all his early work and all his fine material by putting the rest of it together any which way?

Yet that is what you do when you stop LOOKING FORWARD at 30 or 40, and decide thereafter to just grow old any which way. You throw away the wonderful model on which you have been building, you take the finest material in the world, and let your workmen put it together any way they like. In fact, you do worse than that. You tell them you don't expect much from them any more. That any sort of a patched up job they put together after that will be about as good as you can look for.

Man alive! What would you expect from ordinary workmen to whom you talked like that? Your inner workmen are no different. You will get from them just what you look for—no more, no less.

"Your time of life" should be the best time you have yet known. The engineer who has built forty bridges should be far more proficient than the one who has built only a few. The model you are passing on to your Master Chemist now ought to be a vastly more perfect model than the one you gave to him at twenty. Instead of feeling that your heart is giving out and your stomach weak, you ought to be boasting of how much better a heart you are now making than a few years ago, how much more perfectly your stomach is functioning than before you learned that you were its boss.

Of one thing you can be sure. God never decreed a law of decay and death. If there is any such law, it is man-made—and man can unmake it. The Life Principle that came to this planet thousands or millions of years ago brought no Death Principle with it. For death is like darkness—it is nothing in itself. Death is merely the absence of life, just as darkness is merely the absence of light. Keep that life surging—strongly.

In the Book of Wisdom, of the Apocryphal writings, you read: "For God made not death; neither hath He pleasure in the destruction of the living.

"For He created all things that they might have being; and the generative powers of the world are health-some, and there is no poison of destruction in them, nor hath death dominion upon the earth.

"For righteousness is immortal:

"But ungodly men with their works and words called death unto them.

"For God created man to be immortal, and made Him to be an image of His own proper being.

"But by the envy of the devil came death into the world."

"Whosoever liveth and believeth in me (understandeth me)," said Jesus, "shall never die."

And again—"If a man keep my saying, he shall never see death."

Universal Mind knows no imperfection—no decay—no death. It does not produce sickness and death. It is your conscious mind that has decreed these evils. Banish the thought—and you can banish the effect. Life was never meant to be measured by years.

I remember reading a story of a traveler who had journeyed to a land of perpetual sun. Since there was no sunrise and no sunset, no moons or changing seasons, there was no means of measuring time. Therefore to the inhabitants of that land, time did not exist. And having no time, they never thought to measure ages and consequently never grew old. Like organisms with a single cell, they did not die except by violence.

There is more truth than fiction to that idea. The measurement of life by the calendar robs youth of its vigor and hastens old age. It reminds me of the days of our grandparents, when a woman was supposed to doff her hat and don a bonnet at 40. And donning a bonnet was like taking the veil. She was supposed to retire to her chimney corner and make way for the younger generation.

Men and women ought to *grow* with years into greater health, broader judgment, and mature wisdom. Instead of becoming atrophied, and dead to all new ideas, their minds should through practice hold ever-stronger images before them of youthful vigor and freshness. The Psalmist says—"But thou art the same, and thy years shall have no end."

No one need retire to the chimney corner, no matter how many years have passed over his head. Years should bring wisdom and greater health—not decrepitude. Many of the world's famous men did their greatest work long after the age when most men are in their graves. Tennyson composed the immortal lines of "Crossing the Bar" at the age of 80. Plato still had pen in hand at 81. Cato learned Greek at the same age. Humboldt completed his "Cosmos" in his ninetieth year, while John Wesley at 82 said—"It is twelve years now since I have felt any such sensation as fatigue."

You are only as old as your mind. Every function, every activity of your body, is controlled by your mind. Your vital organs, your blood that sends the material for rebuilding to every cell and tissue, the processes of elimination that remove all the broken down and waste material, all are dependent for their functioning upon the energy derived from your mind.

The human body can be compared to an electric transportation system. When the dynamo runs at full power every car speeds along, and everything is handled with precision. But let the dynamo slow down and the whole system lags.

That dynamo is your mind, and your thoughts provide the energy that runs it. Feed it thoughts of health and vigor and your whole system will reflect energy and vitality. Feed it thoughts of decrepitude and age, and you will find it slowing down to the halting pace you set for it.

You can grow old at 30. You can be young at 90. It is up to you. Which do you choose?

If you choose youth, then start this minute renewing your youth. Find a picture—or, better still, a statuette—of the man you would like to be, the form you would like to have. Keep it in your room. When you go to bed at night, *visualize* it in your mind's eye—hold it in your thought as YOU—as the man *YOU ARE GOING TO BE!*

The Journal of Education had the idea in their story of "The Prince and the Statue" in a recent issue:

"There was once a prince who had a crooked back. He could never stand straight up like even the lowest of his subjects. Because he was a very proud prince his crooked back caused him a great deal of mental suffering.

"One day he called before him the most skilful sculptor in his kingdom and said to him: 'Make me a noble statue of myself, true to my likeness in every detail with this exception—make this statue with a straight back. I wish to see myself as I might have been.

"For long months the sculptor worked hewing the marble carefully into the likeness of the prince, and at last the work was done, and the sculptor went before the prince and said: 'The statue is finished; where shall I set it up?' One of the courtiers called out: 'Set it before the castle gate where all can see it,' but the prince smiled sadly, and shook his head. 'Rather,' said he, 'place it in a secret nook in the palace garden where only I shall see it.' The statue was placed as the prince ordered, and promptly forgotten by the world, but every morning, and every noon, and every evening the prince stole quietly away to where it stood and looked long upon it, noting the straight back and the un-lifted head, and the noble brow. And each time he gazed, something seemed to go out of the statue and into him, tingling in his blood and throbbing in his heart.

"The days passed into months and the months into years; then strange rumors began to spread throughout the land. Said one: 'The prince's back is no longer crooked or my eyes deceive me.' Said another: 'The prince is more noble-looking or my eyes deceive me.' Said another: 'Our prince has the high look of a mighty man,' and these rumors came to the prince, and he listened with a queer smile. Then went he out into the garden to where the statue stood and, behold, it was just as the people said, his back had become as straight as the statue's, his head had the same noble bearing; he was, in fact, the noble man his statue proclaimed him to be."

A novel idea? Not at all! 2,500 years ago, in the Golden Age of Athens, when its culture led the world, Grecian mothers surrounded themselves, with beautiful statues that they might bring forth perfect children and that the children in turn might develop into perfect men and women.

Eleven months from now *you* will have an entirely new body, inside and out. Not a single cell, not a single bit of tissue that is now in you will be there then. What changes do you want made in that new body? What improvements?

Get your new model clearly in your mind's eye. Picture it. VISUALIZE it! Look FORWARD daily to a better physique, to greater mental power.

Give that model to your Subconscious Mind to build upon—and before eleven months are out, that model *WILL BE YOU!*

STUDY GUIDE

XXII *Why Grow Old?*

1. Do you believe that Moses was, in fact one hundred and two years old when he died? What age do you want to be when you die? Why?

2. *"As a man grows older he shouldn't expect to get the same fun out of life that he did in his earlier years"* Do you believe this to be true? Why or why not? Do you believe this is the case with your life?

3. Collier emphasizes that age is a state of mind. How do you feel about your age? Do you feel younger, older or your actual age?

4. Dr. Hornell predicted that babies born in the year 2000 would live to be 200 years old. Now that the year 2000 has come and gone, do you believe this to be true? Why or why not?

5. Collier references a man who was growing his third set of teeth at the age of 105. What do you make of this situation?

6. According to the author there is no biological reason for man to grow old. What do you think of this statement? Is it difficult to fathom?

7. Collier asserts that *"man hastens decrepitude and decay by holding the thought of old age always before him"*. According to Dr. Alexis Carrel, living cells can be kept alive indefinitely, and can, in fact, grow. Do you believe this to be true?

8. Take some time to read M. Metalnikov's "Immortality and Rejuventation in Modern Biology". Why do you think that Collier suggested you read it?

9. How do the Infusorium experiments apply to your life and your believes around aging and death?

The Fountain of Youth

10. If you know that your body is constantly renewing itself, then how much impact do you believe mass consciousness has over you?

11. Collier states that the issue with aging is that *"youth looks forward always to something better. Age looks backward and sighs over its 'lost youth'"*. Is this true in your life? If so, how do you believe it affects you?

12. The author shares several examples of older individuals who are living vital, youthful lives. Research someone you admire who is elderly, but still living a vital life. Call their energy and vitally into your life, asking the Infinite Mind to shift your perception and reorganize your body's cells. Then have faith and anticipate change.

13. According to Collier, your body has a Master Chemist that can tend to be lazy if you overuse drugs. In order for Him to be successful, you need to keep Him functioning and on task. Do you believe this theory to be true? Why or why not?

14. How much do you currently rely on drugs to maintain health? Do you think there is a potential problem in doing so?

15. Looking forward on your life, what are you enthusiastic about for your future?

16. Take five minutes and visualize yourself aging gracefully and vitally. Then write a summary of what you experience in this exercise.

17. With life experience, Collier is suggesting that the model self (your body) that you give your Master Chemist at this time should be an improvement on the one you gave Him when you were twenty years of age. Do you believe this to be true? Why or why not?

18. Death and decay does not exist in the perfection of the Universal Mind, and Collier asserts that life was never meant to be measured by years. Do you get excited with each passing birthday, or do you get discouraged?

19. When your mind slows down, your body will for the mind is the dynamo. On a scale from one to ten (one being very little, and ten being very much so), rate how dynamo your mind currently functions.

    1——2——3——4——5——6——7——8——9——10

20. As Collier suggests, find a picture or statue of an individual you would like to resemble. Keep it in your bedroom and before you go to sleep, visualize it as you. Do this exercise continuously until you feel you physically match your visualization.

21. Collier shares the magical story of the prince who changed his crooked back by focusing on a statue of himself with an erect spine. He states that eleven months from now, you will have an entirely new body, both inside and out. Imagine yourself looking in the mirror and experiencing this wonderful change in the present. Be sure to use your senses and experience it fully. Write about your feelings of gratitude as you note this change.

VOLUME SEVEN

XXIII

The Medicine Delusion

"I find the medicine worse than the malady."
—SHAKESPEARE.

"We are getting rid of the drug illusion," declared Dr. Woods Hutchinson, the noted medical writer of America, at a luncheon given on June 6, 1925, by the English-Speaking Union to 700 American and Canadian doctors assembled in London, England.

"We are willing even to subscribe to the dictum of Oliver Wendell Holmes," the doctor added, "that if 99 per cent of all drugs we possess were thrown into the sea it would be a good thing for the human race, but rather hard on the fishes."

Sir Arbuthnot Lane, Surgeon to King George, seconded Dr. Hutchinson's remarks. "They might say," he went on, "that he was trying to establish a 'suicide club' for doctors. It practically came to that, because as the public became educated in matters of health the medical profession might disappear. It was in fact an anomaly that a medical profession should exist. If people were healthy, there was no reason to have doctors at all."

Twenty-five years ago, the charms of the Patent Medicine fakir and the incantations of the Indian Medicine Man were in the heyday of their popularity. So long as you talked about their aches and pains, their diseases and ailments, people would buy any kind of a nostrum that an unscrupulous fakir chose to palm off upon them. Patent medicine manufacturers made fabulous fortunes selling cheap whisky adulterated with burnt sugar and water, under a hundred different names for $1.00 the bottle. You could hardly pick up a magazine or newspaper without seeing a dozen of their lurid ads.

The day of the Indian Medicine Man and street-corner fakir has passed. And for a time, thanks to the crusade against them led by *Collier's*, and backed by a number of other reputable magazines, patent medicine manufacturers suffered an eclipse.

But they are back again today in a more respectable guise. Pick up almost any small town paper and you will find a dozen "sovereign remedies" for tired women or fretful children or run-down men. Concoctions, most of them, containing just enough alcohol to give you a pleasant sense of stimulation, enough burnt sugar to color them—and a whole lot of water.

But if that were all, no great harm would be done. If the peddling of drugs depended entirely—or even mostly—on Patent Medicine advertisers, the end of it would soon be in sight. But it doesn't. The worst offenders of all are the ones who, of all people, should know better—some of the doctors.

Understand, I don't mean all of them. And I don't mean the best of them. There are thousands of them like Dr. Woods Hutchinson who have the courage to get up and say that medicine itself cannot cure disease. That it never has cured disease. That Nature is the only Healer. Drugs can give you temporary relief from pain—yes. They can cleanse—yes. But as for *curing* anything, the drug is not made that can do it.

The principal good that the administering of a drug has is in its effect upon the mind of the patient. Men have been taught for so many years that drugging is the only way to cure disease, that when you give them something, they BELIEVE they are going to be cured, and to the extent that they believe, they ARE CURED.

The best proof of that is to let two patients suffering from the same complaint go to two different physicians—the one a doctor of the regular school, the other a homeopath. The regular doctor will administer a dose containing ten thousand times as much of the mother drug as the homeopath. In fact, there is so slight a trace of any drug in the homeopath's prescription that it might be called none at all. Yet it frequently happens that his patient will respond just as readily to his denatured dose as the other will to his drug.

Dr. Gour, in a recent issue of *Pearson's Magazine*, said: "A few years ago there appeared an article in the *Atlantic Monthly* written by a young woman physician who was with the Red Cross in Russia. Immediately following the Kerensky revolution, the Russian peasants who, for the first time in their lives, found that they could keep what they earned, began to think of going to doctors for ailments which had afflicted them for years, but which they could never before afford to have treated. Within two weeks' time this young physician exhausted her supply of medicine. But the rush of peasant patients continued and she was reduced to the placebo idea of administering colored waters with a slight amount of a single drug-quinine, if I recall correctly. For several weeks she obtained such wonderful results in every conceivable form of affliction that she said her faith in specific medication was completely lost."

In a dispatch from Rome to the New York *Herald-Tribune*, under date of June 15, 1926, I read:

"Under the skeptical eyes of local doctors Don Luigi Garofalo, a priest in the Quarto sector of Naples, alleges that he is curing all the ills that flesh is heir to, from pneumonia to broken bones, by a practical application of the theory derived from the text, 'Man is of dust and to dust he shall return.' Don Luigi argues that from a homeopathic view point dust should be a curative element. So from dust taken from the reddish earth near Pozznoli, which contains traces of sulphur and copper, he makes pills for the afflicted, but he contends that any other earth will do.

"The cures, most of which have been effected by means of the red earth, include the healing of broken limbs, tubercular cases, toothache, internal lesions, heart diseases, mumps, paralysis and fevers."

Of course, it is not to be inferred from this that reliance can be placed upon red earth—or any other kind of earth—to cure you of any ill. But it shows that even so common; ordinary a thing as a bit of dirt can be used to arouse people from the lethargic condition in which sickness so frequently leaves them, and gives them the power to help themselves.

Take another case. Your doctor prescribes regular doses of some drug. You take it once. It has the desired effect. You take it again. The effect is not quite so pronounced. You keep it up—and in a short time *the drug seems to have lost its efficacy.*

Why? The same chemical elements are there. And if you mix the same chemical elements in a retort, you will get the same results whether you do it once or a thousand times. Why doesn't it work the same way with drugs and your body?

Because the strongest factor in bringing about the desired effect in the beginning was your BELIEF—yours and that of your doctor. But as you kept on and on, your belief began to falter, until presently it died away altogether. You may have *hoped*, but the active belief suggestions to your subconscious mind had stopped carrying conviction.

Dr. Richard C. Cabot, Professor of Medicine at Harvard University, in a recent address, declared, "three-quarters of all illnesses are cured without the victims even knowing they have had them.

"Proof of this contention is to be found in post-mortem examinations, which time after time reveal indelible and unmistakable traces of disease which the subject has conquered all unknowingly. Ninety per cent of all typhoid cures itself, as does 75 per cent of all pneumonia. In fact, out of a total of 215 diseases known to medical science, there are only about eight or nine which doctors conquer—the rest conquer themselves."

He went on to say that—"If nature, assisted by the proper mental and emotional moods, is capable of curing an ulcer in three or four weeks, why isn't it possible for the same force to heal a similar ulcer in a few minutes, when the curative processes have been speeded up abnormally?"

Great physicians have, on numerous occasions, maintained that there is no science in *medicating* people. In Preventive Medicine—yes. In Surgery. In Obstetrics. In a score of different lines that fall under the heading of the medical profession.

But the art of drugging is little ahead of where it was in the Middle Ages, when Egyptian mummies were in great demand among druggists and "powdered Pharaoh" was considered the greatest remedy for any ill that flesh was heir to.

Every day brings the discovery of some new drug, and the consequent dictum that the remedy previously prescribed was all a mistake—that it had little or no real value whatever.

One doctor says: "A medicine that will not kill you if you take an overdose is no good." Another: "The most prominent doctors now claim that there is not a single drug that will do what it has been prescribed for in the past."

Dr. Douglas White, writing in *The Churchman*, sums it up thus:

"All cure of every disease is spiritual. Healing can never be imposed from without by either the surgeon or physician; it is the living organism which, helped by the skill of the one or the other, is enabled to work its way back to health. The whole principle of healing in all cases is the *vis medicatrix naturae*. And when we speak of nature, we are only personifying the principle of life which Christians call God."

In the *Medical Record* of September 25, 1920, Dr. Joseph Byrne, Professor of Neurology at Fordham University Medical School, said:

"At a conservative estimate it may be admitted that of all the ailments for which relief is sought, 90% or over are self limited and tend to get well. It may also be admitted that in over 90% of all human ailments, the *psychic* is the dominating factor."

In other words, Mind is the Healer. Drugs can sometimes make its work easier by removing obstructions, by killing off parasites. But the regular use of drugs is far more likely to harm than to heal. We might well quote to the druggists the old Hindoo proverb:

"God gives the mango;
  The farmer plants the seed.
God cures the patient;
  The doctor takes the fees."

In the Great War, the one drug that most proved its worth was Iodine. And what is Iodine? A *cleanser*. It killed germs. It cleansed wounds. But it has no healing power. And no healing was expected of it. It did all that was asked. It cauterized—cleansed so that Nature (Mind) could do its own healing, unobstructed.

That would seem to be the most that should be expected of any drug—kill the germs of sickness or disease, cleanse so that Nature can then more easily do its rebuilding. And that is where the use of drugs should stop. Mind works best when it is interfered with least—when we throw ourselves entirely upon it for Support, rather than share the responsibility with some outside agency.

Dr. Burnett Rae, a well-known English specialist, addressing a large audience on the subject of "Spiritual Healing and Medical Science," said the term "spiritual healing" was sometimes used in a manner which seemed to imply that there was a form of healing which was of a non-spiritual character, and that spiritual healing was incompatible with, or opposed to, medical practice. Healing could never be regarded as a purely physical process. He would go so far as to say that healing was always effected through the control of the mind, and medicinal remedies only set the machinery of the mind in motion. We are too apt to think of medical science as concerned with drugs or appliances and operations. *These might completely pass away during the next twenty or fifty years.*

It is not through drugs that the medical profession has done so much of good for the world. It is not through drugs that they have improved the general health, cleaned up plague spots, cut down infant mortality, and lengthened the average life expectancy of mankind by fifteen years.

It is by scotching disease at its very source. It is by getting rid of artificially created *unwholesome* conditions, getting back to *natural wholesome* conditions.

What is it causes typhus? Filth—an entirely unwholesome condition, man-made. And how do doctors prevent the spread of typhus? By cleaning up—by getting back to natural wholesome conditions.

What is it causes typhoid? Impure water. And its prevention is simply the purifying of the water—getting back to natural wholesome supply.

Yellow fever has been practically stamped out of existence. Typhus is almost a forgotten plague, except in such backward places as parts of Russia and Asia.

Malaria has been conquered. And doctors predict that in another generation tuberculosis will be an almost forgotten malady.

How were these wonderful results brought about? Not through drugs—but by cleaning up! Cleaning out swamps and filth. Purifying water. Building drainage systems. Making everything round about as clean and wholesome as Nature herself. Cleanliness—Purity—Sunshine!

God gave us in abundance all that is necessary for perfect health—clean air, pure water, clear sunshine. All we need to do is to keep these pure and clean, and to use all we possibly can of them. The greatest good the medical profession has done mankind is in discovering the value of these gifts of God and showing us how to use them.

The Chinese have long had the right idea—they pay their physicians to keep them well, not to cure them of sickness. And the thing that made the reputation of such men as Gorgas, Reed, Flexner, Carrel, was not their *cure* of disease—but their *prevention* of it.

That way lies the future of medicine—bringing our surroundings back to the natural wholesome conditions for which we were created. That way lies health and happiness for all—cleanliness inside and out, clean air, pure water, plenty of sunshine—*and right thinking*!

In the next Chapter, I shall try to show you how you can apply the illimitable power of Mind hopefully towards the successful treatment of disease.

STUDY GUIDE

XXIII *The Medicine Delusion*

1. Collier opens this chapter with the statement that it would be a good thing if 99 percent of all drugs were thrown out to sea. What are your current beliefs about modern day medicine?

2. Medicine began with fakirs and Indian Medicine Men selling concoctions mostly made of alcohol. He says that they have since been replaced by some wayward doctors. Our society puts great power and belief in modern medicine, drugs in particular and yet, there is evidence that placebo tests show little effectiveness of drugs over none. The healing comes from the mind's belief that a cure has been administered. On a scale from one to ten (one being very little, and ten being very much so), rate how much faith you have in modern medicine, drugs in particular.

   1——2——3——4——5——6——7——8——9——10

3. Why do you believe that drugs lose their efficacy over time? Do you concur with Collier's theory on this—that your original belief brought about the desire effect? Why or why not?

4. Dr. Richard C. Cabot claimed that *"three-quarters of all illnesses are cured without the victims even knowing they have had them."* Do you believe this to be true? Do you believe your body has a strong curing mechanism within it?

5. Do you concur with Dr. Douglas White that all cures are spiritual? Why or why not?

6. In the Great War, Iodine most proved its worth. Collier states that it cleansed the wound, so that nature could do the curing. Disease has weakened in the world because we have gotten back to natural wholesome conditions: purified water, cleanliness and sunshine. Could you stop relying on modern medicine and trust in clean air, pure water and clear sunshine to cure your ails?

7. Like the Chinese medical system, you should focus on prevention of disease over treatment of it. Right thinking plays a part in good health as well. Have you found that when you are emotionally or physically run down, you are more prone to getting sick? What additional steps can you take to maintaining good health?

XXIV

The Gift of the Magi

"Sweep up the debris of decaying faiths;
Sweep down the cobwebs of worn-out beliefs,
And throw your soul wide open to the light
Of Reason and of Knowledge. Be not afraid
To thrust aside half-truths and grasp the whole."
—Ella Wheeler Wilcox.

All over the world, sick, weak and devitalized men and women are searching for health and strength. By the hundreds of thousands, they drag their weary and aching bones around, or languish on sick beds, waiting for someone to bring health to them corked up in a bottle.

But real, lasting health was never found in pillboxes or medicine bottles. There is one method—and only one—by which it can be gained and kept. That method is by using the power of the Subconscious Mind.

For a long time the doctors pooh-poohed any such idea. Then as the evidence piled up, they grudgingly admitted that nervous troubles and even functional disorders might be cured by mind.

Even now there are some who, as Bernard Shaw put it, "Had rather bury a whole hillside ethically than see a single patient cured unethically. They will give credit to no method of healing outside the tenets of their own school."

Yet, as Warren Hilton has it in "Applied Psychology":

"All the literature of medicine, whether of ancient or modern times, abounds in illustrations of the power of the mind over the body in health and in disease. And medical Science has always based much of its practice on this principle. No reputable school of medicine ever failed to instruct its students in practical applications of the principle of mental influence at the bedside of their patients. A brisk and cheery manner, a hopeful countenance, a supremely assured and confident demeanor—these things have always been regarded by the medical profession as but second in importance to sanitation and material remedies; *while the value of the sugar-coated bread pill when the diagnosis was uncertain, has long been recognized.*

"The properly trained nurse has always been expected to supplement the efforts of the attending physician by summoning the mental forces of the patient to his aid. She, therefore, surrounds the patient with an atmosphere of comfortable assurance. And by constantly advising him of his satisfactory progress toward speedy recovery she seeks to instill hope, confidence and mental effort.

"To quote Dr. Didama: 'the ideal physician irradiates the sick chamber with the light of his cheerful presence. He may not be hilarious—he is not indifferent—but he has an irrepressible good-nature which lifts the patient out of the slough of despond and places his feet on the firm land of health. In desperate cases, even a little harmless levity may be beneficial. A well-timed jest may break up a congestion; a pun may add pungency to the sharpest stimulant.' Dr. Oliver Wendell Holmes reduced this principle to its cash equivalent when he said that a cheerful smile might be worth five thousand dollars a year to a physician.

"Today, psychotherapy, or the healing of bodily disease by mental influence, has the unqualified endorsement of the American Therapeutic Society, the only national organization in America devoted exclusively to therapeutics. It has the enthusiastic support of men of such recognized international leadership in the scientific world and in the medical profession as Freud, Jung, Bleuler, Breuer, Prince, Janet, Babinski, Putnam, Gerrish, Sidis, Dubois, Munsterberg, Jones, Brill, Donley, Waterman and Taylor.

"The present attitude of reputable science toward the principle that the mind controls all bodily operations is, then, one of positive conviction. The world's foremost thinkers accept its truth. The interest of enlightened men and women everywhere is directed toward the mind as a powerful curative force and as a regenerative influence of hitherto undreamed-of resource."

The more progressive physicians everywhere now admit that there is practically no limit to how far mind can go in the cure of disease. As Dr. Walsh of Fordham University puts it: "Analysis of the statistics of diseases cured by mental influence shows that its results have been more strikingly manifest in organic than in the so-called nervous or functional diseases."

Everyone admits that the mind influences the body somewhat; for everyone has seen others grow pale with fear, or red with anger. Everyone has felt the stopping of the heartbeats at some sudden fright, the quickened breathing and the thumping of the heart caused by excitement. These and a hundred other evidences of the influence of mind over matter are common to all of us, and everyone will admit them.

But everyone does not know that our whole bodies seem to be nothing more or less than the outward expression of our thought. We sit in a draught, and education teaches us we should have a cold or fever. So we *have* a cold or fever. We eat something which we have been told is indigestible, and immediately we are assailed with pains. We see another yawn, and our impulse is to follow suit. In the same way, when we hear of sickness round about us, the fear of it visualizes it in our own minds and we, too, have it. The *fear* of these things seems to bring them about, the mental suggestion sent through to our subconscious minds. We have been educated in a medical age to think that most diseases are infectious or contagious. So the mere sight of a diseased person makes most of us withdraw into ourselves like a turtle within his shell. We fear we shall catch it—when one of the great dangers of disease is that very fear of it.

For years it has been accepted as an acknowledged fact that anyone trapped in a mine or other air-tight compartment would presently die of carbon dioxide poisoning—lack of oxygen. Now comes Houdini to prove that death for lack of oxygen is not necessary at all!

"Fear, and not poisoning by carbon dioxide, causes the death of miners and others trapped in air-tight compartments," in the opinion of Houdini, according to an Associated Press dispatch of August 6, 1926.

Houdini had himself sunk in a sealed coffin in a swimming pool, without chance for a breath of outside air to reach him, and stayed there for an hour and a half, although, according to all previous scientific belief, he should have been dead at the end of four minutes. Yet Dr. W. J. McConnell of the United States Department of

Mines, who examined Houdini before and after the experiment, reported no marked physical reactions from the test, and Houdini himself said he felt only a slight dizziness when he was released from the coffin!

"Anyone can do it," said Houdini. "The important thing is to *believe that you are safe.*"

The Chinese have a saying that when the plague comes, 5,000 people may die of the plague, but 50,000 will die of the fear of it.

Did you ever hurt a limb, or a finger, so that you thought you couldn't move it? And then, under the stress of some sudden emotion, forget all about the hurt and presently wake to find yourself using the finger or the limb just as readily and as painlessly as though there had never been anything wrong with it?

I have before me a clipping from the New York *Times* of March 29, 1925, telling of a cripple who had been paralyzed for six years, but under the spur of sudden fear, he ran up a stairway unaided, without crutch or cane. He had been treated in a number of hospitals, but because of an injury to his spine received in an auto accident, had been unable to walk without crutches or canes for six years. The patient in the bed next his own suddenly went crazy and attacked him, and in his fear this paralytic leaped from his bed and ran up a flight of stairs. According to the report, *the sudden fright cured him!*

Take the miracles of Lourdes, or of St. Anne of Beaupre, or of any of the dozens of shrines that dot the world. What is it that affects the cures? Two things—*Desire* and *Faith.* "What wouldst thou that I should do unto thee?" the Saviour asked the blind man who kept following and crying out to him. "Lord that I should receive my sight." And again of the cripple at the Pool of Bethesda Jesus asked—"Wouldst thou be made whole?"

Sounds like foolish questioning, doesn't it? But you remember the story of the famous Saint of Italy, who traveled from town to town healing the lame, the halt, and the blind. A pilgrim hastening to a town where the Saint was expected met two lame beggars hurrying away. He asked them the reason for their haste, to be told, to his astonishment, it was because the Saint was coming to town. As they put it—"He will surely heal us, and where will our livelihood be then?"

So it is with many people today—not beggars, mind you—but people in every walk of life. They have become so wedded to their ailments; they "enjoy poor health" so thoroughly, that they are secretly a bit proud of it. Take away their complaints and they would be lost without them.

You must have the *sincere desire first.* That is prayer. Then the faith—the kind of faith that Jesus meant when he said—"Whatsoever ye ask for when ye pray, believe that ye *receive* it, and ye shall *have it.*" Mind you, not "believe ye are *going* to receive it." "Believe that ye *receive* it"—*now*—this very minute. Know that the REAL you, the image of you held in Universal Mind—in short, the *Truth* concerning every organ in your body—is perfect. *"Know the Truth."* Believe that you HAVE this perfect image. On the day that you can truly believe this—carry this sincere conviction to your subconscious mind—on that day you WILL BE perfect.

This is the faith that Jesus meant when he said—"Thy faith hath made thee whole." This is the faith that is responsible for the miracles of Lourdes, for miraculous healings everywhere. It matters not whether you be Catholic or

Protestant, Jew or Gentile. Desire and faith such as these will heal you.

A month or two ago I read in the newspapers of a farmer, blind for two years, who went out in the field and prayed, "that he should receive his sight." At the end of the second day, his sight was completely restored. He was a Protestant. He went to no shrine—just out under the sky and prayed to God.

Today I have before me a clipping from the New York *Sun* of February 23, 1926, telling of Patrolman Dennis O'Brien of the Jersey City police force, who at the end of a Novena to Our Lady of Help at the Monastery of St. Michael's in Union City, recovered the use of his legs, which had been paralyzed since the time, two years before, when a bullet had entered the base of his spine, severing the cord of motor and sensory nerves. He was a Catholic.

Then here is one from the New York *Sun* of June 26, 1926, telling how Miss Elsie Meyer of the Bronx, New York, was healed *overnight* of a tumorous growth that had troubled her for months:

"I realized last fall that there was an unusual growth on my body," she said. "It might have resulted from the strain of lifting a trunk. I wanted to know what it was, and I first went to a doctor, who informed me it was a tumorous growth and likely to become serious.

"But I would not be frightened and refused to receive any medical remedies in the way of cure. I have been a believer in faith healing and member of the Unity Society, a branch of the New Thought organization, for a number of years, so I went to a New Thought practioner. While this seemed to help me, the tumorous growth remained. I guess my faith wasn't strong enough at the time. That was last fall.

"I came to the congress with the same growth, apparently unaffected by any attempts to cure it. But after attending the healing meeting at the congress yesterday I left with firm faith that I would get the healing I had asked for. When I retired I noticed the tumor was still on my body, but when I awoke this morning it had disappeared."

The chronicles of every religion are full of just such miracles. And the reason for them is the same in every case—*prayer* and *faith*. Given these, no healing is impossible.

Suppose we go back for a moment to the lowly Amoeba, the first bit of animal life upon the earth. I know not whether you are Fundamentalist or Evolutionist. The facts are a bit harder to prove from the Evolution side of it, so let us argue from that angle.

The Amoeba, as you will recall from Chapter I, is the lowest form of animal life known to scientists, a sort of jelly-fish with but a single cell—without brains, without intelligence, possessing only LIFE. No one would ever contend that this jellyfish could improve itself. No one would argue that it developed the next form of life out of its own mind or ideas.

Yet, according to science, the next form of life did develop from this jelly-like mass. The Amoeba certainly was not responsible for doing it. And it couldn't develop itself. So the conclusion is forced upon us that some outside Intelligence must have done it.

But there were no other living creatures. The Amoeba was alone of all animal life upon the planet. The condition of the water and atmosphere was such that few if any other forms of animals could have sustained life at that time. So the Intelligence, which developed the next form of animal life, must have been the same that created the Amoeba—that first brought LIFE to this Planet. That Intelligence is variously called God, Providence, Nature, the Life Principle, Mind, etc. For our purposes here let us call it Universal Mind.

Having formed life here on earth, Universal Mind proceeded to develop it. Starting with a single cell, It built cell upon cell, changing each form of life to meet the different conditions of atmosphere and environment that the cooling of the earth crust brought about. When the multi-cellular structure became complicated, It gave a brain to it to direct the different functions, just as you put a "governor" on a steam engine. When land appeared and the receding tides left certain animals high and dry for periods of hours, It gave these both lungs and gills—the one for the air, the other for the water.

When the creatures began to prey upon one another, It gave one speed, another a shell, a third an ink-like fluid, that each in its own way might escape and survive.

But always It progressed. Each new stage of life was an improvement over the previous one. And always It showed Its resourcefulness, Its ability to meet ANY need.

Finally, as the culmination of all Its efforts, It made MAN—a creature endowed not only with a brain like that of the lower animals, but with the power of reason—"made in His image and likeness," sharing Infinite Intelligence—himself a Creator and a part of Universal Mind.

All through the creation—from the time of the one-celled Amoeba right up to Man—every scientist will admit that the directing intelligence of Universal Mind was on the job every minute, that It formed the models on which each new and different kind of animal was made, that each of these models was perfect—the one model best fitted to cope with the conditions it had to confront.

Certainly when It came to Man, It is not likely to have been any less successful in forming a perfect model than it was in making the tiger or the elephant. So we can take it, I assume, that all will admit that Man as formed by Universal Mind is perfect—that the idea of Man as it exists in Universal Mind is perfect in every particular.

And Universal Mind, from the very beginning, has never taken a step backward, has never stood still. Always it has PROGRESSED. So it would seem safe to assume that man is not going backward now—that he is a more perfect creature than he was 5,000, 10,000 or 100,000 years ago—that he is constantly drawing nearer and nearer the likeness of his Creator.

The next step seems just as logical. If there was inherent in even the earliest and lowest forms of life the power to develop whatever means was requisite to meet each new emergency, such as a shell or lungs or legs or wings—if this power is still inherent in the lower forms of life such as the Plant Parasites referred to in a previous chapter, does it not seem a certainty that we have the same power within ourselves, if only we knew how to call it forth?

Jesus proved that we have, and his disciples and followers added still further proof. After the third century of the Christian era, that power was allowed to lapse through disuse, but of late years thousands have been taking advantage of it for themselves and for others through psychology or religion. A new Church has been founded upon the words of James: "Faith without WORKS is dead." It differs from most Churches in that it teaches that Jesus meant ALL that he said when he commanded his disciples to—"Go, preach, saying, the kingdom of heaven is at hand. *Heal the sick,* cleanse the lepers, raise the dead, cast out devils; freely ye have received, freely give." The sick, the lame, the halt and the blind have flocked to it literally by the hundred thousands. That thousands have been cured is beyond dispute. That many were cases, which had been given up by the medical fraternity, the doctors quite frankly admit.

And the basis of all these cures is that there is nothing miraculous about the cure of disease at all. That it is "Divinely Natural." That it requires merely understanding. That Mind is the only Creator. And that the only image Universal Mind holds of your body is a perfect image, neither young nor old, but full of health, of vigor, of beauty and vitality. That all you have to do when assailed by disease is to go back to Universal Mind for a new conception of its perfect image—for the Truth concerning your body. Just as you would go back to the principle of mathematics for the Truth concerning any problem that worked out incorrectly. When you can make your subconscious mind copy after this Universal image—the *Truth*—instead of the diseased image you are holding in your thoughts, your sickness will vanish like the mere dream it is.

Does that sound too deep? Then look at it this way:

When you think an organ is diseased, it is your conscious mind that thinks this. Inevitably it sends this thought through to your subconscious mind, and the latter proceeds to build the cells of that organ along this imperfect, diseased model. Change the model—in other words, change your belief—and your subconscious mind will go back again to building along right lines.

Your body, you know, is simply an aggregation of millions upon millions of protons and electrons, held together by mind. They are the universal substance all about us, the plastic clay from which the sculptor Mind shapes the forms you see.

To quote the New York *Sun*: "Man's body is made up of trillions of miniature solar systems, each with whirling planets and a central sun. These tiny systems are the atoms of modern Science. The atoms of all elements are made up of protons and electrons in varying quantities and arranged in various ways.

"But what are protons and electrons?

"The masters of physics have succeeded in weighing and measuring them. We know that they carry the smallest possible charges of electricity, and we are learning much about the way they behave; but students are beginning to doubt that they have real substance that they are anything one could hit with a Lilliputian hammer. Dr. H. G. Gale of the University of Chicago, addressing the Ohio Academy of Science the other day, said there was good reason to believe; that electrons were composed entirely of electricity and that their mass or weight was only a manifestation of electrical force. According to this view, *nothing exists in the Universe except electricity*—and perhaps ether."

Your subconscious mind partakes of the creative power of Mind and because of that, it is daily, hourly, changing the particles of electrical energy, which constitute your body, to conform to the image you hold before it.

The clay cannot reply to the sculptor. No more can these tiny particles of electricity. Your body has nothing to say as to whether it shall be diseased or crippled. It is MIND that decides this. Jesus understood this, and it was on the basis of this understanding that he was able to cure any and all manner of disease. He was not a magician or occult wonder-worker, aiming to set aside the laws of nature. He was a TEACHER, demonstrating those laws. He didn't pick the learned Scribes and Pharisees and let them in on the secret of his wonder working. On the contrary, the men he chose were simple fisher folk, and to them he gave the UNDERSTANDING that enabled them, too, to cure the sick, the halt and the blind.

For what is sickness? An illusion, a mortal dream—merely the *absence* of health. Bring back that health image, and the sickness immediately disappear. Universal Mind never created disease. The only image it knows of man is the Truth—the perfect image. The only idea it has of your body is a perfect, healthy idea. "For God is of purer eyes than to behold evil."

Then where does disease come from? Who created it? *No one did.* It is a mere illusion—just as, if you think a pin is sticking you, and you concentrate your thought on the pain, it becomes unbearable. Yet when you investigate, you find that no pin was sticking you at all—merely a hair, or bit of cinder lodged against the skin. How often have you had some fancied pain, only to have it promptly disappear when your physician assured you there was nothing wrong with you at all. It would be the same way with all sickness, all pain, if you would understand that it is merely fear or suggestion working on your conscious mind, and that if you will deny this belief of pain or sickness, your subconscious mind will speedily make that denial good. Don't render that mind impotent by thoughts of fear, doubt and anxiety. If you do, it is going to get like a working crew, which is constantly being stopped by strikes or walkouts or changes of plans. It will presently get discouraged and stop trying.

To quote Dr. George E. Pitzer again—"In proper, healthy or normal conditions of life, the objective mind and the subjective mind act in perfect harmony with each other. When this is the case, healthy and happy conditions always prevail. But these two minds are not always permitted to act in perfect harmony with each other; this brings mental disturbances; excites physical wrongs, functional and organic diseases.

"Our unconscious is a tremendous storage plant full of potential energy which can be expended for beneficial or harmful ends. Like every apparatus for storing up power, it can be man's most precious ally, if man is familiar with it and, hence, not afraid of it. Ignorance and fear, on the other hand, can transform a live electric wire into an engine of destruction and death."

Even as long ago as Napoleon's day, men had begun to get an inkling of this. "Think that you are well," said the astute Tallyrand, "instead of thinking that you are sick." And the formula of the Quakers is that an energetic soul is "master of the body which it loves."

So keep in mind the one basic fact that covers the whole ground—that *Mind is all*. There is no other cause. When you drive the belief in disease from your subconscious mind, you will drive away the pain and all the other symptoms with it.

Few sick people have any idea how much they can do for themselves. There is an old saying that every man is "a fool or his own physician at 40." When the science of Mind is more generally understood, that saying will become literally true. Every man will find within himself the Mind, which "healeth all thy diseases." For every function of your body is governed by your mind. When sickness or pain assails you, *deny it!* Cling steadfastly to the one idea that covers all—that Universal Mind made your every organ perfect;

that the only image of each organ now in Universal Mind is this perfect image; and that this perfect idea is endowed with resources sufficient to meet any need.

Jesus' command—"Be ye therefore perfect, even as your father in Heaven is perfect,"—was meant to be taken literally. And it can be followed literally if we will model our bodies upon the image He holds of us in Universal Mind. We are all sculptors, you know, but instead of marble or clay, our material is the plastic energy—protons and electrons—of which we and everything in this world about us are made. What are you making of it? What image are you holding in mind? Images of sickness? Of poverty? Of Limitation? Then you are reproducing these in your life.

Banish them! Forget them! Never let them enter your thought, and they will never again manifest themselves in your life. You admit that mind influences your body to some extent, but you think your physical organs hold the preponderance of power. So you depend upon them, and make yourself their slave.

"Know ye not," says Paul, "that to whom ye yield yourselves servants to obey, his servants ye are to whom ye obey?"

By holding before yourself the thought that your organs are the masters, you make them your master, and deprive yourself of the directing intelligence of your subconscious mind. When an organ ceases to function properly, you try to doctor it, when the part that needs attention is your mind. If you are running an electric machine, and the current becomes weak or is switched off, you don't take the machine part, or oil it or tamper with it to make it run better. You go to the source of the power to find what is wrong there.

In the same way, when anything seems wrong with the functioning of your body, the place to investigate is your subconscious mind. Your stomach has no intelligence, nor your heart, nor your liver, nor any other of your organs. Your liver, for instance, could never figure out how much sugar should be turned into your blood every minute to keep your bodily temperature at 98 degrees, when you are sitting in a room that is warmed to only 65 degrees. It doesn't know how much more sugar is required to keep that temperature normal when you go out into a driving gale 10 below zero. Yet it supplies the requisite amount—neither too much nor too little. And it does it instantaneously. Where does it get the information? *You* don't know it. No mortal man could figure it out in a year's time.

It gets it from your subconscious mind. It gets both the information and the directions to use it. And every other of your bodily organs gets its information in the same place. Your muscles are not self-acting. Take away mind and those muscles are just like any other bit of matter—lifeless, inert. They have nothing to say as to what they shall do. They merely obey the behests of mind.

Have you ever seen one of those great presses at work in a newspaper plant? They seem almost human in their intelligence. At one end, great rolls of paper feed in. At the other, out comes the finished newspaper, folded, ready for delivery. Everything is automatic. Everything as perfect as machinery can be made. The "fingers" that fold the papers seem almost lifelike in their deftness.

But shut off the life-giving electric current—and what happens? The machinery is powerless. Take away the directing human intelligence, and how long before that wonderful machine would be a mass of scrap—mere bits of steel and rubber? How long could it function of itself?

So it is with your body. A wonderful mechanism—the most complicated, yet the most perfect in the world. But switch off the current of your mental dynamo; take away the intelligence that directs the working of your every organ, and what is left? A bit of bone and flesh—inert and useless.

In the final analysis, your body is merely a piece of mechanism—dependent entirely upon mind. It has no power, no volition, of its own. It does as mind tells it to, insofar as mind believes itself to be the Master. Your eyes, for instance, are merely lenses, which transmit light from the outer world to the brain within. They contract or elongate, they open or close, just as mind directs. And mind, in its turn, keeps them constantly nourished with new, life-giving blood, replacing old tissue, old cells, as fast as they wear out, rebuilding ever, so that your eyes may continue to function perfectly as long as your conscious mind is dependent upon them for its impressions of outer objects. It doesn't matter how old you may be or how much you use them. Your eyes are like any other muscles of your body—they improve in strength with use. Give them but enough rest intervals for mind to repair and rebuild the used tissue, keep before your subconscious mind the perfect image of eyes on which you expect it to rebuild, and you need never fear glasses, you need never worry about "your eyes going back on you."

What is it happens when your muscles refuse to work—fail to perform their functions properly? You are what has happened. You have switched off the current from some particular part. You have been holding the belief so long and so firmly that the muscles have the preponderance of power that your subconscious mind has come to believe it, too. And when the nerve or muscle suffers an injury, the subconscious mind—at the suggestion of your conscious mind—gives up all dominion over it.

All disease, all sickness, all imperfections of the human body are due to this one cause—your belief that your body is the master, that it can act, that it can catch cold, or become diseased, without the consent of mind. This is the procuring cause of all suffering.

One disease is no different from another in this. They are all due to that one erroneous belief.

If you will deny the power of your body over your mind, you can destroy all fear of disease. And when the fear goes, the foundation of the disease is gone.

The way to begin is to *refuse to believe* or to heed any complaint from your body. Have no fear of climate or atmosphere, of dampness or drafts. It is only when you believe them unhealthy that they are so to you. When your stomach sends a report of distress, when it tells you that something you have eaten is disagreeing with it, treat it as you would an unruly servant. Remind it that it is not the judge of what is or is not good for it. That it has no intelligence. That it is merely a channel through which the food you give it passes for certain treatment and selection. That if the food is not good it has but to pass it through to the eliminatory organs as speedily as may be.

Your stomach is entirely capable of doing this. Every organ you have is capable of withstanding any condition—given the right state of mind to direct it. The only reason that they succumb to sickness or disease or injury is because you tell them to. Men have fallen from great heights without injury. Men have taken the most deadly poison without harm. Men have gone through fire and flood and pestilence with not a scratch to show. And what men have done once they can do again. The fact that it *has* been done shows that your body does not need to suffer injury from these conditions And if it does not *need* to, then it would seem that the only reason it ordinarily suffers is because your fear of injury is the thought you are holding before your subconscious mind and therefore that is the thought that it images on your body.

In a dispatch from Stockholm to the New York *Herald-Tribune* dated January 18, 1926, I read that Dr. Henry Markus and Dr. Ernest Sahigren, Stockholm scientists, have been able, through hypnotic suggestion, to offset the effect of poisons on the human system to a marked degree.

The scientists put three subjects into hypnotic sleep and then administered drugs, carefully recording the effects on blood pressure and pulse, both with and without "suggestion." When a drug, which acts to increase blood pressure, was administered without "suggestion," the blood pressure readings ranged between 109 to 130 and pulse readings from 54 to 100. But when the drug was administered with the "suggestion" to the mind of the patient that it was merely so much harmless water, the blood pressures were from 107 to 116 and pulse readings all less than 67. From which one would judge that it was the patient's *belief*, which affected him, far more than any power in the drug.

Bear this in mind when anyone tells you that certain foods are not good for you. You can eat what you like, if you do it in moderation. Just remember—no matter what you may eat—if you relish it, if you BELIEVE it to be good for you, *it will be good for you!*

But, you may say, is not this like the tenets of a well-known religion? What of that? If another has uncovered certain fundamental truths why not use them, regardless of whether or not we agree with the philosophy from which they are taken.

To quote again from Dr. Richard C. Cabot of the Harvard Medical School:

"There need be no conflict. There is opportunity for all sincere, humble-minded effort. Let us have no persecutions and no interference with the spread of truth and light from any source. Indictments against movements as powerful and sincere as Christian Science and Preventive Medicine are anachronistic. Let us all get busy along our own lines. 'With malice towards none, with charity for all, let us bind up the nation's wounds.'"

It has often seemed to me that if all the churches would take a leaf out of the book of ordinary Business Practice, forget their differences over dogma, and simply profit by the example that Mary Baker Eddy, Discoverer and Founder of Christian Science, has given them of building up an enormous following almost overnight, they would be much the better off thereby.

For what was it brought men and women into the Church in such vast numbers in the early day of Christianity? *Healing*! What was responsible for the phenomenal growth of the Christian Science Church? The *healing* of thousands of people of any and every kind of ill. What is it that people go to any Church for? To pray—*and to find how to get an answer to their prayers.* Show them the way to do this, show them the way to *heal* themselves of all their ills and lacks, and you will need to worry no more about the crowded theaters and the empty churches.

"If this be treason, make the most of it."

The moment any symptom of illness shows in your body, vigorously deny its existence. Say to yourself—"My body has no intelligence. Neither has any germ of disease. Therefore neither my body nor the disease can tell me I am sick. Mind is the only cause. And Mind has not directed them to make me sick. The only image of my body that Mind knows is a perfect, vigorous, healthy image. And that is the only image I am going to build on." Then forget the image of disease. It is only an illusion, and can be dispelled like any other illusion. Keep in your mind's eye the image of perfect health, of vigorous, boundless vitality.

Your body cannot say it is sick. Therefore when the belief of sickness assails you, it must come either from your conscious mind or from outside suggestion. In either event, it is your job to see that no belief of sickness reaches your subconscious mind, that no fear of it, no thought of it, is imaged there.

To treat one who has already succumbed to the belief of sickness, explain to him, as I have explained to you here, that his body has no power for sickness or for health, any more than a log of wood has. That his body is merely an aggregation of millions of electrons—particles of electrical energy, really—subject wholly to his mind. That these particles of energy have neither substance nor intelligence; that they are constantly changing; and that the forms they take depend entirely upon the images he holds in his own mind.

His body is, in short, a mental concept. It is an exact reflection of the thought he is holding in mind of it. If he has been sick, it is because he has been holding sickly, weak and unhealthy thoughts in his mind. If he wishes to get well, it is first necessary for him to change his thought. Instead of doctoring the machine, he is to go direct to the powerhouse and change the current. Let him repeat to himself, night and morning, this little formula:

"There is no permanence to matter. The one surest thing about it is *change*."

Every cell, every tissue in my body is constantly being renewed. The old, worn out tissues are being torn down and carried away. New, perfect ones are replacing them. And the model on which those new organisms are being re-built is the perfect model that is held in Divine Mind.

"For God made man in His image. That image was perfect then—is perfect now. It is the only image that Divine Mind knows of me. It is the only image on which my subconscious mind is ever again going to pattern its re-building. Every minute of every day I am growing more and more into the image of God—the *True Likeness* He holds of me in His thought."

If he will do that, if he will bear in mind that matter as such has no feeling, no intelligence; that it is the mind that feels, the mind that directs, and therefore he has nothing to fear from any external causes, his fear of the disease will vanish. And the patient does not exist who will not speedily recover when his fear of the disease is gone.

"Verily, verily, I say unto you," said Jesus, "if a man keep my saying, he shall never see death." And again—"This is the life eternal." "*Is*," you will notice, not "shall be."

"The subconscious mind is God's way of utilizing His energy," says the Rev. William T. Walsh, Rector of St. Luke's Church, New York City, in his book "Scientific Spiritual Healing." "God evolved the subconscious mind. It is His gift to us like all else that we possess, and because it is from Him we should give thanks and learn to use it intelligently.

"God has so fashioned us that we do not have to give conscious attention to the vital processes. He has given us what is called the subconscious mind, which looks after all the vital functions. This mind can receive commands from us and has wonderful ability to carry them out, for it is a law that *every thought tends to realize itself* subconsciously in the body.

"If you allow evil thoughts to remain, they are received by the subconscious which tends to realize them in the body just as much as though they were good, wholesome, health-giving spiritual thoughts. For remember, the subconscious does not reason and judge. It only receives and obeys." When you have an accident, don't immediately think that you must be hurt. On the contrary, deny at once that you can be hurt. The denial will take away the creative power of your thought from any damaging condition. More than that, if you will immediately call to mind the fact that the only image of your body that Universal Mind holds is a perfect image, and that this is the image on which your subconscious mind is building, you will find: that this subconscious mind will speedily rebuild any damaged parts in accordance with that image.

As a matter of fact, if we could thoroughly realize that our bodies are made up merely of vortices of energy subject wholly to the control of mind, it should hurt us no more to run a knife through them than it does to run it through water. The water immediately resumes the shape of the vessel that holds it. Just so, our bodies should immediately resume the shape that mind holds them in.

But even with our present imperfect understanding, we can perform what the uninitiated would call miracles with our bodies. And each victory we win gives us a bit more of power over them. To conquer one diseased condition makes it easier to ward off or to conquer other diseased conditions. The body cannot oppose us. It is only the bias of education and the suggestions of those about us that we have to combat.

There is no necessity for disease. There is no necessity even for fatigue. "They that wait upon the Lord shall run and not be weary; and they shall walk and not faint." Those words from Holy Writ were meant literally—and they can be applied literally if you will govern your body by mind, and not let custom and popular belief make your body the master. Whatever it is right for you to do, you can do without fear, no matter if it entails long-continued toil, hardship or danger. Depend upon it, your mind can call to your aid all the forces of Nature if they are necessary to your emergency.

"Therefore I say unto you," quotes the Master, "take no thought for your life, what ye shall eat, or what ye shall drink; nor yet for your body, what ye shall put on. Is not the life more than meat and the body than raiment?"

Diet, exercise and rules of health never kept any one well of themselves. Often they attract the mind to the subject of sickness and thereby foster it.

Dieting is good insofar as it prevents gluttony. Temperance is just as important in eating as in the drinking of alcoholic liquor. But you can eat in moderation anything you like, anything that you relish and BELIEVE to be good for you, without fear of its disagreeing with you.

Reasonable exercise, too, is fine for both the body and the mind. Provided you do not make a fetish of it. It isn't the exercise that keeps you well—it is the mental image you hold in your thought.

The exercise merely helps to impress that mental image on your subconscious mind.

Electrical treatments, skin tonics, alcohol rubs, etc., all are useful only to the extent that they center the attention of the subconscious mind upon the parts affected. Exactly the same results, even to that pleasant little tingling of the skin, can be affected by mind alone. I remember reading an article by Mrs. Vance Cheney, telling how she cured herself of paralysis of the legs in just that way. After lying for months under the care of doctors and masseurs, she tired of them and decided to depend entirely upon mind. So, several times a day, she would utterly relax in every nerve and muscle, and then consciously send her thought down along the nerves of her legs to her feet. Presently there would be that little tingling sensation in her feet—evidence of increased circulation—followed after a time by a feeling of drowsiness. A few weeks of these treatments completely restored the use of her legs.

The same effort can be made to throw off any physical trouble. Put your hand upon the part affected. Try to visualize that organ, as it should be. See it functioning perfectly. BELIEVE that it IS working normally again! Your thought brings the blood to the affected part, clears up the trouble, provides new cells, new tissue, while your belief that the organ IS functioning properly will bring about that normal condition.

This is a treatment, however, that must be used with discretion, for to consciously interfere in the regular functioning of the body without any real need for such interference results in confusion rather than help. It is like going down a flight of stairs rapidly. Pay no attention to the movement of your feet, and they flit over the steps with never a sign of hesitancy or faltering. But try to watch them step by step, and you will either have to slow up or you will presently miss a step, stumble or fall.

"The centipede was happy quite,
Until the toad, for fun,
Said, 'Pray, which leg goes after which?'
This stirred his mind to such a pitch,
He lay distracted in a ditch,
  Considering how to run."

There is one rule that will help anyone keep healthy. That rule is to forget your nerves, throw away your pills and your medicine bottles, and hold before your mind's eye only the perfect image that Universal Mind has of your body. That is the surest way to keep free from sickness.

And if you are already sick, the same rule applies. Know that Universal Mind never created disease—which it is but an illusion of your conscious mind. Know that mind is the only creator that as Shakespeare puts it, "There is nothing, either good or bad, but thinking makes it so." Know that you have the say as to what that thinking shall be. Know, therefore, that by holding a perfect image of your body in your thoughts you can make your body perfect.

Have you ever cut your finger? Who was it coagulated the blood, stopped the gash, wove new skin? Who was it called upon the little phagocytes to come and kill the septic germs?

Not your conscious mind, certainly. Most people don't even know there are "any such animals." Their conscious minds don't know the first thing about healing. Whence comes the information? Whence the directing genius? Where but from the same intelligence that keeps your heart and lungs on the job while you sleep, that regulates your liver and your kidneys, that attends to all the functions of your body?

That intelligence is your subconscious mind. With the proper co-operation on your part, your subconscious mind will attend to these duties indefinitely, keeping your every organ perfect, your every function regular as clockwork.

But it is exceedingly amenable to suggestion. Worry about sickness or contagion, hold before it the thought that you are getting old, or that some organ is becoming feeble, and it will be perfectly agreeable to bringing about the condition you suggest. Convince it that there is no danger from contagion, hold before it the thought of health and strength, and it will be just as prompt in manifesting them.

So what you must realize is this: Before anything can be made, there must be a model for it in mind. Before a house can be built, there must be a plan, a blueprint from which to build. Before you were created, Universal Mind held in thought the model on which you were made. That model was perfect then—is perfect now. The only idea of you that Universal Mind knows is a perfect model, where every cell and organism is formed along perfect lines. True, many of us have built up imperfect models in our own thoughts, but we can get rid of them just as rapidly as we get rid of the fear of them.

Your body is changing every moment. Every cell, every organism, is constantly being rebuilt. Why rebuild along the old, imperfect lines? Why not build on the lines held in the thought of Universal Mind? You CAN do it! But the essence of it lies in the words of the Master: "Whatsoever things ye desire when ye pray, believe that ye RECEIVE them, and ye SHALL HAVE them."

It matters not what your ailment may be. It will respond to that treatment. Suppose, as an example, that your stomach has been troubling you, that you cannot eat what you would like, that you cannot assimilate your food, that you are weak and nervous is consequence. Every morning when you awake, and every night just before you drop off to sleep say to yourself—

"My stomach has neither intelligence nor feeling. It functions only as mind directs it. Therefore I need have no worry about its being weak or diseased, for the only image that Mind knows of stomach is Its perfect image. And that perfect image can assimilate or remove anything I may put into it. It is perfect, as everything that Universal Mind makes is perfect. And being perfect, it can do anything right I may ask of it without fear or anxiety."

Concentrate on the one organ at a time, and repeat this formula to yourself night and morning. Say it, feel it, BELIEVE it—and you can do what you please with that organ. "As thy faith is, so be it done unto thee."

"Suffer Little Children to Come Unto Me"

"I can believe all you say about my fears and worries being responsible for my 'own illnesses," write many people, "but how about infants and little children? They have no fear. Why do they sicken and die?" What many people do not understand is that the subconscious mind is just as amenable to suggestion from those round about you as it is from your own conscious mind. Otherwise you would be in no danger from anything you did not consciously know of. And the more ignorant you were, the safer you would be.

Suppose, for instance, you took a draught of what you believed to be pure "bootleg" whisky, but which in reality was no more than wood alcohol. Many others have done it. Your conscious mind would expect no harm from it—any more than did theirs. You would have no fear of the result.

No more did they. So, you would say, you should experience no harm.

Yet you would probably die—or at least go blind—as have these others. Why? Because your subconscious mind would know the wood alcohol for what it is. Your own conscious belief, and the preponderance of opinion of those about you, has instilled the conviction in your subconscious mind that wood alcohol is dire poison. Therefore when you pour this poison into your system—even though you do not consciously recognize it as such—your subconscious mind proceeds to bring about the effects you would logically expect such a poison to produce.

It is the same with contagion, with the hundreds of diseases which most people scarcely know the names of, but to which they are constantly falling victims. They don't know they have been exposed to contagion. They don't know that their systems are in such condition that certain diseases logically follow. But their subconscious minds do know it. And they have so thoroughly educated those minds to believe in the necessity for ill health, in the inevitability of sickness under certain conditions that the subconscious proceed to work out the contagion or the condition to its logical conclusion.

Grown people can change these subconscious convictions by the proper counter-suggestions, consciously given. But young children cannot reason. They accept the beliefs that are held by the generality of mankind, or that are strongly suggested to them by those nearest to them.

That is why babies and young children fall such easy victims to the fears of disease and contagion of their parents and those about them. That is why worry over a seeming epidemic so often results in the children catching it, even when they have apparently been in no way exposed to the contagion.

"Man," says a famous writer, "often has fear stamped upon him before his entrance into the outer world; he is reared in fear; all his life is passed in bondage of fear of disease and death and thus his whole mentality becomes cramped, limited, and depressed, and his body follows its shrunken pattern and specification. IS IT NOT SURPRISING THAT HEALTH EXISTS AT ALL? Nothing but the boundless Divine Love, exuberance, and vitality, constantly poured in, even though unconsciously to us, could in some degrees neutralize such an ocean of morbidity."

But the remedy is just as simple. Know that your children are primarily children of God. That the image He holds of them is perfect. His perfect image has within itself every power necessary to ward off disease of any kind.

Put your children actively under His care. Throw the responsibility upon Him. Depend upon it, when you do this in the right way, no harm can come near them. Whenever fear assails you, whenever your children are exposed to danger or contagion, realize that "He shall give His angels (his thoughts) charge over them, to lead them in all their ways."

If your children are sick or ailing, read these thoughts aloud to them just as though you were talking to a grown person. Only address yourself to their subconscious minds. Read over the past few pages. Repeat to them the little formula outlined above, adapting it to their own particular need. Above all, BELIEVE it! Your faith will work just as great wonders for your children as for yourself.

Never doubt. Never fear. Go at your problem just as you would approach a difficult problem in mathematics. In mathematics, you know that the problem does not exist for which you cannot find the solution, provided you follow the rules and work in the right way.

As long as you do your part, the principle of mathematics will do the rest. It is the same in all of life. Don't worry. Don't fret. Go at your problem in the right way, no matter how difficult it may seem; follow the rules herein laid down, and you can confidently look to the Principle of Being to bring you the answer.

L'Envoi

"The Kingdom of Heaven is like unto a treasure hid in a field; the which when a man hath found, he hideth, and for joy thereof goeth and selleth all that he hath, and buyeth that field." This field is your own consciousness—a treasure you find within yourself—, which others cannot see. But you know it for the in-dwelling Spirit—"the Father within you"—and are willing to sell all that you have because this treasure is worth more than all other possessions.

If you have begun to realize this treasure, and use it even in a small way, the most wonderful thing that can happen to anyone on this planet has happened to you. What does it mean? It means that an ordinary human being, afflicted with all the sufferings and fears and worries and superstitions of the average man, has learned the Law of Being. It means that he has acquired a power above all that of his would-be destroyers. It means that he has put his foot upon the Rock of Life that the Doorway of Heaven is open before him, that all of Good is as free to him as the air he breathes.

"There hath not failed one word of all His good promises." "And we declare unto you glad tidings, how that the promise which was made unto the fathers, God hath fulfilled the same unto us."

Surely we have every reason to be grateful for all the good round about us. Surely we should be thankful for the infinite power that has been given to us.

And being truly grateful, by the way, is the surest evidence of real faith that there is. Faith, you know, is "the substance of things hoped for, the evidence of things not seen," Remember, when Jesus raised Lazarus from the dead, how He first prayed, *and then thanked the Father for answering His Prayer?* There was not yet any material evidence that the prayer had been answered. But Jesus had perfect faith in the Father. And it was justified. Immediately He had given thanks, Lazarus *came forth from the tomb!*

The world today is so much more wonderful than it was to former generations. Mankind has begun to glimpse its illimitable powers. The whole world is plastic and sensitive to new ideas. The soul of man is finding itself, and learning its relation to the Infinite. The veil between the visible and the invisible is being drawn aside. Through seeing the "Father do the works," we are becoming more assured of our own power, beginning to assert "the Father that is within us." We know that, given the right understanding, the works that Jesus did we can do also. We recognize his "miracles" as divinely natural laws, part of God's continuous plan.

So let us go with Him unto the Mount of Vision, taking as our motto His words—"See that thou make all things according to the pattern showed thee in the Mount."

STUDY GUIDE

XXIV *The Gift of the Magi*

1. What call to action does Ella Wheeler Wilcox's poem invoke in you?

2. It is said that the properly trained nurse instills a sense of progress in the patient. In doing so, she instills hope and a greater sense of well-being in the individual. Do you believe her care can have as much effect on a patient that drugs? Why or why not?

3. A cheery disposition is also encouraged among physicians. Is your doctor positive and enjoyable? Do you believe that being so is important for a doctor? Why or why not?

4. As Collier references Freud and other psychotherapists, we are reminded that this book was written when the practice of psychology was new. Thus Collier was a true pioneer in this work. If you were to be a pioneer in a field of expertise and there were no limitations, what would that field be?

5. Does the sight of someone sick in your presence set you into panic or concern about becoming sick yourself?

6. Houdini is an example of an individual who defied the science of his time. While we should have been dead after 4 minutes of submersion under water, I stayed there for one and a half hours. He said that *"The important thing is to be believe that you are safe"*. Take some time to study Houdini and uncover how he was able to remain calm during such submersions.

7. Collier shares examples of individual who, under stress or sudden emotion were able to break free of their ailments,

and acted as if they were not ill. Have you ever experienced or witnessed such an event? If so, describe it? If not, if you are interested in doing so, go to the Internet and research videos of such phenomenon.

8. Desire and faith are the reasons behind miraculous healings at places like Lourdes, according to Collier. Study such a healing place and write about your findings.

9. Some are wedded to their ailments, or often see the ailment as part of their self-identity. They are lost without their complaints. Are you at all wedded to your ailments, or do you know of anyone who is? What would you/they have to face or endure if they were totally healthy?

10. You must first have sincere desire, and then believe that you are going to receive healing. Then believe that you have the perfect image of yourself as healthy and whole. Once you do this, you will then be perfect. Do you believe yourself to be perfect? If not, why not?

11. Collier shares the story of the farmer who prayed for his sight and regained it. If there was some physical healing you could pray for, what would it be? Take time now to pray for it, seeing it as healed and experiencing complete gratitude for the shift. Note any insights you gain by doing this exercise.

12. Starting with the creation of the first one-celled Amoeba through to the birth of man the intelligence of the Universal Mind was at working, creating. Collier states that man is evolving and drawing nearer and nearer to the likeness of his Creator. Where do you see evidence of this in the world today? Might you find it in a comparison from early man to present? If so, how has man progressed. Provide examples.

13. When combating illness, shifting your mind back to the perfection of who you are, will make sickness vanish. If you were naturally born with a healthy body and organs,

then your mind knows that healthy state. Thus, all that needs to be done is to remove the clouds so that the light of the sun can shine through. Do you agree with this premise? Why or why not?

14. How would you hold an image of health in your mind's eye, if your body is in pain?

15. Have you ever found yourself discouraged when bad health arose? If so, how did you pull yourself out of the negativity?

16. If medication helps you pull out of sickness, is it beneficial? Why or why not?

17. The Quakers have a saying, *"master of the body which it loves"*. Research the Quakers and that saying. Then summarize what you learned.

18. Collier asserts that *"When you drive the belief in disease from your subconscious mind, you will drive away the pain and all the other symptoms with it."* Try this with a pain or ailment you feel in your body, seeing the pain as merely a belief and not a reality. Then note whether or not this experiment was successful.

19. You are encouraged to deny pain or sickness when it arises. Does this suggestion create any uneasiness within you? Would your tendency be to reach out to a doctor? Do you believe it is wrong to do so? Are you conflicted at all on this subject? If so, perhaps you can research it further to alleviate the conflict. Record your findings.

20. Do you believe you are slave to your organs? Why or why not?

21. You are encouraged to go to your subconscious to investigate any illness or disturbance in the body. Take a few minutes to check in with your subconscious, and ask if there are any imbalances in your body of which you need to become aware. Then write a list of the areas that arise.

22. Now that you have been guided by your subconscious, call in the Universal Mind and set an intention for all imbalances to go back into equilibrium. At least once a day, visualize your body as perfect and in balance. See and feel it as radiant, strong and whole. Write about any insights or shifts in thoughts, feelings and health that arise from practicing this visualization.

23. While each organ functions perfectly when healthy, none of them possess intelligence. They all function naturally and instantaneously under the care of the subconscious mind. Without the mind, it is an inert mechanism. Imagine your body as it was when you were born – perfectly balanced and in harmony. See your cells youthful, and re-generating easily, naturally and effortlessly. Do this exercise especially when you begin to feel energetically depleted or fatigues. Write down your findings.

24. How is your eyesight? The author prescribes that you give them rest so that they can repair and re-build themselves. See your eyes as healthy and perfect. Focus on your desire for perfect eyesight, seeing it as if it already exists. Do this exercise as your subconscious suggests and write about your findings.

25. *"All disease, sickness, all imperfection of the human body are due to this one cause – your belief that your body is the master, that it can act, that it can catch cold, or become disease, without the consent of mind."* Until now, have you believed that your body is its own master? Are you ready to see your mind as the master? If not, what is blocking you from doing so? If you don't know, call upon your subconscious mind to guide and direct you.

26. On a scale from one to ten (one being very little, and ten being very much so), rate how fear you have about disease taking over your body.

    1——2——3——4——5——6——7——8——9——10

27. To start to eliminate your fears, *"refuse to believe or to heed any complaint from your body. Have no fear of climate or atmosphere, of dampness or drafts. It is only when you believe them unhealthy that they are so to you."* Do you get anxious with climate or atmospheric changes? If so, imagine your body being exposed to such changes and maintaining equilibrium, realizing that the Universal Mind of perfection is your body's master. Practice this technique until you no longer feel anxious.

28. If your stomach acts distressed, *"treat it as an unruly servant. Remind it that it is not the judge of what is or is not good for it. That it has no intelligence. That it is merely a channel."*

29. In the Stockholm experiments, patients were hypnotized into believing that the poisons they ingested would not harm them.

30. If someone tells you that a certain food is not good for you note that if you believe it to be good for you, it will be.

31. Collier shares that the work of Mary Baker Eddy, Discoverer and Founder of Christian Science supported healing. If you are not familiar with her, research and the healing that she has encouraged. Then write a summary of your findings.

32. The author suggests that when any symptom of illnesses arises in your body, you recite the following:

"My body has no intelligence. Neither has any germ of disease. Therefore neither my body nor the disease can tell me I am sick. Mind is the only cause. And Mind has not directed them to make me sick. The only image of my body that Mind knows is perfect, vigorous, healthy image. And that is the only image I am going to build on."

Forget the image of illness and then note how you feel after reciting this affirmation.

33. If another comes to you with health issues, would you feel comfortable sharing this information with him or her? Why or why not?

34. It is suggested that one repeat this formula to himself morning and night: *"There is no permanence to matter. The one surest thing about it is change."* Collier asserts that if the individual say this and practice having faith in their perfection, that his fear of disease will vanish, along with disease. Have you ever known someone who lives this mindset? If so, what are your thoughts and feelings about him or her?

35. Rev. William T. Walsh states that the subconscious mind is God's gift to us. Take a moment and express gratitude to the Creator for your subconscious mind. Write a poem, narrative or prayer in honor of the power and genius inherent in it.

36. If your body is in an accident and damaged in any way, according to the author, holding the perfect image of your body will support your subconscious mind to speedily rebuild any damaged parts. You may wish to experiment with this process and write about your findings.

37. While diet prevents gluttony, the author does not encourage it. Reasonable exercise is fine for both the body and mind, but excessive is unnecessary. All treatments are useful only to the extent that they center the attention of the subconscious mind on the parts that are affected. If you eat certain foods because you feel good doing so, then continue. If you enjoy exercise because you feel you are doing something good for your body, then continue. Just be aware of the power of your mind, and that it has true reign over all aspects of your body. List the foods and exercises that you enjoy most.

38. Collier cautions you to use treatments with discretion, for *"to consciously interfere in the regular functioning of the*

body without any real need for such interference results in confusion rather than help." Be sure to call upon your subconscious so that you are not overdoing these practices. Then trust in yourself and Infinite Mind.

39. Shakespeare's quote, *"There is nothing, either good or bad, but thinking makes it so."* Judgmental thinking can be toxic, especially if you feel bad about doing it. Write a list of things you have deemed as bad and see if you can shift your perception to neutral.

"Suffer Little Children to Come Unto Me"

40. Regarding illness in children, Collier states that the *"subconscious mind is just as amenable to suggestion from those round about you as it is form your own conscious mind."* What thoughts or feelings does this realization raise within you?

41. While you may not consciously know that you've been exposed to a contagion, your subconscious mind does. You, in turn may have so thoroughly educated your subconscious mind of the inevitability of sickness that it prevails. The good news is that you can change these convictions by the proper counter-suggestions.

42. Young children cannot reason; thus they are affected by the beliefs and fears of their parents and others in their environment. To remedy their situation, know that they are children of God and that the image He holds of them is perfect. Put the child under His care. Whenever you are fraught with fear, call upon God to protect your child and then have faith that it is done. Have you ever practiced calling upon the divine to assist you with your children? If not, practice doing so and note the peace of mind that comes with releasing fear and having faith.

L'Envoi

43. The quote that opens this segment, speaks of a treasure. Have you found a treasure within the teachings of this book? Are you excited about the power of the Universal Mind and your ability to shift your life?

44. Collier states that *"all of the Good is as free to him as the air he breathes."* Do you see the freedom that can come with applying this information and these techniques? What is the most powerful lesson you have learned in reading this book?

45. The author re-emphasizes the power of gratitude as her reiterates the story of Lazarus and how Christ expressed gratitude before Lazarus had risen. While you have practiced gratitude throughout this study guide, take a moment to write or speak words of gratitude to Robert Collier, the publisher, the Universe and whatever impetus within your psyche nudged you to read this book and apply its lessons to your life.

46. Collier ends the book stating that the world is so much more wonderful now than it was to former generations. *"The whole world is finding itself, and learning its relation to the Infinite. The veil between the visible and invisible is being drawn aside."* Write a list of the ways in which you are finding yourself. Then make a list of the ways in which you see the world as a whole finding itself.

47. As you *"go with Him unto the Mount of Vision"*, speak aloud or write an affirmation on the perfection of you, the perfection of everyone that you know and love, and the perfection of the world as a whole. Then envision this perfection. Have faith and know that it is so!

Index of Scriptural References and Quotations

These passages are quoted from the King James Version of the Bible. Authorized, Revised, and from various modern translations.

According to your faith—Matthew 9:29, vol. ii, vol. iii, vol. iv, vol. vii
Acquaint now thyself with Him—Job 22:21, vol. v
All things are yours—I Corinthians 3:22, 23, vol. v
All that thou commandest us—Joshua 1:16, 17, vol. v
All things were made by Him—John 1:3, vol. iii,
And God said, Let us make man—Genesis 1:26, 27, vol. ii, vol. iii, vol. iv, vol. v, vol. vi, vol. vii
And Moses was an hundred and—Deuteronomy 34:7, vol. vi,
And whatsoever ye do, do it heartily—Colossians 3:23, vol. v
And the second is like unto it—Matthew 22:39, vol. iv
And we declare unto you glad—The Acts 13:32, 33, vol. vii
And when thou prayest, be not—Matthew 6:5, vol. ii
Are not two sparrows sold—Matthew 10:29, 30, 31, vol. i
Ask and it shall be given—Matthew 7:7, vol. iii
Ask and ye shall receive—John 16:24, vol. iii, vol. vi
As a man thinketh in his heart—Proverbs 23:7, vol. iii, vol. iv, vol. v, vol. vi
As the rain cometh down and—Isaiah 55:10, vol. vi
Beauty for ashes, the oil of joy—Isaiah 61:3, vol. ii
Because thou hast made the Lord—Psalms 91:9, 10, 11, vol. v
Before Abraham was, I am—John 8:58, vol. iv

Index of Scriptural References and Quotations

Behold I stand at the door—Revelation 3:20, vol. ii
Behold, the kingdom of God-Luke 17:21, vol. i, vol. ii, vol. iii, vol. v, vol. vi
Believe that ye receive it—Mark 11:24, vol. v, vol. vi
Beloved now are we the sons—I John 3:2, vol. i
Be not afraid—Matthew 14:27, vol. iii
Be still, and know that I am. God—Psalms 46:10, vol. iv
Be ye therefore perfect—Matthew 5:48, vol. vii
Blessed are they which do hunger—Matthew 5:6, vol. ii
Blessed is the man whose delight—Psalms 1:2, 3, vol. iii
But thou are the same—Psalms 102:27, vol. vi
But thou, when thou prayest—Matthew 6:6, vol. ii,
But where shall wisdom be found?—Job 28:12, vol. v
Cast thy bread upon the waters—Ecclesiastes 11:1, vol. iv
Come ye to the open fountain—Revelation 7:17
Commit thy works unto the Lord—Proverbs 16:3, vol. v
Consider the lilies—Luke 12:27, vol. iii
Delight thyself also in the Lord—Psalms 37:4, vol. v
Do men gather figs of thistles? —Matthew 7:16, vol. iv
Every good gift and every perfect—James 1:17, vol. ii
Except ye turn and. become as—Matthew 18:3, vol. iv
Faith without works—James 2:17, vol. iv, vol. vii
Fear not little flock—Luke 12:32, vol. iv
For God made not death—Apocrypha, Book of Wisdom 1:13, 18, vol. vi
For herein is the Father glorified—John 15:8, vol. iii
He shall give His angels charge—Psalm 5 91:11, vol. vii
He that believeth on me—John 14:12, vol. ii vol. iv
Hewers of wood—Joshua 9:27, vol. v
Ho, every one that thirsteth—Isaiah 55:1, vol. i
I came that ye might have life—John 10:10, vol. iii
I can of mine Own self—John 5:30, John 14:10, vol. ii, vol. iv, vol. v,
If ye have faith as a grain—Matthew 17:20, vol. ii
If ye abide in me and my words—John 15:7, vol. ii

If a man keep my saying, he shall—John 8:51, vol. vi
I have given you power—Luke 10:19, vol. iv
In all thy ways acknowledge—Proverbs 3:6, vol. v
In returning and rest—Isaiah 30:15, vol. v
Jacob wrestles with the angel—Genesis 34:24-26, vol. v
Know that ye are the temple—I Corinthians 3:16, vol. iii
Know ye not that to whom ye yield—Romans 6:16, vol. vii
Lazarus raised from the dead—John 11:1-44, vol. v, vol. vii
Let this mind be in you—Philippians 2:5, vol. ii, vol. iv
Lo I am with you always—Matthew 28:20, vol. iv
Lord that I may receive—Luke 18:41, vol. vii
Now he that planteth and he—I Corinthians, 3:8-9, vol. v
Ninety-first Psalm—vol. iii
O taste and see that the Lord—Psalms 34:8, vol. iii
Prophetic sons of God—Hosea 1:10, vol. iii
See that thou make all things—Hebrews 8:5, vol. vii
Seek ye first the kingdom—Matthew 7:33, vol. iii
Son thou art ever with me—Luke 15:31, vol. iii, vol. iv
Suffer the little children—Mark 10:4, vol. vii
The earth is full of the—Psalms 33:5, vol. iii
The earth is the Lord's—Psalms 24:1, vol. iv
The Father that dwelleth in me—John 14:10, vol. iii, vol. vii
The kingdom of heaven is like—Matthew 13:44, vol. vii
The loaves and fishes—Luke 9:12-17, vol. iv
The manna from heaven—Exodus 16:15, vol. v
The mount of Vision—Exodus 24:13, 18, vol. vii
The pillar of fire—Exodus 13:21, vol. v
The sea rolled back—Exodus 14:21-22, vol. v
The substance of things—Hebrews 11:1, vol. iv, vol. vii
The thing that I greatly—Job 3:25, vol. iv
The tribute money—Matthew 17:27, vol. iv
The water from the rock—Exodus 17:6, vol. v
The water turned into wine—John 2:1, vol. v
The waters which came down—Joshua 3:16-17, vol. v

Index of Scriptural References and Quotations 391

Therefore I say unto you—Matthew 6:31-33, vol. iii, vol. vii
There hath not failed one—I Kings 8:56, vol. vii
There is that scattereth—Proverbs 11:24, vol. iv
They that wait upon the Lord, shall win—Isaiah 40:31, vol. vii
They shall obtain joy and—Isaiah 35:10, vol. iii
This is life eternal—John 17:3, vol. vii
This one thing I do—Philippians 3:13, vol. v
Thou art of purer eyes than to behold—Habakkuk 1:13, vol. vii
Thou shall love the Lord—Matthew 22:37, 38, vol. iv
Thou wilt show me the path—Psalms 16:11, vol. iii
Thy faith bath made thee whole—Luke 8:48, vol. vii
To him that hath—Matthew 25:29, vol. ii
To know aright is life—John 17:3, vol. v
Trust in the Lord and—Psalms 37:3, vol. iv
Twenty-third psalm—vol. ii
Verily, verily I say unto you—John 8:51, vol. vii
We shall see Him as he is—I John 3:2, vol. i
What eye never saw—I Corinthians 2:9, vol. iii
What things so-ever ye—Mark 11:24, vol. ii, vol. v, vol. vi, vol. vii
What wouldst thou that I—Mark 10:51, vol. vii
Where there is no vision—Proverbs 29:18, vol. iii
Who hath measured the waters—Isaiah 40:12, vol. v
Who healeth all thy diseases—Psalms 103:3, vol. vii, page 593
Whosoever shall be great—Matthew 20:26, 27, vol. iv
Whosoever liveth and believeth—John 11:26, vol. vi
Whosoever shall compel thee—Matthew 5:41, vol. iv
Whosoever will let him take—Revelation 22:17, vol. i
With all thy getting—Proverbs 4.7, vol. i, page 70; vol. iii
Work out your own salvatioii—Philippians 2:12, vol. iv
Wouldst thou be made whole—John 5:16, vol. vii
Ye shall ask what ye will—John 15:7, vol. ii
Ye shall know the truth—John 8:32, vol. iv, vol. vii
Your Father knoweth that ye—Luke 12:30, vol. iii

www.ingramcontent.com/pod-product-compliance
Lightning Source LLC
Chambersburg PA
CBHW052008070526
44584CB00016B/1671